# Praise for Michael Hodgson

Here's what reviewers say about *Camping For Dummies*:

"Once again, Michael Hodgson proves himself to be the consummate guide to the outdoors. *Camping For Dummies* is full of insightful tips and gentle reminders, without being condescending — or worse, boring. When it comes to gearing up and heading out, Hodgson's been there, and it shows. If he writes, 'I have always found it helpful to...' you'd better get out the yellow highlighter."

> — Daniel Glick, special correspondent for *Newsweek*

"His witty and concise information for novice (and not so novice) campers is superb. Parents will be especially grateful for the section on camping with kids. I'd gladly share a tent with Michael anytime!"

> — Bruce Ward, Director, Continental Divide Trail Alliance and former President, American Hiking Society.

"An adventure is sometimes called an outing that goes wrong. The way to prevent your camping trip from becoming an outing epic is to do what the Boy Scouts have always told us: plan and prepare. *Camping For Dummies* will help you do just that."

> — Rick Ridgeway, President, Adventure Photo & Film

"*Camping For Dummies* is not only a 'must read' for newer campers but a must for all lovers of the outdoors. From the Camp Crafter to the Peak Bagger, we all can gain from this well written and common sense book. A fun read!"

> — Lou Whittaker, President, Rainier Mountaineering, Inc.

# Camping

## FOR

# DUMMIES®

by Michael Hodgson

WILEY

Wiley Publishing, Inc.

**Camping For Dummies®**

Published by
**Wiley Publishing, Inc.**
111 River Street
Hoboken, NJ 07030
www.wiley.com

Copyright © 2000 by Wiley Publishing, Inc., Indianapolis, Indiana

Published by Wiley Publishing, Inc., Indianapolis, Indiana

Published simultaneously in Canada

**Trademarks:** Wiley, the Wiley Publishing logo, For Dummies, the Dummies Man logo, A Reference for the Rest of Us!, The Dummies Way, Dummies Daily, The Fun and Easy Way, Dummies.com, and related trade dress are trademarks or registered trademarks of John Wiley & Sons, Inc. and/or its affiliates in the United States and other countries and may not be used without written permission. All other trademarks are the property of their respective owners. Wiley Publishing, Inc., is not associated with any product or vendor mentioned in this book.

LIMIT OF LIABILITY/DISCLAIMER OF WARRANTY: WHILE THE PUBLISHER AND AUTHOR HAVE USED THEIR BEST EFFORTS IN PREPARING THIS BOOK, THEY MAKE NO REPRESENTATIONS OR WARRANTIES WITH RESPECT TO THE ACCURACY OR COMPLETENESS OF THE CONTENTS OF THIS BOOK AND SPECIFICALLY DISCLAIM ANY IMPLIED WARRANTIES OF MERCHANTABILITY OR FITNESS FOR A PARTICULAR PURPOSE. NO WARRANTY MAY BE CREATED OR EXTENDED BY SALES REPRESENTATIVES OR WRITTEN SALES MATERIALS. THE ADVICE AND STRATEGIES CONTAINED HEREIN MAY NOT BE SUITABLE FOR YOUR SITUATION. YOU SHOULD CONSULT WITH A PROFESSIONAL WHERE APPROPRIATE. NEITHER THE PUBLISHER NOR AUTHOR SHALL BE LIABLE FOR ANY LOSS OF PROFIT OR ANY OTHER COMMERCIAL DAMAGES, INCLUDING BUT NOT LIMITED TO SPECIAL, INCIDENTAL, CONSEQUENTIAL, OR OTHER DAMAGES.

For general information on our other products and services or to obtain technical support, please contact our Customer Care Department within the U.S. at 800-762-2974, outside the U.S. at 317-572-3993, or fax 317-572-4002.

Wiley also publishes its books in a variety of electronic formats. Some content that appears in print may not be available in electronic books.

*Library of Congress Cataloging-in-Publication Data:*

Library of Congress Catalog Card No.: 99-69710

ISBN: 0-7645-5221-X

Printed in the United States of America

10 9 8 7 6 5 4 3 2

1B/QR/QW/QV/IN

# About the Author

Recognized nationally for his poignant writing style, humor, and knowledge of the outdoors, award-winning journalist and author **Michael Hodgson** constantly seeks the wilder side in search of a good story or rip-roaring adventure, like when he captained Team Media in the inaugural Eco-Challenge 360-mile adventure race in Utah.

Michael currently works as a content editor for Planet Outdoors and is a founding partner in GearTrends LLC — www.GearTrends.com — the premier information Web site for new products and trends in the outdoor sport, snow sport, fitness, paddling, and bike markets. His other Web site — www.adventurenetwork.com — was recognized in 1999 as a USA Today Hot Site, a Featured Expert award winner, and a Golden Globe award winner.

Michael served as the gear editor for *Men's Health* magazine from 1997 to 1999 and during that time was also the on-air talent covering gear and trends for the nationally syndicated weekly program *Outside Radio Network.*

Michael's articles have appeared in *Backpacker, Outside, Men's Journal, Adventure Journal, Field and Stream, Outdoor Life,* and *The Christian Science Monitor,* among other periodicals. He has published 18 books on the outdoors. Prior to becoming a fulltime writer in 1988, Michael worked as mountain guide, outdoor education instructor, and Nordic ski instructor; as general manager of Western Mountaineering, an outdoor specialty store and sleeping bag manufacturer; and as a store manager for Adventure 16, a highly successful chain of outdoor specialty stores in Southern California.

When not behind a computer working on his Web sites, books, or magazine articles, Michael can be found paddling oceans, running trails, climbing mountains, or wandering the backcountry by himself or with his daughter Nikki and wife Therese. In other words, he gets paid to play — it doesn't get much better than that, does it?

# Dedication

For my mother, who encouraged my first steps outdoors; my father, who guided my feet on wild trails as I was growing up; my daughter, Nikki, who inspires me by seeing everything through fresh eyes; and my wife, Therese, whose loving smile and sparkle are my favorite hiking companions.

# Author's Acknowledgments

With any camping trip, there must be a beginning, and so it was with this book. I must thank Mark Reiter, my agent with the International Management Group, who saw in me the perfect *dummy* for this book. I'm grateful to Stacy Collins at Wiley who agreed with Mark that I was the right one for a project she had wanted to see completed for over a year before my assignment.

My friend Kristin Hostetter, equipment editor of *Backpacker* magazine, deserves more thanks than I can possibly offer here for taking on the challenge of technical editing. Because of her, this book is more accurate, more useful, more practical, and simply much better than I could ever have hoped for had I done it alone.

This book never would have been possible had it not been for many folks who over the years had enough faith in me to be my friends and my advisors. I can only name a few and apologize now to the hundreds who I count as friends and hope that a collective thank you — and you know who you are — will suffice. There are a number of individuals whom I need to single out for special thanks, though. Tim Rowell, who helped me guide many trips in the mountains with paying clients — imagine that — and stood at my side as best man — twice. Mark Jenkins, with whom I still hope to complete a trip worthy of our friendship and mutual sense of adventure, for being a fellow traveler in the field of words. Marcus Woolf, for being there through thick and thin and for helping me learn, by trial and error, the better ways to camp — no, I will never forget a stove repair kit again. Jim Ward, my first editor at a small, free paper — *Footprints* — distributed all over Southern California to Adventure 16 patrons. Tom Shealy, editor of *Backpacker* magazine, who, upon reading my first submission to a "big name" publication, returned it with thoughtful editing and suggestions on improving the piece. Thanks for having enough belief in me that you published that article the second time around and, in effect, gave me the confidence to continue. Mic and John Mead for giving me a chance to find my wings in the outdoors at Adventure 16. Joan Alvarez for taking a chance with me and helping me become a better outdoor writer while I was at Outdoor Retailer. Wendy Geister, who showed me that editing is an art form worth appreciating. Tom Stienstra, who embodies the ideal outdoor writer — from the beard and hat right down to his boots. And Bob Woodward, who has become my friend and partner in the business of fun.

## Publisher's Acknowledgments

We're proud of this book; please send us your comments through our online registration form located at www.dummies.com/register.

Some of the people who helped bring this book to market include the following:

*Acquisitions, Editorial, and Media Development*

**Project Editor:** Norman Crampton

**Acquisitions Editor:** Stacy Collins

**Copy Editor:** Donna Frederick

**Technical Editor:** Kristin Hostetter

**Acquisitions Coordinator:** Lisa Roule

**Editorial Manager:** Pam Mourouzis

*Production*

**Project Coordinator:** Maridee Ennis

**Layout and Graphics:** Amy Adrian, Tracy K. Oliver, Shelley Norris, Brent Savage, Jacque Schneider, Brian Torwelle, Erin Zeltner

**Proofreaders:** Corey Bowen, John Greenough, Susan Moritz, Joel Showalter

**Indexer:** Steve Rath

**Illustrators:** Shelley Norris, Brent Savage

*Special Help*
Amanda M. Foxworth

*Publishing and Editorial for Consumer Dummies*
**Diane Graves Steele,** Vice President and Publisher, Consumer Dummies
**Joyce Pepple,** Acquisitions Director, Consumer Dummies
**Kristin A. Cocks,** Product Development Director, Consumer Dummies
**Michael Spring,** Vice President and Publisher, Travel
**Brice Gosnell,** Associate Publisher, Travel
**Suzanne Jannetta,** Editorial Director, Travel

*Publishing for Technology Dummies*
**Richard Swadley,** Vice President and Executive Group Publisher
**Andy Cummings,** Vice President and Publisher

*Composition Services*
**Gerry Fahey,** Vice President of Production Services
**Debbie Stailey,** Director of Composition Services

◆

The publisher would like to give special thanks to Patrick J. McGovern, without whom this book would not have been possible.

◆

# Contents at a Glance

# Cartoons at a Glance

## By Rich Tennant

page 285

page 5

page 323

page 97

page 209

page 131

**Fax:** 978-546-7747
**E-mail:** richtennant@the5thwave.com
**World Wide Web:** www.the5thwave.com

# Table of Contents

# Introduction

• • • • • • • • • • • • • • • • • • • • • • • • • • • • • • • • • • • • • • • • • • • • •

*W*e all need to go camping more. Life becomes simplified and pure in the wild places of our earth. Among the mountains, rivers, woods, and open spaces, city-bound inhibitions, dot-commonisms, and lifestyle complications slip away like excess baggage. The outdoors plucks at the fiber of instinct and rekindles a familial longing to breathe deeply the fresh pine-scented air and smile at the simple sound of wind whispering through trees.

But too often we head outdoors practically insulated from the natural world by a barrier of technology that was intended only to make our time outdoors safer and more pleasurable. Taken at face value, there is nothing wrong with breathable fabrics, portable ovens and pizza makers, full meals that reconstitute from nothing, backpackable espresso makers, and two-pound tents the size of a small house. Still, amid all the technology available, we must be careful not to lose sight of why we head outside in the first place.

By constantly fighting to protect ourselves from the elements and soften the edges of wilderness, are we in fact losing touch with the wildness we leave the city to find? This book helps you stay in touch with a wilder side and slow down your need-for-speed mentality so that you can find a personal listening point.

I hope that as you thumb through these pages, you find the time to seek the lessons and gifts the wild places of our earth have to offer. I pray that you get to enjoy, as I frequently do, the feel of a spring shower on your face, the sensation of a snowflake on your tongue, and the playful tug of a mountain wind through your hair. After you discover your personal sense of wildness, you will be able to draw inspiration and meaning from it time and again, whether you're standing on a city corner waiting for the traffic light to change or hunching over a campfire watching a sunset's warm rays trace wistful lines up a canyon wall.

## Why You Need This Book

Going camping has never been so easy — or more confusing — than it is now. The product choices available to you are mind-boggling, to say the least. There are literally hundreds of stoves, tents, jackets, shoes, lights, packs, sleeping bags, and more, all made from space-age materials that claim to do marvelous things — short of actually setting up camp for you and serving dinner on a platter.

If you're a novice who's just starting to put together a camping kit, then you can depend on *Camping For Dummies* to cut through all the techno-garble you're likely to hear in stores and online and to point you to the right purchases for your needs and budget. And even if you're the kind of person who has trouble telling north from south (and perhaps left from right on occasion), I can help you to navigate the wilderness — and live to tell about it.

If you're a more experienced outdoor adventurer and already have all the gear you need, more power to you. In that case, you can depend on *Camping For Dummies* for tips and technique advice to help you become the star of any camping trip. No, I can't promise to turn you into a modern-day John Muir or Daniel Boone. I can, however, teach you how to prepare a delicious dinner over coals, anticipate weather changes before a storm hits, repair a broken tent pole, or start a fire with one match (just don't use this book as a fire starter). Throughout the book, I suggest resources that can help you find all the maps, new gear, repair information, guidebooks, and camping reservation assistance you can stomach.

# How to Use This Book

*Do not read this book in one sitting!* If you do, I'll be forced to smack you with a copy of the book, should I run into you at a campground or trailhead. *Camping For Dummies* is designed as a pick-and-choose resource for you. It is *not* the next great American novel. I trust that you will skim, poke, and probe the pages, seeking out the information that interests you and leaving the rest to remain as ink stains on bound paper — at least for now. Thumb through the pages, letting the catchy icons — explained in a bit — garner your interest or the section titles grab your attention. The Table of Contents is very detailed to help you decide what is of the greatest importance to your experience, plans, and needs. A very comprehensive index at the back of the book helps you search for topics by keyword.

# How This Book Is Organized

Here's a part-by-part synopsis of what you can find in each section of the book:

## Part I: Planning Your Escape

Every trip has to start somewhere, and this section is all about beginnings. Here I share resources for finding maps, making camping reservations, and deciding where to go and what to do anywhere in the United States or Canada. I also include information about what you need to pack for almost any kind of camping adventure and how to dress for your outing to make sure that you maximize comfort and minimize suffering. The bonus in Part I, "Wintering, Paddling, Biking," is designed to stretch the imagination of more experienced campers.

## Part II: Getting There Is Half the Fun

Too many trips end as soon as they begin simply because one essential factor is not anticipated and planned for: the trip to the destination. I smooth the path with advice on how to prepare your vehicle so that it gets you where you want to go, how to properly pack all your gear so that Grandma doesn't have to hold the camp stove and straddle the kayak all the way there, and even how to keep the kids (or people who just act like kids) amused while journeying to the campsite. I also include tips for picking a campsite and selecting the best spots for tents, kitchens, and more.

## Part III: Camping Skills, Food, and Fun

Camping is *not* about eating burnt food. In this part, I show you how to plan a menu, prepare a meal, and even clean and serve fresh fish, whether you are cooking over a camp stove or open flames. Not sure of your camping skills? No worries, mate. From coping with wildlife to repairing gear and tying knots, I teach you enough campcraft skills to have you dreaming of living off the land — almost. I also explain how to enjoy a walk through nature without wrecking the wilderness and how to entertain the troops with fun and games that can make every outing a memorable one.

## Part IV: Staying Safe, Staying Found

Going camping isn't much fun if you don't stay safe. In this part, you learn enough navigation skills to see you into the wild and back again — safely. I also show you how to predict weather patterns, which is eminently useful if you're planning a hike or a climb from base camp. And no part on safety would be complete without a first-aid chapter that helps you deal with minor scrapes, bumps, blisters, and bites — as well as more serious injuries.

## Part V: The Part of Tens

Lists are great because they're so easy to scan and glean information from. In this part, you can find lists for my ten favorite camping recipes, ten camping essentials, ten great camping destinations in North America, ten top camping resources, ten low-impact camping rules to live by, and a ten-times-two bonus: Hodgson's 20 Laws of Camping.

## Part VI: Appendixes

Understanding outdoor-speak can be a challenge sometimes, so I compiled a list of camping and outdoor terminology often heard and sometimes used in this book. In this part, you also enter checklist nirvana. Checklists for planning a trip, taking a trip, planning a menu, preparing your vehicle — the only thing I might have forgotten is a checklist of checklists.

# Icons Used in This Book

This icon highlights special suggestions that can help you protect the land and its resources for all to enjoy.

This icon marks words to the wise from my years of experience in the outdoors — sometimes philosophical, sometimes practical, but always useful.

This icon points to routine camping matters to file away for everyday reference.

This icon points out handy tips and tricks that can make your life outdoors more fun — and certainly more comfortable.

This icon draws your attention to health and safety advice — such as "Don't run with sharp sticks, or you'll put someone's eye out."

This icon zeroes in on advice that caters to kids' special interests and needs to help families get the most out of their camping experiences.

# Part I
# Planning Your Escape

The 5th Wave                    By Rich Tennant

"This looks like a good spot to camp. The ground is flat, we're protected by trees, and this is as far as the extension on the VCR stretches from the RV."

## In this part. . .

*E*very trip has to start somewhere, and this section is
all about beginnings. In Chapter 1, I show you how to
obtain maps, make camping reservations, and decide
where to go and what to do anywhere in the United States
or Canada. For a broad discussion on camping gear,
including everything you need for a backpacking outing,
peruse Chapter 2. There, I offer buying guides and discuss
each item of equipment with an eye to making your camping experience more efficient and enjoyable. Of course,
unless you're thinking of camping naked, you probably
want some advice on dressing for outdoor comfort, no
matter what the weather, and you find that and more in
Chapter 3. Chapter 4 is all about gearing up for specialized
trips such as winter camping, bike touring, and paddling.
In that chapter, you find tips for choosing gear and clothing and planning your specialized activity.

# Chapter 1

# What to Do and Where to Go

## In This Chapter

▶ Deciding what to do on your camping trip

▶ Figuring out where to go

▶ Camping with your family and Fido

*E*very camping trip has a beginning and an end. How you remember the end depends a lot on how much planning and preparation go into the beginning.

"How do you know where to . . . ?" and "How do you know how to . . . ?" are questions I get asked all the time. The answers are what this chapter is all about.

First off, let me assure you that camping is a simple pursuit — well, at least it should be. Granted, bureaucracy has added a layer of modern paperwork to the endeavor, but believe me when I tell you that anyone can go camping.

The first thing to pack is common sense. The second is patience. The third is flexibility. And the fourth? Well, the fourth is the wild card — a sense of humor. If you load up on all four, and add a few necessary permits and other trappings of the civilized world, you'll have a grand old time every time no matter the weather or the surprises Mother Nature may choose to unveil.

As you gain more camping experience, the planning becomes easier and easier, this I promise. In fact, sometimes I don't plan at all anymore, letting spontaneity rule the day. Granted, some of my "spontaneous" adventures lead me down roads that are best remembered for their trials and tribulations, but that is to be expected when planning entails simply snatching a pack from the garage and heading outdoors.

But I digress. This is a beginning for you and we'd best begin to plan a successful camping trip from start to finish.

# Determining Your Interests and Needs

Knowing what you want to do is just as important as knowing where you want to go. In fact, determining what you want to do should be the first item on the planning agenda because the answer may very well determine what choices you have in camping destinations. No sense planning a camping trip to the desert if fishing is high on the agenda — no matter how beautiful the spring wildflowers may be.

To make the planning process the most productive, ask yourself the following questions:

- ✔ What activities am I interested in — fishing, hiking, scrambling, climbing, swimming?
- ✔ Am I seeking solitude, exercise, group interaction, or photographic opportunities?
- ✔ How important is seeing wildlife — deer, bear, squirrels, skunks, raccoons?
- ✔ Is studying the stars or viewing vast fields of wildflowers important to me?
- ✔ What is the maximum hiking, paddling, biking, or skiing distance I and the members of my group can handle?
- ✔ How near to the parking area or car do I want to be in case of emergencies?
- ✔ What kind of temperatures and weather can I tolerate — fog, sun, rain, snow?
- ✔ What kind of terrain am I looking for — rolling, flat, mountainous, swampy?
- ✔ Is my group interested in historical events or the historical significance of particular areas such as the Yukon Goldrush, the Donner Party, or the Cumberland Gap?

# Choosing Your Destination

While flexibility and a positive attitude are important in any adventurous endeavor, choosing an appropriate destination for your trip should reign supreme and can go far in minimizing potential pitfalls.

I love the planning stages of a camping outing — books open, notes scribbled, maps spread from wall to wall, dreams gaining inspiration. Spend as much time as you can poring over everything available about particular areas you would like to visit. Magazines, books, park flyers, travel logs, and state or provincial promotional brochures are all excellent resources for initial exploration. For detailed guidebooks about particular destinations, check your local specialty outdoor outfitter's book department. And see Chapter 17, "Ten or So Camping Resources."

In the following sections, I help you figure out what camping destination is right for you.

## Timing is everything

Few of us can simply pick up and take off for the wilds at a moment's notice. Scheduling time to recreate, as distasteful as that sometimes feels, is the norm. That said, it is important to find out when to visit and when not to visit the particular areas you may be considering. If you are seeking solitude, for example, you would be ill advised to plan a camping trip to Yosemite in June or to any park in the Northeast during the peak of fall colors. Likewise, if Death Valley is high on your list, summer is *not* a time to think about visiting — unless you savor temperatures hot enough to melt shoes to rock.

Want to know when the best time is to visit a particular park, wilderness, or campground? Call the park or managing agency for the areas you are planning to visit and ask them. Rangers are a helpful lot and happy to steer you away from overcrowded, overheated, freezing, or otherwise less desirable times to visit.

Another resource for determining the best time to visit is a guidebook. Most guidebook authors will add "best times to visit" notes in their descriptions. Of course, their idea and your idea of a best time to visit may not jibe, but it is a starting place.

Two other factors to consider are the length and difficulty of the drive to and from the chosen site. This may not seem like a major matter, but try sitting in a car for too many hours with children craving to "get there" and you have a recipe for frustration, frayed tempers, and outbursts like, "I hate this — why didn't we just stay home?!" Not an ideal way to begin a family outing to the wilderness.

## Getting some breathing room

Some parks are rarely crowded. Nearly 170 such parks are highlighted in "Lesser Known Areas of the National Park System." For a copy of this useful publication, send a check or money order for $1.50 payable to the Superintendent of Documents, Consumer Information Center, Department 134b, Pueblo, CO 81009.

## Talk to those who know

After you decide on a potential area from reading and researching, try talking to people who have been there. Find out from them what the area is really like. Firsthand experience is invaluable for obtaining specific information about the location of such things as hidden hot springs, the best place to fish, the ideal campsite, seasonal insect populations, bear or other animal precautions, and the difficulty of the terrain.

Where can you find such folks? Try the online community (see Chapter 17 for leads) or, if virtual chat rooms and bulletin boards aren't your game, then strap on your boots and wander over to the local outdoor store. Inside you're likely to find a few staffers who, in addition to looking as though they live outdoors, actually do live outdoors whenever their days off allow. These experts are a great source of "where to" and "how to" information. Also, most specialty stores have bulletin boards — the old kind with cork and thumbtacks — which are used to announce when local hiking, paddling, or camping clubs are meeting and where. Such outing clubs are another fantastic source of firsthand information . . . and perhaps new camping partners.

## Are you sure?

After you select a potential destination, take one final look at the information you've compiled and compare it honestly against your group's physical and emotional abilities. Is the destination feasible, and is it a good choice for maximum fun and safety? If the answer remains "Yes," then your destination selection is locked in and the firm planning begins. If the answer is "No" or "Not sure," then choose something a little less ambitious for this trip. After a few more camping trips, you may find that you're ready for your dream destination.

Many of the National Parks can provide assistance to visitors who have visual, auditory, or other physical limitations. Most have parking lots, restrooms, and other features that are accessible to disabled persons. If accessibility is important to you, however, inquire in advance.

# Beginning the Firm Planning

Your dreams of a great adventure are taking shape, but unless you want to end up like Gilligan, who only intended on a three-hour tour, you need to sweat the details. That means maps, permits, camping reservations, emergency planning, and more. Read on and I'll lead you through the maze.

## Obtaining maps of the area

Once you decide on the destination, you need to obtain detailed information regarding the area if you haven't already. Purchase U.S. Geological Service (USGS) topographic survey maps, National Forest Service maps, trail guidebooks, and other privately produced maps of the area if available. (See Appendix C for a list of resources.) You can't have too much information in this planning stage.

## Making campsite reservations and obtaining permits

The best-laid plans can be tossed to the winds unless you first ensure that you'll have a place to sleep. Most public lands, including National Parks, Forest Service land, Bureau of Land Management (BLM) land, and Canadian Park land require you to obtain a permit before entering. Which permit you need depends on the camping experience you desire. Contact the officials managing the park or public land you want to visit to find out what their rules and regulations are regarding camping and campsite reservations. If you are campground camping, then a simple camping reservation will suffice. (Many public campgrounds offer camping sites on a first-come-first-served basis. However, if you want to guarantee that you'll be able to stay when and where you want, reserve your campsite.)

Anyone entering wilderness or backcountry areas needs a wilderness permit. You can obtain such a permit via reservation or, often, by simply showing up. In the more popular backcountry sites, expect to see people form a line outside the ranger station at dawn to obtain the few permits available each day.

You can visit the National Park Service Campground Reservation Service online at `www.nps.gov/pub_aff/camping.html`. There are 25,700 campsites in 548 campgrounds found at 77 areas of the park system. These campsites can accommodate almost every camping style, from tent camping and recreational vehicle spaces to more primitive backcountry camping. Most parks administer their campgrounds on a first-come-first-served basis. The easiest way to get more specific information is to contact the park directly.

## A few words on roads

From the air, many of our parks and wild lands appear to be etched with roads. In fact, the U.S. National Forest Service has more miles of road than all the paved state and federal highways combined. Add to that all the BLM roads and an infinite number of ranch roads, mining roads, and timber company roads and our country begins to look rather like a tangled mess of twine that a cat has scattered all over the living room floor.

## Make the Visitor Center your first stop

Try to make the Visitor Center your first stop at any park. There you can find information on attractions, facilities, and activities, such as scenic drives, nature trails, and historic tours. Descriptive literature and exhibits will acquaint you with the geology, history, and plant and animal life of the area. The park staff will answer questions about accommodations, services, and accessibility of attractions.

If your trip takes you onto the many unimproved and wilder roads that criss-cross the land in the U.S. and Canada, treat all official and unofficial terminology on maps — even recent ones — such as "improved," "graded," "primitive," "graveled," and so on, with a healthy dose of skepticism. While the road that leads into the great backcountry campground you heard about may very well have earned an "improved" designation several months ago, recent storms may have turned it into a rutted, soupy, quagmire capable of eating trucks, RVs and any other vehicle you choose to place on the menu.

I always recommend checking in with the locals before heading off down a dirt road, improved or not. They travel, hunt, camp, and use the roads frequently and will be able to offer you accurate and up-to-date information.

Many National Park Service areas charge entrance fees. If your trip will take you to several parks, you may save money buying an entrance fee passport. Senior citizens are eligible for a discounted lifetime pass, and disabled persons qualify for free passes. All such passports are available at any park that charges an entrance fee.

## *Plotting your route carefully*

After you make the arrangements for your camping trip, plot your route carefully on the maps (obviously, if you're only car-camping in park campgrounds, this is not necessary). Many of the USGS topographic maps were last surveyed in the early to late 1950s, and revisions and updates (often visually checked only by aerial survey) are slow in coming. Transcribing detailed information regarding trails, roads, and other man-made landmarks from Forest Service maps, private maps, and guidebooks to the topographic maps is most helpful. Most private maps available for sale — such as National Geographic's Trails Illustrated maps — are reproductions of the USGS maps with all the necessary trail and hiking data updated and transcribed for you. See Appendix C for a list of map resources.

---

## National Park area camping facts to remember

The National Park system provides campsites to hundreds of thousands of people every month. Here are some pointers on using the system.

- Campsite use fees vary.

- Some parks offer year-round camping, while others have specific dates of operation.

- Backcountry camping requires a permit.

- You are allowed to camp only in designated areas.

- Developed area campsites have drinking water, toilets, fire containment devices, tables, refuse containers, and limited parking spaces. Generally, utility hookups are not available.

- Gathering of firewood is generally restricted, except in certain areas (check with a park ranger). In some parks, the use of campfires may be restricted to protect air quality or due to extreme wildfire danger.

- In parks where bears are present, the superintendent may designate areas where food must be stored in a specified manner to prevent its loss or to avoid an encounter with a potentially dangerous wild animal.

- Maximum lengths for trailers, campers, and motorhomes vary from park to park. The average maximum length permitted is 27 feet, but some parks can accommodate vehicles up to 40 feet in length. There are no electrical or water hookups at campsites. Some parks may have dump stations. Find out your park's specific maximum length so you won't be disappointed when you arrive.

## *Planning for emergencies*

Always have an emergency plan in place. You never know when a real need or emergency will arise, so it's best to be prepared. Here's a quick checklist:

- Know where the nearest hospital emergency room is in relation to the place you will be exploring.

- Always tell someone responsible where you are going camping, and be sure to notify that person when you return so that she or he doesn't worry (or notify authorities to begin an unnecessary search).

- Learn basic first aid and CPR. Being in an emergency and having no idea how to proceed or what to do is a helpless feeling. The Red Cross is a good place to look for instruction in first aid.

Check out Chapter 13 for more detailed health and safety information.

Involve your children in every plan that you make if they are camping with you. Kids are never too young to hear how to take care of themselves.

# Planning to Camp with Your Family

Camping with children is an outstanding way to share a love for the outdoors without breaking the budget. While family backpacking or camping does take a great deal of planning and loads of patience, it is a rewarding activity for both you and your children. If you have gone camping before, you will quickly realize that to go camping with children requires added responsibility and alertness on a parent's part. Common sense and good judgment are the rule. If you have never been camping before, what are you waiting for? — you're missing all the fun! Not surprisingly, the crucial point to a successful camping trip with parents and children is often rooted in their first experiences outdoors together. In this section, I highlight some things to consider when planning an outdoor adventure with your family.

## Deciding when your child is old enough to go camping

The question most often posed to me is, "When is my child old enough to begin hiking and camping?" The answer depends on your child. No two personalities are the same; no two children the same. What may work for my family may not work for yours.

The following guidelines can help you decide when and where to introduce your child to the great outdoors, but please remember that the only firm guide is each child's particular personality and physical condition. Whatever the activity, you must let her pace herself.

- **Infant:** Pediatricians recommend that parents wait until the child is 5 months old before venturing out. This is when a child can easily sit up and support his own weight and has fallen into a fairly regular sleep pattern. Use a sturdy child carrier that is safe and secure for the child and comfortable for you.

- **Toddler:** Between the ages of 2 and 4, children are still getting used to the idea of being on two points of balance and not four. Short hikes between half a mile and 2 miles are ideal as long as the terrain is flat and secure to walk on. Take regular walks in a neighborhood park to get a feel for your child's attention span. Expect a focused attention span of around 10 minutes for younger children and up to 30 minutes for older children.

✔ **Ages 5-9:** Longer hikes at an easy pace over easy terrain are now possible. Children are beginning to develop more physical and mental durability. This is an ideal age to begin allowing your child to become involved in most aspects of the trip, from planning and packing to helping lead. The older your child is in this age group, the more likely moderate goal setting will be effective. Just make sure that the goals are shared and not an unrealistic attempt on the parent's part to "motivate" the child up an impossible hill or over a 10-mile endurance test.

✔ **Ages 10-13:** Children are becoming increasingly conditioned physically. Emotionally, they are more likely to be able to handle moderately challenging situations, but they are also more likely to question the worth of anything extremely difficult. Hikes up to 10 miles are possible as long as the terrain is not too hilly or mountainous. Children in this age group thrive on being the leader — diplomatic and judicious support from parents is key. Menu planning, route finding, cooking, and camp setup are reasonable tasks to assign to kids at this age, but be careful that they do not take on too much and begin to feel like all they are doing is working.

✔ **Ages 14-18:** Distances up to 12 miles become reasonable in this age group (although personally I prefer to hike no more than 8 miles myself). Terrain choices and goal setting can become more challenging, but the axiom remains the same: Any choice must be a group choice, or the parent risks making the children feel dragged along.

Children are encountering growth spurts during this period and are definitely vulnerable to stress and overuse injuries. Use caution and listen to your children — they may need to back off a hike.

## *Beginning with a day-trip together*

No matter how old your children are or how much or how little you have experienced the outdoors yourself, if anyone in your family has yet to spend his first minute in the great outdoors, then you would be wise to proceed slowly. The foundation of an outdoor adventure experience must be laid carefully. Plan some simple day trips to local parks and wilderness preserves. Just walking, skiing, biking, or wandering outdoors, drinking from a canteen, carrying a day pack, wearing hiking or ski boots, or eating trail food will all be new to your family.

On your first day-trip, you have much to do and consider. Do your family members have the right clothes? How do their shoes and packs fit? Did everyone bring plenty of water? How about snacks and a trail lunch? Does everyone have rain gear — just in case? Who is carrying the first-aid kit? Who knows how to use the first-aid kit? Is the hike, ski, or bike trip you have selected well suited to all the participants? How is the walking, skiing, or biking pace?

## Experience the outdoors as a child

Be prepared to get down and dirty with your children. Experience the outdoors with them — don't just watch them. I wince when I see parents scolding their children for getting up close and personal with a mud puddle, dirt, a bug, or more. Become childlike in your pursuit of the outdoors and your children will appreciate even more the time you spend together in the wilds. This is not to say that you have to get filthy to appreciate being in the outdoors. However, a little dirt should not hold you back — whether you're a grown-up or a child.

Even though you must assume leadership because you are the parent, it is important to remember that this is supposed to be fun and relaxing for everyone — including you. Don't be the only one running around frantically trying to make sure that everything is getting done. Assign responsibilities. Put someone in charge of the first-aid kit — preferably an older child or another parent. Designate a "cook," even though this will be a sack lunch, to plan and pack the meal. Get everyone involved in checking gear and making sure the daypacks are equally loaded, with no one carrying too much or too little.

Above all, listen to your family. Set the pace of the hike to the slowest member (often, although not always, that will be the youngest member) of your hiking team. This is not to embarrass that person but to ensure that the pace is appropriate and nobody gets pushed beyond her limits. When selecting this member, diplomacy is crucial. Don't give playmates an invitation to tease if a weakness is suspected. Whatever reason you give, pick a positive one.

## Choosing a destination for your first campout

Choosing a destination is perhaps the most difficult task of all. Everyone has a favorite memory, most spectacular view, and most unbelievable campsite. But what is incredible to one person may not be worth the effort to another. This is especially true with children. Parents quickly learn that fantastic views are not enough to stimulate children into oohs and aahs. Children seem to prefer lakes to splash in, streams to wade through, meadows to romp around, trees to climb up, hills to roll down, easy rocks to scramble on, mud to play in, and someone to play with.

## Bring a friend along

Children want and need peers with them. I encourage you to plan on bringing a close family playmate or include another family with children to enjoy the outdoors with. Having friends along makes things much more fun and will usually make the hike that much smoother for you — you won't have to plan so much entertainment.

## Deciding how far to hike

On a hiking trip, deciding how far and how fast often becomes a guessing game contingent upon the mood of the hikers, the weather, the difficulty of the terrain, and the interest of the terrain. You really can't do much about the hikers' moods, short of keeping an excellent sense of humor. You also can't do much about the weather except to be prepared for anything with the appropriate clothing and gear. However, you can plan and control the difficulty of terrain as well as the visual interest of the terrain to be traveled through.

Plan easy hikes, especially for those group members who may have their doubts about whether hiking is really going to be fun. Under most circumstances, I recommend planning a hike with no more than 500 feet elevation gain and loss and a distance of less than five miles. To virtually guarantee that everyone will have a wonderful time, the hike itself and not just the destination must be memorable. Huffing, puffing, and wheezing are memorable — but labored breathing is not the kind of memory most children are anxious for. Take frequent rest breaks, eat plenty of snacks, splash through a stream or two, and play entertaining games — anything to have fun.

## Observing your family members' moods

Always have a plan in place that will allow you to adapt the destination or length of the trip should anyone in your family group begin to grumble, mope, mumble, and whine because he is too tired to go on. If the reasons are right, no one will regret a decision to turn around and shorten a trip. The mountain or lake will always be there for another try. Your family and children may not be persuaded to go again if the last outing was so miserable that they never want to risk a repeat. Not surprisingly, most of the camping horror stories I hear from adults and children revolve around someone dragging them uphill, both ways, through deep snow and over ice-covered peaks in search of "a really cool place."

A sense of humor and patience are musts. Without them, your efforts to share the outdoors with your children will be seriously hampered. Laughter, fun and games, silly pranks, and unexpected occurrences are part of being outdoors with children. Go with the flow and enjoy every moment together. If you can learn to laugh off a child who is covered with mud and expecting a ride home in the family car, then you are ready to proceed as an outdoor leader. Good luck!

# And the survey says . . .

Over the years of being a parent, a guide, an outdoor education instructor, and a camp counselor, I have asked children many questions to find out what they like and don't like about camping. I also asked my daughter, Nikki, to poll her friends at summer camp over the years about their likes and dislikes. While not a statistically official poll, I think you'll find the responses enlightening and useful in planning your next family camping escape.

**The best things about camping are:**

- The food tastes better than the food at home.
- I don't have to worry about staying clean.
- I get to stay up late.
- I get to sleep under the stars.
- I like breathing the fresh air.
- The outdoors is peaceful.
- I get to see wildlife.
- Camping is never boring.

**The worst things about camping are:**

- Mosquitoes
- Ticks
- Noisy, drunk people
- Bears and trash
- Nagging parents

- Park ranger trucks kicking up dust
- Rain
- Burnt food
- Sleeping in the cold
- Having to go to the bathroom in the dark and cold by yourself

**Adults drive kids nuts when they do the following:**

- Go to the next camp to ask for toilet paper
- Spray bug repellent all over us
- Cover us with goopy sunscreen that just collects dirt
- Cram the whole family into one tent to save money
- Tell us what to bring as if we were 2-year-olds
- Take surprise photographs
- Make us eat gross camping food
- Hike too fast
- Hike too far
- Get too enthusiastic
- Spend forever talking to people along the trail and in camp so you never get to where you are going on time

# Taking Fido Along

Taking your dog camping is a great way for the two of you to spend some quality time together. Not only does your favorite pet get a great opportunity to enjoy a controlled romp and play outdoors, but you will appreciate the time, too — it beats laps around the block on a leash any day.

Not every park welcomes dogs, however, and even in those that do, leash laws are often enforced — thankfully — restraining you and your dog's wandering freedom.

One of the chief reasons parks restrict dogs is that dogs think of parks as simply big backyards, full of animals to chase and new sounds to bark at. Another reason is that dogs can transmit diseases to wild animals such as nesting birds or marine mammals. Also, the scents dogs leave behind can disrupt the behavior of the native animals which parks want to protect.

In parks where Fido is allowed to romp unrestrained (all parks require dogs to be leashed within parking, picnic, and camping areas), certain points of etiquette and safety must be considered:

✔ **Not all dogs are good hikers.** Just like humans, dogs must be conditioned to the trail. Don't expect your pet to get up and hike easily over hill and dale with you if the backyard has been the extent of his exploration thus far. Remember that your dog will always try to keep up with you even if he is overheating or in physical pain.

✔ **Be sure that your dog's vaccinations are up to date.** Rabies, parvo, heartworm, and more await your unprotected friend. Consult your veterinarian.

✔ **A good ID tag hanging from your pet's collar is a must in case he manages to get lost.** Only because of an ID tag, a good friend of mine had his dog returned several days after the two were separated in the woods. The tag should have your name, the dog's name, and your phone number with area code engraved on it.

✔ **Always clean up after your dog.** Beyond the obvious fact that no one likes to step in poop, the smell drives off wild animals, creates an urban experience for whoever views it, and is one of the problems that causes park administrations to crack down on dog privileges. If your dog brought it in, you carry it out — no exceptions.

✔ **Do not let your dog chase wildlife.** Reports of dogs chasing squirrels, deer, or other wildlife is reason enough for park officials to close a park to dog use.

✔ **Dogs must yield to all trail users.** Always leash up when encountering horses, cattle, bicyclists, and other trail users. Obeying any leash law is critical, because if citations stack up, the various boards and administrations may close parks to dogs.

✔ **Carry water for both yourself and your dog — especially in the summer.** Dogs do not tolerate heat as well as humans do.

✔ **Carry a first-aid kit for both yourself and your dog.** Your veterinarian can offer tips for treating common injuries.

✔ **Dogs will pass poison oak, ivy, and sumac to you if they manage to run through it or roll in it.** If your dog encounters one of the poisonous plant triumvirate — ivy, oak, or sumac — do not cuddle or pet her until you clean her. Immediately wash her with warm water and dog shampoo. If you forgot to bring soap, steer clear of your mutt until you get home.

✔ **Check your dog for ticks periodically.** If you find one, grasp it close to the head with tweezers and pull out firmly. Check to make sure that you have not left the head behind. If you have, watch the area closely to ensure that it does not get infected. If infection sets in, head to the vet. Using a good flea and tick spray as well as a flea and tick collar will help to prevent ticks.

# Is your dog welcome?

In general, you can expect agencies to have the following dog regulations:

✔ **All Parks:** Seeing-eye dogs and dogs assisting those with disabilities are allowed in all public places and in all public buildings.

✔ **National Parks:** No dogs are allowed except those on leashes within campgrounds.

✔ **National Forests:** Dogs are allowed, but consult ranger stations governing each National Forest area for specific guidelines.

✔ **Bureau of Land Management:** Dogs are allowed, but consult each district for specific regulations governing each management area.

✔ **State Parks:** No dogs are allowed except those on leashes within campgrounds, with a few exceptions.

# Chapter 2

# Outdoor Gear and Gadgets

- - - - - - - - - - - - - - - - - - - - - - - - - - - - - - - -

*In This Chapter*

▶ Selecting tents, sleeping bags, and back packs

▶ Taking care of your sleeping bag

▶ Loading a pack and hoisting it aboard

▶ Assembling a camper's kitchen

▶ Shedding light on the whole scene

- - - - - - - - - - - - - - - - - - - - - - - - - - - - - - - -

*B*efore heading out on any camping adventure, you need to equip your-self. Equipping yourself means selecting among many choices, poten-tially a tough task. To make it easier for you, I cover some basic considerations and guidelines in this chapter.

You can begin by researching what equipment is available for the type of trip you have in mind. Talk to friends about what they like and where they like to shop. Check out magazines that evaluate camping gear such as *Backpacker*, *Canoe & Kayak*, or *Outside*. Head to your local specialty outdoor store and talk to a salesperson about your needs.

After you collect and evaluate enough product information, you will be able to narrow your choices and make fairly educated decisions about buying or borrowing the gear you need. Many outdoor specialty stores rent sleeping bags, tents, backpacks, stoves, and even child carriers. Some also rent boots, although I would discourage renting footwear — no two feet are quite the same, and "walking in someone else's shoes" implies achy feet. The advice I give you within these pages is current and will not be outdated soon. However, I also recommend that if you have access to the Web you log onto www.adventurenetwork.com for the most up-to-date equipment buying sug-gestions, advice, and helpful hints. You should also check out www.GearTrends .com for the latest gear updates directly from the manufacturers.

# Tenting Tonight!

Any person's camping domicile had better be a secure and roomy place to spend the night, or that individual will be one very grumpy camper indeed. So, all the time you invest in selecting the right camp shelter and the money you pay for it will be time and money well spent.

A good shelter must be able to slip the wind without caving in, shed the rain without leaking, offer decent ventilation so you don't feel as if you are sleeping in a steamy locker room, and be relatively easy to set up and take down.

Don't take the stated tent capacity too seriously. The tentmaker may say that the tent sleeps three, but most times that's really pushing the definition of comfortable sleeping in my experience. Tents for mobile camping use — backpacking, cycling, paddling, adventure travel — should be as light and compact as possible. On the other hand, if your objective is to shelter, for example, four or more adults at a campground, opt for the biggest tent money can buy — short of purchasing a big top.

Buy the best camping gear your budget can afford. Remember that you can't return something when you're in the middle of the wilderness.

## Family shelter

If any of the adults in your tribe like to camp without the kids along on some occasions, you may have to decide between buying two tents or one that is sometimes too small or too large. I solved this dilemma by buying a relatively roomy two-person tent, which we used under slightly cramped conditions until daughter Nikki reached age 4. I then added a large nylon tarp to our gear — it didn't add much weight to my backpack. The tarp provided an "extra room" for me (I was protected even in the worst rain) while my wife and daughter slept in the tent. The tarp also provided an extra benefit — a place for us to sit and cook in wet weather.

After Nicole turned 8 and began bringing a friend along for the fun, I opted for another lightweight two-person tent. Nicole and company slept under one roof and my wife and I under another — sometimes several hundred yards apart depending on how brave Nikki was feeling on a given evening. Now that my daughter is 16, she and I head out on adventures, just the two of us, and we're back to a two-person tent or — when we're thinking very lightweight and have no fear of mosquitoes — a tarp.

# A tent buying guide

Buying a tent is like buying a home — you have to decide what you must have and what you are willing to give up.

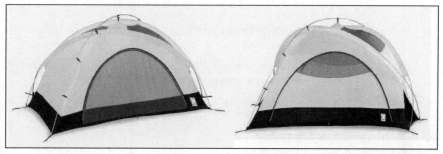

**Figure 2-1:**
Tents for backpacking, car camping.

*Courtesy of Sierra Designs*

## Basic features

Every tent should have basic features (see Figure 2-1) to make your life easier:

- Collapsible tent poles of aluminum, high-strength aluminum, carbon fiber, or tubular fiberglass.

- Freestanding structure that sets up easily on sand, rocks, snow, or anywhere it is difficult to get a stake into the ground. You still need to stake a tent down, however, to avoid turning it into a very expensive, disposable kite.

- Storage pockets inside for organizing.

- Nylon or polyester fabric for durability and lightest weight.

- One-piece floors to increase waterproofness.

- Steep walls to increase the useable interior space, shed precipitation better, and help vent out humidity.

- Waterproof rain fly that clips to poles and requires only minimal additional stakes.

- Mesh windows and doors with zippered closures for battening down the hatches when things get blustery and damp.

- Same-length poles or color-coded poles (each color corresponds to a specific pole sleeve on the tent). This feature makes it easier to set up the tent in less-than-ideal conditions.

- Tent body of yellow, white, or beige to let the most light in.

- Gear loops inside the tent to hang flashlights and other stuff.

- Beefy nylon webbing stake loops at each pole end on the tent body.

Buy a tent with a vestibule. It's the mudroom of the tent and works great for keeping boots and socks dry when the weather turns wet — which you know will happen at some point.

### Summer tent

A summer tent is ideal if you camp only in hot climates.

- ✔ Generous amounts of mesh in the tent body — the breezier the tent, the better it ventilates.
- ✔ Rain fly that stops several inches above the ground, allowing for maximum protection combined with maximum ventilation.
- ✔ Two-pole construction for weight savings.

### Three-season tent

This tent is useful to camp in everything from light snow to a hot climate.

- ✔ Three-pole, high-strength aluminum construction to stand up to strong winds and heavy rains.
- ✔ Full-coverage rain fly that extends to the ground.
- ✔ Sturdy guy-out points sewn to the rain fly for tying down the tent should things get downright blustery.
- ✔ Design that allows setup of the rain fly by itself for the ultimate in weight savings and go-light travel.
- ✔ Inside gear loft that attaches to roof for additional storage.
- ✔ Large vestibule, adding room for wet boots and damp dogs.
- ✔ Two doors or extra-large door, providing easier entrance and egress without risking stepping on your partner's face.
- ✔ Skylight window in the rain fly for additional light.

### All-season tent

This type of tent is commonly called a convertible tent because it works in all seasons, but isn't intended for hard-core winter mountaineering.

- ✔ Skylight window in the rain fly for additional light.
- ✔ Four high-grade aluminum poles, freestanding construction. One-pole-removable option to conserve weight.
- ✔ Sturdy guy-out points sewn to the rain fly for tying down the tent should the wind blow up.
- ✔ Design that allows setup of the rain fly by itself for the ultimate in weight savings and go-light travel.

✔ Removable vestibules for additional weight savings.

✔ Generous mesh with zip-out panels for added ventilation when you need it or full closure when you require maximum protection.

### Winter camping/mountaineering tent

The mountaineering tent is the bomb shelter of the portable domicile world. You should use it for harsh conditions only.

✔ Four to five high-grade aluminum poles, freestanding construction.

✔ Full-coverage rain fly.

✔ Steep sidewalls to shed wind and snow.

✔ Two doors on opposite ends or sides of the tent with vestibules for maximum gear storage and entrance or egress versatility in the face of anything Mother Nature tosses your way.

✔ Vestibules that have their own poles for support.

✔ Sturdy guy-out points sewn to the rain fly for tying down the tent in high winds.

✔ Rain fly that pitches separately from tent so you can use it as a roof for a modified snow cave shelter to save weight and space.

### Single-wall tent

When you purchase a single-wall tent, it's best to stick with name brands that include Bibler, Marmot, Integral Designs, and Dana Design.

✔ High/low ventilation ports for maximum flow-through of air even when the hatches are battened down.

✔ Vertical sidewalls for maximum interior space and shedding precipitation.

✔ Freestanding design.

✔ Sturdy guy-out points sewn to the tent body for tying down the tent for those blustery winds.

### Size does matter

Just because a manufacturer says a tent will sleep three doesn't make it so. How much space you require inside a tent is a personal thing that needs to take into account how tall you are, how wide you are, how much "toss and turn" room you need, and how much extra sitting-up room you desire. I've seen "two-person" tents that won't even accommodate two full-sized ThermaRest sleeping pads side by side without overlapping. Unless you particularly enjoy sleeping two stacked into a space the size of a twin mattress, opt for a few more inches in roominess.

### *The add-on purchase*

You should add a ground cloth to your purchase. Using nothing more than clear polyethylene sheeting available at most hardware stores by the roll, you can make a trim-to-fit ground cloth that is slightly smaller than the footprint of your tent's floor. The tough plastic subfloor will save your harder-to-replace tent floor from the wear and tear of earth and grit abrasion.

When purchasing a tent, buy quality. Blown stitches, waterproof coatings that leak like a sieve, cheap fiberglass poles, and torn fabric are all candidates for the nightmare weekend. Be sure that the tent is roomy enough that you don't feel like the filling in a nylon burrito, but not so roomy that you need porters to carry it. My three-person tent and large tarp for group camping have a combined weight of nine pounds.

# The Ins and Outs of Sleeping Bags

The key choice in sleeping bags (see Figure 2-2) is between synthetic fill or down. Down is lighter in terms of a weight-to-warmth ratio. Down is also more compact. However, only synthetic fills like PolarGuard 3D, Lite Loft, Hollofil, or Quallofil will maintain loft and warmth even when wet. Down turns into a heavy, soggy, cold mess that takes forever to dry out. I recommend synthetic fill for children at all times. I use a down sleeping bag because of the size and weight, but I am very careful to keep it protected from the elements — even to the point of storing it in a waterproof stuff sack.

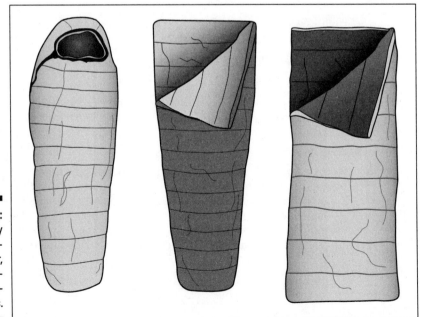

**Figure 2-2:**
Mummy (left), semi-rectangular, and rectangular sleeping bags.

# The truth about temperature ratings

A number of summers ago, in Alaska, I spent a night or two testing a synthetic sleeping bag rated to 20 degrees. Granted, it was raining, although the bag stayed dry. Sure, I was tired from a 16-hour trek in chilly conditions. But in 35-degree night air, feeling chilled inside the bag while wearing dry Thermax underwear, dry socks, and a hat was not my idea of accurate temperature rating. Understand — I can regularly slumber comfortably at 10 degrees in a 20-degree-rated down bag. What's up with temperature ratings?

First the facts. It is not uncommon for users judging a minimum comfort limit to differ by 20 degrees when testing an identical sleeping bag. I know of at least one case in which two users judged the same sleeping bag more than 30 degrees apart. Even without the variables of environmental factors such as clothing worn, food eaten, pads used, body size, fitness, and so on, the perception of "comfort" varies wildly.

Use temperature ratings as a guide only. If you tend to sleep colder at night, piling on the blankets even in warm temperatures , then you will likely need to find a bag rated 10 to 20 degrees warmer than the most extreme temperatures you expect to encounter. If you sleep warm at night, you will most likely find the temperature ratings on a bag to be adequate. Be sure to add a very good sleeping pad to your purchase, and never, ever, sleep in the same clothing you spent the day in — that is a surefire way to sleep cold.

# A sleeping bag buyer's guide

If you're desperately seeking the one ideal sleeping bag that will meet all of your outdoor needs, forget it! There isn't such a beast. However, there is a bag out there that will keep you snug and happy through most of your adventuring dreams — a three-season mummy with a temperature/comfort rating of around 10 to 20 degrees Fahrenheit. A good three-season bag should see you through the odd frosty evening in late October, provide a snug cocoon during a late spring dusting of snow in April, and not overheat you during a warm night in July. If your inclination is more to winter camping, then opt for a bag rated to below 0 degrees Fahrenheit. Winter mountaineering requires temperature ratings of minus 15 to minus 40 degrees Fahrenheit. If all you do is camp in the summer when the sun is shining and the birds are singing, you will do just as well with a bag rated to plus 35 or 40 degrees Fahrenheit.

Mummy-shaped bags are more efficient at keeping the body warm. However, some people find them constricting. Don't be afraid to ask the salesperson to lay out the bags you are considering so that you can climb into them. Also, be sure that if you are buying bags to zip together, the zippers are compatible and you purchase a right and left zipper. The other choices of shape are semi-rectangular and rectangular. Most bags are constructed of nylon, polyester, or nylon blends inside and out.

Sleeping bags with cotton insides, quilted rectangular shapes, and Pokémon or other entertaining figures printed on them are not recommended for backpacking or remotely serious outdoor use.

When you buy any sleeping bag, take the time to "kick the tires." Climb inside each one, roll around, zip it up, stuff it, unstuff it, compare lofts, and then choose the one that seems to best meet your needs for space, warmth, and features.

### General features all sleeping bags need

All sleeping bags need some of the same general features, which are in the following list:

- A lining of taffeta or other softer non-cotton material is more comfy, warms quickly, and breathes supremely.

- A two-way zipper offers more ventilation and flexibility options. Be sure to buy a right- or a left-side zipper that is compatible with the other bag if you desire companionship.

- You want a differential cut — the inner lining is sewn smaller than the outer shell — which allows insulation to loft to its maximum. If there is more loft, there is more warmth.

- An insulated draft collar helps to seal in the warmth and keep out the cold around your neck and shoulders.

- Hook and loop tabs cover the zipper toggle by the hood, preventing unplanned unzipperings whilst you slumber.

- A multisectioned or shaped hood cups the head naturally.

- Ample draft tube that hangs from the top of the bag and covers the zipper to seal out cold air.

- You want man-made fibers or down for insulation. Down is lighter and more durable. Synthetic fills will fare best when the bag gets wet.

- A windproof and water-resistant outer shell. DryLoft is my favorite and the most downproof.

- Semirectangular cut for sleepers who toss and turn. Mummy-style bag for sleepers who manage to stay put.

- Dark colored lining. This absorbs heat better and the sun's rays most efficiently should you need to dry out your bed.

- Highly desirable option: a fleece-lined stuff sack. Turn it inside out for a comfy pillow when stuffed with a parka or your extra clothes.

### Points to consider when comparing sleeping bags

- Look at the foot section, hood area, and draft tube. How are they designed? Are there any obvious cold spots? How do they compare with the other bags? The draft tube runs the length of a sleeping bag's zipper and is a small tube filled with insulation that is designed to block air movement through the zipper. The tube should cover the zipper completely on the inside. An exposed zipper is an obvious cold spot. As for other cold spots, stay alert for areas where the insulation feels thinner or clumped — a sign the insulation quality is not very good.

- How much insulation is in the bag? Consider that physically larger bags require more insulation to equal the insulating properties of smaller or narrower-cut bags.

- Concerning down bags, do the compartments feel firm? That's a good sign because firm compartments prevent cold spots from forming — by minimizing down shift. Be wary of bags with compartments that feel soft and fluid, permitting down to move around the tube and create cold spots. The only exception to this test is a bag designed for the user to deliberately shift down from top to bottom to adjust for temperature fluctuations.

### Bags for cold nights

Sleeping bag designers generally agree that a cold weather bag must have the following features to keep the occupant really warm: zipper draft tubes and shoulder collars, hoods that cup the head and insulate without being claustrophobic, and a temperature rating of 0 Fahrenheit or below (in the winter it is far better to err on the side of warmth).

What insulation do designers prefer? Believe it or not, the response was virtually unanimous: Down, with a 650-power fill rating or above, is best for weight-to-warmth ratio and for longevity. The fill power of down indicates the amount of actual downy feather and quill. The lower the fill number, the more quill and less feather. The higher the number, the less quill and more feather. Down would be the perfect insulation if it retained its loft when wet. Synthetics are best if you are worried about moisture compromising the insulation.

How big should a winter bag be? Buy it long. Most mountaineers with whom I have spoken recommend against regular-sized bags and opt for bags that offer at least an extra 8 to 10 inches of space at the foot after you are nestled comfortably inside. That's so there will be adequate space to store cameras, water, boots, and such items that you don't want to freeze for whatever reason. In addition, bags with a wider cut can offer more warmth because they give you room to add clothing without constricting the bag.

### *Bag systems*

Bag systems — bags with several layers you can add or pull off — have become more visible in the marketplace, but some folks do wonder whether systems are a compromise. After all, isn't a specific bag for a specific temperature a far better idea?

While I don't deny that bag systems are a compromise, for many campers this choice may be an intelligent compromise. Sure, a specific bag that addresses a specific use is better than a system approach. After all, a system will generally weigh more and be more bulky than a single-purpose bag. But not everyone can afford the extra bags that may be needed for a specific adventure. I have many different bags myself (most down, some synthetic), and I could probably argue the case that I need a couple more.

For many campers, my multiple-bag approach may not be viable, which is why some manufacturers have created the bag system. A bag system is essentially an upgrade program allowing you to purchase the bag you want initially, and then if you decide you want to warm it up a bit, you can purchase an upgrade and zip it in, adding 20 degrees.

## *Care and feeding of your sleeping bag*

There comes a time when every sleeping bag, down or synthetic, needs cleaning. Accumulated body oils, trail dust, and grime all serve to decrease the effectiveness of a bag's insulation and increase the effective range of obnoxious aromas. You have two washing choices and one drying method.

- ✔ **Machine wash.** Wash the bag in a front-loading machine. Wash warm, rinse cold. For down bags, use a mild soap or special down soap (available at outdoor stores). For synthetic bags, use a mild detergent or special synthetic cleaning product such as Nikwax Tech Wash. Use the minimum amount of cleaning agent. I recommend that you scrub the head and foot section before you wash the entire bag. Get all the soap or detergent out of the bag by using at least two rinse cycles.

- ✔ **Bathtub hand-wash method.** Wash the bag in warm water in your bathtub using Nikwax Tech Wash. Knead water through the bag thoroughly. I recommend scrubbing the head and foot before doing the whole bag. After you have determined the bag is clean (don't expect to remove stains from the shell and never use a stain remover), drain the tub. While the water is draining, press the soapy water out of the bag with your hands. Do not lift the bag and do not wring it. Rinse thoroughly, making sure all of the cleaning agent is out of the bag. Refill the bathtub with clean, cold water at least three or four times to be sure you have adequately rinsed out all the detergent. You must get all the soap out of the down bag; otherwise the down will mat when it dries.

✔ **Drying.** After you complete the final rinse, gently roll the bag up to press out as much water as possible. Do not wring the bag! Carefully place the wet bag into either a large pillowcase or a plastic clothesbasket. If you try to lift a bag without support, you risk tearing the baffles and ruining the bag. Grab several dollars worth of quarters and head to the nearest self-service laundry. Tumble dry in a large commercial dryer on medium-low heat. The dryer must be large enough for the bag to flop freely around. Be patient and dry slowly and thoroughly. Toss in several terry cloth towels and two tennis balls while the bag is drying. The terry cloth will minimize static electricity and speed the drying process while the tennis balls help to fluff up the fill. Plan on waiting two to four hours for your bag to dry. Bring a good book and a lot of quarters.

If you haven't paid close attention to the list on how to wash your sleeping bag, let me repeat, because this is important to the integrity of your sleeping bag. Here is a list of the big don'ts in bag washing:

✔ *Don't* use a top-loading washing machine.

✔ *Don't* use strong soap or detergent.

✔ *Don't* use your home dryer.

✔ *Don't* attempt to lift your bag from one end when wet (lift the entire bag all at once).

✔ *Don't* hang it to dry in the sun (the ultraviolet rays will damage the nylon).

✔ *Don't ever* dry clean your synthetic fill bag. Dry cleaning will irreversibly damage the fill.

## *Making sure your bag purchase lasts for years*

Want to extend the useable life of your sleeping bag? The following are a few tips to help you:

✔ **Always stuff your sleeping bag, never roll it.** Stuffing is actually easier on the fabric and fill.

✔ **Be gentle with your sleeping bag when removing it from the stuff sack; never yank it.**

✔ **Store your bag uncompressed in a large, breathable storage sack — a king-sized pillowcase works well.** Hanging it or storing the bag flat also works.

✔ **Wear a T-shirt, shorts, and socks to bed.** The clothing will act like a sheet and protect the inside of your bag from damaging sweat and body oils.

> ✔ Never lay your bag directly on the dirt; use a ground cloth.
>
> ✔ Air out and fluff your bag after each use and never leave it compressed for long.

### *Bivy sacks*

Bivouac sacks — "outer garments" for sleeping bags — offer a compromise shelter for the minimalist adventurer or an additional line of protection for the winter traveler who wishes to ensure his or her sleeping bag stays dry. In addition to offering protection from the elements, a bivy can extend the temperature rating of a bag by up to 5 degrees.

Bivies are an important component in the sleeping bag system because no matter what material the sleeping bag shell is made of, a sleeping bag is not an outer garment, but a Gore-Tex bivy sack is, functioning at times like a weatherproof tent for the individual mountaineer.

Note that a bivy is not a foolproof piece of gear. The user and the user's metabolism are responsible for how a bivy performs, often judged by how well the bivy manages moisture and by how well water vapor is pumped through the waterproof/breathable membrane. Campers who sleep "wet" and churn out perspiration may find that they overload the membrane and, in cold climates, soak their bags quickly. In a very cold setting, sweat production can lead to ice buildup inside a bag, a potentially dangerous combination.

*Vapor barrier liners (VBLs)* can help to prevent this buildup of moisture, but VBLs come with their own guidelines and challenges. For one, sleeping in a VBL is akin to napping inside a giant plastic baggie and, oftentimes, about as pleasant. Managing airflow, however minimal, and minimizing excessive heat buildup to reduce perspiration generation is essential and an art in itself.

Drawbacks to bivies? As additions to a sleeping bag system during the winter when you use them in conjunction with a tent or snow cave, there are few. When you use them as minishelters, however, the drawbacks of bivies mount up. For one, it's darn tough to cook inside a bivy sack should the need to cook arise. Also, a bivy provides absolutely no shelter for gear and can become a nylon prison if you have to wait out a long storm or bad weather.

### *Pad your sleep*

You use a ground pad for several things: insulation from the ground, for certain, because otherwise you pump heat into the ground in cold weather; moisture protection to a very minimal degree; comfort to a high degree. So deciding whether to carry a pad comes down to the choice between reducing weight and bulk or adding insulation and comfort.

If you are sleeping directly on the ground and not in a tent, you and your sleeping bag are more likely to absorb moisture wherever the bag contacts the ground. Is a pad the guaranteed answer? Unless you are an incredibly still sleeper, even a full-length pad won't entirely do the job because your sleeping bag will most likely extend over the pad to the sides and may even slide off from time to time. I recommend full-length pads only if you are sleeping on snow and insulation is your main motive. Although you can save weight on a full length by opting for the thinner versions, I must say the weight saving is not enough for me when I look at the comfort lost. I use a regular three-quarter length ThermaRest most often. Add to the package a nylon ground cloth or, my favorite, a Gore-Tex bivy sack, and you have moisture protection from above and below. You can then tuck the pad into the bivy to minimize nocturnal slipping and sliding.

 To get creative, you can pack along a sleeping pad of ensolite (closed cell foam) about 2.5 feet long to place under your feet and lower legs when cold becomes an issue. That same bit of ensolite makes a perfect seat, protecting the posterior from cold and the hard ground. Excellent, too, when sitting on snow during a snack break while skiing or snowshoeing.

To pad your head, you can create a pillow by filling a stuff sack with your parka and other items of clothing. You now have comfort, insulation from the ground, and ready access to your clothing in the morning.

# Backpacks

Backpacks come in hundreds of styles, and everyone has a favorite. But just because your best friend likes his backpack, that doesn't mean you will feel comfortable in the same model. Try on any backpack that you are considering. Have the salesperson load 30 to 40 pounds of stuff into each pack you try so that you can compare.

## Remember, you have to carry it

If your backpack is large enough, you will fill it. With that in mind, consider that the pack you choose should be as small and streamlined as you can possibly get away with. Experience has shown me that between 1,000 and 1,500 cubic inches is about right for short day trips where all you will be carrying is the "Ten + One Survival Essentials" gear (see Chapter 14) and perhaps a few extra items. Look for a padded back, well-padded and contoured shoulder straps, and a sturdy waistbelt to keep the load from bouncing around. Some daypacks come with padded waistbelts, which add weight and bulk and not all that much in terms of support. The bottom line here though, as with all other packs: Buy what feels best on your back with a load in it. If you're shopping for a daypack, I suggest asking the salesperson to fill the pack with about 10 to 15 pounds of weight using actual gear so that you can get a good feel for the pack's comfort claims.

If you are heading out for a weekend jaunt or are going to be carrying gear for a large group including several children on a daylong adventure, you will want to opt for a weekend pack in the 3,000- to 4,500-cubic-inch range. Here, the suspension system becomes a little more critical to the overall carrying comfort of the pack. Well-padded and contoured shoulder straps with a sternum strap (fastens across your breastbone and takes some of the pressure off your shoulders by keeping the straps from slipping to the outside) are essential. Look for a padded back with some kind of stiffening framesheet to aid support and pack shape, and a padded, stiffened, and contoured waistbelt.

If you are planning on trekking overseas or heading out for multi-day trips, then I recommend a more substantial pack with an internal or external frame. Overall, I prefer internal frames because they are easier to travel with, more flexible, and offer better balance, which is useful when you are ducking and weaving through trees or moving over loose scree. Sizes between 4,000 and 6,000 cubic inches should prove adequate in this range.

Some people prefer fanny packs. They rest the load on your hips and are basically a small pack sans shoulder straps. The problem with fanny packs is their size, although I have used a fanny many times for all-day trail runs when size and weight are crucial and I am not carrying more than water, snacks, and a few emergency items. If you do opt for a fanny pack, look for one that has accessory straps built in on the underside (so that you can attach a jacket or other articles of clothing) and sturdy lash points on the top (for securing a hiking pole, camera tripod, or even a small insulated pad to sit on).

I also recommend buying your pack from a reputable outdoor specialty store whose staff is well versed in backpacks and even use them. Do this, and you improve your chances of achieving a good fit and the best pack for the type of use you intend.

Don't put anything more in your pack than you are willing to carry. Light is right, and if you can learn to live without something, you'll walk lighter and happier. Frankly, a heavy pack is neither a sign of strength nor virility, but rather a clue that you haven't yet figured out to leave the extras at home. Either that or someone is slipping rocks into your pack.

## Packs for children

Buying a backpack for a child is a little less complex. I recommend that children under 8 carry nothing more than a daypack. If you can find one with a waist strap to help prevent the pack from bouncing around on your child's back, your child will find it much more comfortable to carry. As your child gets older and expresses an interest in carrying more (usually between the ages of 8 and 10) it is time to consider buying a child-sized frame pack. Tough Traveler, JanSport, Kelty, Osprey, and Camptrails make decent external frame and internal frame packs for children that have a certain amount of adjustability built in to allow the pack to grow with the child.

Be very careful of buying a pack that does not fit well and ends up bouncing and swaying around on your child's back. A loaded pack that does not fit is extremely uncomfortable and top-heavy, creating a potentially miserable child and a ruined outing. The top of the shoulder straps and bar they are attached to should rest, when the pack is loaded, between the top of the shoulders and the base of the skull. The waist belt should comfortably cup the hips, not so high that it compresses the stomach or so low that it sits on the buttocks.

Rent camping gear when and where you can. Many specialty stores rent tents, backpacks, sleeping bags, stoves, and even child carriers. Avoid renting boots.

## A backpack buying guide

When buying a backpack, the first decision will be whether to go with an internal frame or external frame (see Figure 2-3).

**Figure 2-3:**
Internal frame (left) and external frame backpacks.

*Courtesy of Kelty, Inc.*

*Internal frame backpacks* have a streamlined shape because the frame, a flexible one, is inside the backpack. Because the pack is flexible and carries close to the body, it offers a comfortable fit, a low center of gravity, flexibility, and a relative freedom of movement to the user. Those features make internal frame packs an ideal choice for rock scrambling, off-trail work, winter ski touring, and mountaineering. The drawback with internal frames is that they do not carry unwieldy loads easily and can become quite unstable and uncomfortable if you end up lashing large amounts of gear to the outside of the pack.

*External frame backpacks* feature rigid, rectangular frames, typically made of aluminum. The weight carries higher than a pack with an internal frame, so correct loading is essential. The frame carries the pack away from your back, improving ventilation and making the pack a cooler choice. Because the pack frame is somewhat rigid, it tends to restrict moment. External frame packs also typically have a higher center of gravity, making them feel a bit top-heavy unless you load them properly. However, unlike an internal frame pack, the rigid external frame can carry ridiculously awkward loads quite comfortably and offer numerous lash points for attaching items. This feature may be appealing to the parent carrying almost all the gear while the other carries the child. External frame backpacks are ideal for very large and bulky loads and for long backpacking trips. But they're not for mountaineering or skiing.

### Backpack features

Some features that you should covet in a backpack are the following:

- Accessory pockets to customize a pack by function and volume.
- Compression straps placed so you can reduce loads or compress a pack when it is not full.
- Contoured shoulder straps with designs that accommodate women's curves too.
- Cupped or canted hip belts with designs that accommodate women's curves too.
- Daisy chain — a series of webbing loops sewn into a chain running vertically — on the front, offering multiple lash points.
- Durable, coated fabrics that repel sharp objects, resist tears, and turn back raindrops.
- Floating top pocket on internal frame packs.
- Heavy-duty zippers.
- Hydration bladder installed, with drinking hose.
- Hydration pockets that will accept all sizes of drinking bladders.
- Load lifter straps to ease the weight on the shoulders.
- Padded back with wicking synthetic fabric for comfort.
- Reinforced pack bottom to protect the end that gets abused the most.
- Shovel pocket — great for stuffing extra clothing and gear into.

✔ Storm collar that extends between 8 to 12 inches for loads you don't want to comprehend.

✔ Travel packs with removable daypacks that are securely attached when in place.

### Loading choices in packs

Have you ever watched professional movers load a van? Loading a pack is the same idea — top loads, side loads, some things stowed last because they come off first — and everything arrives in good shape. Choose the right pack with the most appropriate loading system for you and your camping needs, as follows:

✔ **Top-loading:** Features one top opening into which you load, cram, and stuff your gear. Many top-loaders have an extension collar or tube that adds additional volume should you need it and a floating top pocket to fit over the main compartment. This is the most water-resistant of all the pack designs simply because there are fewer openings and zippers. Top-loading packs are ideal for backpacking, mountaineering, and winter camping.

✔ **Panel-loading:** This pack is for those who want easy access to their gear. You can open a horseshoe-shaped zipper and see all that is inside the pack. This particular style will not hold as much as other styles and if a zipper fails — oy vey! Panel-loading packs are ideal for backpacking and adventure travel.

✔ **Hybrid or combination-loading:** This type of pack offers the best of both packs: top-loading for stuffing to the gills and panel-loading for seeing what is inside without rummaging. More openings mean less water resistance. A raincover for this type of pack is a must. Combination-loading packs are ideal for adventure travel, backpacking, and hut-to-hut skiing.

## Fitting your pack each time, every time

Perhaps you have experienced the minor discomfort or frustration of a backpack that doesn't fit perfectly or work quite the way you thought it would when you made the purchase. Not to worry! Help is on the way.

Establish a routine for adjusting your pack every time you put it on. Loosen the shoulder straps, load-lifter straps (the ones pulling off the top of the shoulder strap), and hip-stabilizer straps (ones attached from the frame to the waistbelt) slightly.

Bend your knees, swing the pack up onto your thigh, slide one shoulder into an available shoulder strap, and then the other. Lean forward, hunch your shoulders to lift the pack slightly, and cinch the waistbelt.

# What's a hydration system? Do I want one?

A hydration system is a collapsible reservoir that rides in your pack. You take sips of liquid from the reservoir using a flexible tube running from the reservoir and fitted with a little valve. This system supplements, and on some jaunts replaces, water bottles and canteens, but it never diminishes the importance of those tried-and-true containers in the world of hydration.

A *hydration pack* contains a pocket incorporated into the pack design which will accept either specific models or generic-sized water bladders with a capacity up to 70 ounces, typically.

Studies have shown that the human body absorbs and derives more immediate benefits from water if it is consumed in small sips with increased frequency as opposed to stopping at regular rest breaks and guzzling. A hydration system appears to encourage this sip-and-go philosophy.

Because a water bladder is flexible, it molds to fit available space — impossible with a rigid water bottle. Bladders allow people to carry more water far more efficiently and comfortably. A 70-ounce bladder carries the equivalent of three wide-mouth 32-ounce Nalgene bottles against the back and centered. As a bladder drains, it collapses, taking up less space. As a water bottle drains, it simply fills with air and takes up the same space. Also, with a bladder there is virtually no sloshing of water, which means more quiet when hiking, riding, skiing, or running.

Finally, there is the versatility factor with hydration systems. Take a bladder out of a pack and fill it with hot water for use as a hot water bottle inside a sleeping bag (risky if it should spring a leak, however.) Add an accessory hose and use the bladder as a hanging shower system. Use a bladder as a pillow.

Are bottles becoming obsolete? Not at all! There are those who find it more difficult to fill a bladder than a bottle — certainly true when attempting to mix drink flavorings or add ice cubes to the mix. Bladders also require a bit of maintenance to keep clean, especially if you start adding flavored drinks to the mix, something that's rarely a problem with a bottle. A number of bladder manufacturers, and many adventure racers I know, even mention that they carry a bottle or two strictly for preparing and sipping mixed drinks (juice crystals, energy drinks, KoolAid, etc.) The bladder then becomes the primary water source.

Also, in mountaineering situations, bladders freeze solid unless meticulously protected from the cold — very difficult if not impossible to do. Bottles, in very cold environments, hold a most distinct advantage: You can store them upside down and still drink out of them, even if the water begins to freeze.

How can you prevent freeze-ups? This is the big challenge for hydration systems. New designs incorporate insulation in the packs or sleeves covering the bladders, neoprene or foam coverings over the drinking tubes, and so on. But the only guaranteed way of keeping your bladder (that's the one you're wearing, not the one you're born with) from freezing means wearing a layer of clothing, such as your outer shell, on top of the bladder. The drinking tube should be routed up near your neck, remaining under the outer layer until it is time to drink. By drinking in small but regular intervals, the fluid will not freeze. In bitterly cold temperatures, blow air back into the tube, forcing water back into the bladder. Ice may then coat the inside of the drinking tube, but it won't freeze shut.

(For more on the water topic, see Chapters 6 and 13.)

Stand up, settle the pack onto your hips, and pull the shoulder straps snug. Buckle the sternum strap (the strap across the chest between shoulder straps) if you have one — it should be only snug, not so tight that it restricts your breathing.

Finally, tighten the load-lifters and hip-stabilizer straps to control the pack's penchant for swaying or pulling you backward. Ease up some of the tension on the shoulder straps (placing more weight on your hips), and you're ready to go.

## Customizing your pack's fit and performance

There is no such thing as a waterproof pack — unless the pack features sealed seams and a roll-top design, which only a few manufacturers make. In most cases, you have to rely on a pack cover of some kind to keep your gear dry in a rainstorm. Specialty outdoor stores sell a ready-made waterproof nylon cover that fits to your pack. Budget-conscious hikers often prefer a version made of a heavy-duty garbage bag with slits cut for the shoulder straps.

Never trust the flimsy split rings that come with many frame packs. Head to the hardware store and exchange them for the tighter and stronger variety of split ring.

Add extensions to all the pack's zipper pulls to make opening and closing your pack's zippers easier when you're wearing gloves or have cold fingers. Shower hooks, twist ties, or a split ring through the zipper-pull hole all work well.

If you rent or borrow the pack, the waistbelt may feel a tad loose. Fill in the gaps with small pieces (maybe three inches wide by four to six inches long) of ordinary closed cell foam. Should your waistbelt become too loose because of usual weight loss on an extended trip, make do with a rolled sweater or other soft material to fill in the extra space.

Some packs have accessory pockets attached to the waistbelt, allowing ready access to necessary snacks, maps, and water while on the trail. If you don't have a pocket, don't fret. Simply wear a small fanny pack turned towards the front.

The added beauty of the fanny pack is that when you take off your backpack, the fanny pack stays on, minimizing the chance of misplacing important gear. The fanny pack also creates an ideal carrying pouch for short jaunts.

# Loading and fitting your external frame pack

Use these guidelines to help ensure that your pack is properly fitted before you buy or rent it from a retail operation. Here are some guidelines on how to load an external frame pack:

- ✔ You should load heavy gear like stoves, water bottles, and tents to the top and against the frame of the pack — near your shoulders.

- ✔ Midweight gear like clothing and pots should take up the middle space.

- ✔ You should load the lightest gear to the outside and toward the bottom of the pack. Your sleeping bag goes under the pack.

- ✔ A woman needs to load her pack with the weight lower and the sleeping bag attached at the top (because a woman carries her center of gravity lower than a man).

The fitting of your pack is very important. To ensure that your external frame pack fits properly, follow these guidelines:

- ✔ Put the pack on. The hipbelt should cup the hips and the padded section should comfortably wrap around the torso leaving a little gap in the front. If you have less than a few inches of gap, the belt is too big. If you have more than a few inches of gap, the belt is too small.

- ✔ If the pack's lower bar grinds into your back, try moving the belt up or down on the frame.

- ✔ The shoulder straps should anchor to the frame level with the crest of the shoulders, unless the pack has load lifters, in which case the straps should anchor to the frame just below the crest of the shoulders.

- ✔ Load lifters should attach to the straps just below the collarbone and attach to the frame just at ear level, forming roughly a 45-degree angle.

- ✔ If the top bar of the frame bumps your head once the adjustments are made, or if you can't let out the shoulder straps enough, the pack is too small. If the top towers above you or the shoulder straps are completely cinched down against the adjustment buckles, the pack is too big.

# Loading and fitting your internal frame pack

You should make sure that your internal frame pack is loaded correctly for your comfort and safety. Follow these guidelines to insure correct loading:

When you load your pack, build from the sleeping bag on up, keeping heavy items close to the back of the pack (against the framesheet). Middleweight items need to occupy the middle of the pack with light items nesting to the outer edges and top of the pack.

You need to make sure that your pack fits properly. The following guidelines will help you get a good fit:

✔ After you load the pack, the hipbelt should cup your hips. As with external frames, the padded section should comfortably wrap around the body, with a few inches of gap in the front. More or less gap and the belt is either too big or too small.

✔ Position the attachment point of the shoulder strap suspension so that the straps curve over your shoulders and attach to the pack approximately two inches below the shoulder's crest.

✔ Cinch the straps down. If the end of the shoulder straps sits more than four inches below the armpit or bottoms out against the adjustment buckles, find a smaller suspension.

✔ Load lifter straps should meet the framesheet at your ears. If they are lower than that, you need a larger pack. Adjust the load lifters so that they pull off the straps just below the collarbone.

✔ Adjust the pack stabilizers (those that pull off the hipbelt and pack bottom) to pull the pack snuggly in without distorting the hipbelt.

✔ Move the sternum strap up or down so that it sits approximately two to three inches below the collarbone.

# Child Carriers

Introducing children to the outdoors before they can walk any distance is a great way to get them excited about camping. You become the mule and papoose carrier, of course. But if the thought of adding extra and very shifty weight to an already heavy load sends shudders down your spine, here's a word of comfort: The gentle rocking rhythm of a walking parent is often enough to put the squirmiest child to sleep.

A good child carrier is not cheap, but it is worth its price for the carrying comfort, support, and versatility provided to both parent and child. The two basic types of carrier are the soft snuggle sack that hangs in front of the parent, for children too young to sit up, and the frame-supported carrier that attaches to your back, for older children of up to 35 pounds.

## The snuggle sack

The soft snuggle sack is probably best typified by the Snugli brand of carrier. Its crisscross carrying design is quite comfortable. The baby is supported by an adjustable seat and rests inside a soft, cotton-lined pouch. You wear the carrier slung in front for very young babies and over the back for larger infants. The main limitation is its soft design, affording no real support for the parent during extended carries and virtually no place to pack extra gear, not that you would want to. I found this system ideal for my newborn, but quickly moved into something with more support once Nikki could sit up.

## The frame-style child carrier

Larger, frame-style child carriers come in a wide variety of designs and an equally wide variety of comfort levels. The best way to decide what works best for you and your child is to try the carriers — with the child on board — and compare the fit and feel. Your choices will vary from a simple plastic frame with minimal shoulder straps and a basic seat sling to intricate aluminum or composite frames with sturdy and well-padded suspensions similar to the most advanced expedition pack.

Most child carriers are designed so that the child is facing forward. This puts the child closer to your center of gravity, which translates into a more natural gait and stride for you. And because the child can easily see ahead, he or she is more comfortable and more at ease, often putting a head on your shoulder to rest. There are several downsides to carrying children, however. One is the wandering little hands that love to pull hair, stick fingers in your mouth, and inadvertently poke eyes. The second is potentially dangerous. A child who is squirming and shifting, perhaps while turning around repeatedly to see the parent walking behind, creates a rather unwieldy load that can cause stumbles and make hiking less than pleasurable. Nikki learned to shift her weight at calculated moments, causing Dad to stumble and giving her the thrill-a-minute giggles and Dad an extra rush of adrenaline! Following one particularly close call where I nearly completed a headfirst swan dive off the trail and into a gully, Nikki was told in no uncertain terms that shifting and bouncing were *not allowed!*

Before you decide on a particular model, make sure that the system you choose is sturdily built and comes equipped with a safety belt to strap your child in. An untimely trip or fall by you could catapult an unbelted child into space, resulting in a nasty injury. Also, choose a carrier that has a built-in fold-out stand that will support the carrier upright on the ground. You may find this feature wonderful for quick rest stops — although you should never leave your child unattended in a carrier for any reason. Finally, choose a carrier that also has attached pockets and pouches for carrying extra gear and perhaps also a place to secure a sleeping bag or two if needed. Tough Traveler, Madden, Lafuma, L.L. Bean, and Kelty all make very good models of child carriers.

# Stoves

Once upon a time, campfires were the way to cook and stoves were for convenience or backup. Today, firewood remains in heavy demand and is sometimes unavailable at campsites. With so many people enjoying the wilderness heritage, cooking on stoves is the more ecologically responsible decision. Stoves leave no scarring fire rings, no charred wood scattered around, and no reduction in vital deadwood from the environment.

Your choice of stoves begins with choice of fuel: liquid fuel, such as white gas, or pressurized canister fuel, such as butane or propane. White gas stoves typically burn hotter, will boil water more quickly, and can be pressurized with an external pump. On the down side, you have to prime white gas stoves, the pumping can be a hassle, and units require more frequent cleaning and maintenance. Butane/propane stoves are more convenient to use. You turn on the gas and light them. However, because cartridges are self-pressurized, efficiency and heat output drop in cold temperatures and when a cartridge is nearly empty.

Never light a stove in a tent, and do not allow children to operate a stove unsupervised. I also recommend asking a salesperson to show you how to safely light and maintain your new stove before leaving the store.

## Which stove, which fuel, which trip

You have your dual fuels, multi-fuels, single fuels, solid fuels, liquid fuels, gas fuels, and more. Some stoves you have to prime, some stoves you don't. Some fuels burn clean, others don't. The option smorgasbord blur doesn't stop there. Stoves even come with electronic ignition (just like your favorite Chevy — well, not quite) and a battery-powered fan to add glow to the coals on the solid fuel stove. There are two-burner, single-burner, micro, macro — good golly, Miss Molly, just how are you going to get cooking on this topic?

Relax. It's not all that difficult, really. The first thing to determine is what you will be doing — backpacking, car camping, or whatever. If you are going car camping or base camping with a larger number of people, a two-burner stove is probably a good idea. If you're preparing to backpack or trek, think single-burner.

After determining the stove size you need, decide on fuel:

- ✔ **White gas** burns hot and clean and can be used as its own priming agent, but has limited availability outside the United States and Canada.
- ✔ **Butane** is available internationally and requires no priming but loses some performance capability in cold temperatures.

- ✔ **Isobutane and butane/propane blends** offer higher-octane performance than butane alone, solving the cold temperature drawback somewhat.

- ✔ **Propane,** now available for single-burner stoves using larger, heavier cartridges to accommodate the higher pressures, has limited international availability, but offers the very best performance of any of the pressurized gas canister fuels.

- ✔ **Kerosene** is available internationally but can be quite finicky to prime and light, and it burns with a dirty flame. Still, after properly preheated and burning efficiently (don't forget to say your fuel mantras), kerosene has a heat output as good as that of white gas.

- ✔ **Denatured alcohol** is making a comeback of sorts because it burns so cleanly and quietly and is virtually explosion-proof; however, it generates much less heat than pressurized or liquid gas fuels.

- ✔ **Solid fuel stoves,** utilizing twigs and pinecones, are a super alternative for the trekker or backpacker out for a long time where store-bought fuel is unavailable or impractical to carry in the needed quantities. Still, you must be prepared to tinker and fidget with the flame, albeit a very hot one, if and when dry wood is available and legal to use.

I recommend that if convenience is your primary concern, you use any of the pressurized gas canister fuel stoves because electronic ignitions are available with them and you won't have to deal with pressuring or pouring liquid fuels.

## Deciding on a stove model

After you decide what kind of stove and what kind of fuel, you turn to other stove features as well as weight and carrying size. Boiling times, often listed by manufacturers as a means of comparison, should be reviewed skeptically, the same way you look at sleeping bag temperature ratings. Many outfitters I've spoken with who use these stoves almost daily remind customers that many variables affect a stove's operating efficiency, including operator familiarity with the stove, fuel quality, type of pot, stove cleanliness, wind conditions, air temperature, beginning water temperature, altitude, and more. You are most likely to match the stated boiling time if you utilize a full-coverage windscreen (available as an accessory at most outdoor stores) and a pot that is blackened for better heat absorption, with a tightly fitting lid.

## Stove care tips

Getting the most heat from your stove requires a little care. The following are tips for improving stove efficiency:

✔ Always store a stove and fuel away from food, such as in a side pocket of a pack. Many manufacturers offer padded sacks or special stove cases for this purpose.

✔ Take time to test-fire a stove at home. This way you know it works and can teach yourself in a controlled setting about your stove's quirks and features. Another advantage is that you are only a phone call away from a specialty store's help if you encounter any problems — not the case if you discover the problem in the high mountains.

✔ Water (from condensation, typically) and debris (from careless opening and closing of a fuel canister when filling, most likely) can clog a fuel line. Always use a fuel funnel outfitted with a small screen to prefilter fuel going into your stove. Also, before filling a fuel bottle, always check it for debris and water.

✔ Never use old fuel. Fuel stored in a stove's fuel tank for more than a few months begins to break down, producing impurities that clog a stove.

# Kitchen Kit

Assembling a kitchen kit is easy. With a few careful purchases and by borrowing additional items from your home kitchen, you can put together a very serviceable kit. Briefly, the camp kitchen items you choose to pack are a function of your menu. At a minimum, this means two pot sizes, small and large; a griddle; a skillet; a mixing bowl or two; and cooking utensils such as a spoon, fork, spatula, and knife. A cutting board is also very handy. If you plan to grill, bring a grate you can put over the fire — don't assume your campsite will have one. Following are my suggestions for assembling your kitchen kit.

## Pots and pans

The choices for camping pots and pans are simpler than for stove fuel. After you decide on a nested set (pots that sit inside one another for space savings) you need to select from the five basic materials:

✔ **Enamel:** Nothing more than thin steel coated with a kiln-baked enamel finish that looks good, is easy to clean, and hard to scratch. The downside is that this stuff will chip and dent over time and rust appears wherever a chip occurs.

✔ **Aluminum:** It's very light and conducts heat very well, making cooking quite efficient. Health concerns regarding cooking on an aluminum surface have largely been debunked. The one major downside is that burned-on foods stick tenaciously to aluminum, which is why nonstick coatings on fry pans and the like are so popular and such a good idea.

✔ **Stainless steel:** It's extremely durable, cleans quickly and efficiently, and it won't scratch easily. The downside is its inability to conduct heat evenly, leading to scorched food in the pattern of a stove's intense flame.

✔ **Titanium:** It's ultralight, very durable, and very expensive. If you are extremely concerned about weight, this is your choice. If not, you may do better with stainless steel.

✔ **Bimetal combinations:** Combination aluminum/stainless steel pots feature black aluminum outers lined with stainless steel. Durability and heat distribution are enhanced.

Add to your pot-pan ensemble a good pot grip, a mechanical handle that securely grabs the lip of each pot, and a Teflon fry pan with a folding handle and a lid.

### Small bottles

For carrying spices, I recommend buying a number of one-ounce Nalgene bottles with screw-on lids. Also, pick up a few one-ounce bottles with flip-top nozzles for liquids and oils.

### Squeeze tubes

They look like giant toothpaste containers except they're made of plastic and have a clip securing one end. You can fill them with peanut butter, honey, jelly and other spreadables. With the clip removed from the base, the bottles open wide for cleaning and filling.

### Special utensils

From your home kitchen, select an old wooden spoon, a nylon spatula, and several small metal spoons. A tiny whisk is a great item for mixing dried milk, pancake mix, hot cocoa, a so on. A good whisking will help you avoid serving lumpy drinks and food to your camp food critics. I also carry a folding knife that I use only for cooking. The blade stays extremely sharp, locks in place for security, and is inexpensive and light. Add a GI-issue folding can opener for those just-in-case moments when a can of beans makes its way onto the menu.

### Stuff sacks for storage

Pack the pots in one stuff sack, the utensils in another smaller one, and the spices in a very small see-through ditty bag. The stuff sack for the pots helps to prevent the inside of your pack and other items from becoming as black as the pots.

### Gloves for protection

If you are planning to cook over a fire, add a pair of cotton or light leather gloves to your list. They help prevent burns and are definitely worth the extra bulk and weight.

# Personal commissary

Knife, fork, and spoon are essential for everyone. But to lighten the load, consider that a spoon can do almost everything a fork can do, but not vice versa. I leave the fork at home. And if each person carries a pocketknife, you don't need to pack extra knives just for eating.

When deciding to pack eating implements such as plate, bowl, and cup, think light. The kit for each member of our family consists of a wide-bottomed cup and a plastic plate with deep sides that can double as a bowl. Children spill things very easily, so whatever you choose, be sure that it is stable when full of food or drink. Also, the less a child has to hold or worry about, the less likely he or she will spill.

Wooden bowls keep hot food warmer longer and seem more natural in a wilderness setting than metal and plastic.

Plastic, insulated mugs with lids you can drink through are great on camping trips. They keep hot beverages hot, cool beverages cool, and insects out of everything. Plus, they minimize spilling when they (inevitably) get knocked over.

A drinking cup can double as a measuring cup if you simply etch or mark ounces up the side of the cup. I have marked ounces up the side of several cups so that I can quite accurately measure ingredients in the field.

# Furniture

Most experienced campground-goers agree: The one item you're likely to miss if you don't have it is a table. You can sit on rocks and stumps, but when it comes to eating and socializing, nothing beats a good table. Most drive-in campgrounds offer a picnic table at each site, but that's not a guarantee. If you are paddling or visiting a remote site, such as those on Bureau of Land Management lands, you can be virtually assured that camping is a BYOT affair — that's Bring Your Own Table, folks.

A lightweight, portable table makes a great addition to your camping kit. If it turns out that you don't need it, you don't even have to unpack it. But if your site lacks a table, you'll be glad you brought one along!

The same is true of chairs. Rocks, stumps, and coolers can all be used for seating. But portable stools are far more comfortable. Lightweight folding chairs with full back support are even more comfortable, and having one or two at your disposal can really take a load off your feet.

# Coolers

Coolers are a great option to tote along if you are traveling by vehicle or boat. Look for a model that fits the space available in your vehicle and your food-storage needs. You may find that two smaller coolers are a better investment than one house-sized version. A friend of mine once brought home a cooler he couldn't even lift when it was full. I think a 32-quart size suits most needs quite nicely.

## Packing your cooler

When possible, plan on using one cooler specifically for drinks and snacks and one for food supplies that you will open less often. At room temperature, a six-pack or a gallon of liquid melts about one pound of ice just cooling down. Thus, ice will last longer if items packed in coolers are already cold. Also, prechill coolers by placing a few ice cubes inside an hour or so before loading them. Here are some hints on how to pack and service the cooler:

- ✔ Pack foods that you will consume last at the bottom of the cooler. Store first-used and often-used items on top.

- ✔ Cold air travels down. Load cans and bottles first, then cover them with ice for maximum cooling.

- ✔ Keep foods dry by sealing them in plastic containers or sealed plastic bags. Place these items directly on the ice or in the cooler tray.

- ✔ Perishable items like meat and milk should go directly on ice.

- ✔ Water from just-melted ice keeps contents cold almost as well as ice, and preserves the remaining ice much better than air space. So, drain water only when necessary.

- ✔ Ice lasts twice as long when coolers are kept in the shade.

- ✔ Open the lid only when necessary and close it as quickly as possible.

- ✔ While traveling, pack sleeping bags and clothing around the cooler to insulate it even more.

## Cleaning your cooler

After each use, clean all inside and outside surfaces with a sponge using mild soap and water. Leave the lid open for an hour or two to be sure the cooler is completely air-dried before storing. If you need to get rid of a smell, use a diluted solution of chlorine bleach and water. If that doesn't work, wipe the inside of the cooler with a cloth saturated with vanilla or lemon extract. Leave the scented cloth inside the cooler overnight with the lid closed. If it's a stain you need removed, try a little baking soda and water. Pour the baking soda directly onto the stain and add a little water to form a paste. Let it sit for a few minutes, then rub in. Rinse thoroughly with hot tap water. Be sure to run hot water through drain plugs and faucets to remove any residue.

## Water carriers

Collapsible jugs have been around for eons and come in a variety of sizes. I find the most convenient to tote and fill are the 2- to 2.5-gallon models — anything larger gets cumbersome. Keep in mind that collapsible plastic jugs can be a tad hard to collapse and have a nasty habit of developing leaks along the creases after multiple use; perhaps this is why they are so inexpensive. Collapsible plastic jugs also have a penchant for travel — they like to roll off tables and flat surfaces when you turn your back.

For car camping I also carry a five-gallon hard plastic jug with an on/off spigot and a wide-mouth access point at the top for filling and cleaning.

For backpacking, my choice of jug is usually a nylon water bag lined with food-grade plastic. The benefit of a soft water bag is that it is easy to tote inside a backpack and easy to hang from a branch or hook, and it weighs next to nothing when it's empty.

# Lighting the Way

Ever since the first caveman singed his beard trying to chase the night away, man has been fascinated with illumination. If it is dark, it has become man's biological imperative to light up, making the world a safer place by chasing away the ghosts, goblins, and specters of our mind's creation. Never mind that we are often the very ones creating an irrational fear of darkness in the first place. It's light that's right, and here are five of my picks for brightening a slice of your nocturnal life, if not your world.

## Headlamps

What do you do when you need both hands and have to use a flashlight at the same time? While you can clamp your teeth around the back end of a small-enough flashlight, this technique makes it hard to carry on conversations and is not mom-approved — you can't possibly know where that thing's been. What you need is a headlamp. Look for a lamp that is comfortable on your head, is not too heavy, and features zoom or multiple beam (high and low) brightness options.

# *Electric lanterns*

These are perhaps the safest of the lantern options, although the downside is battery consumption. Electric lanterns are certainly the only kinds I recommend for use inside a tent or camper. Some come with optional 12-volt adapters that allow you to plug into a lighter socket in your vehicle, and that's a nice feature to have. I also like the remote-control lanterns by Coleman, especially when camping with children. A quick flick of the remote turns the light out on the picnic table outside the tent when everyone is tucked in for the night. Another quick flick turns the light on to prevent blind stumbling should nocturnal wandering become necessary.

# *Gas lanterns*

Coleman is perhaps the most widely recognized name in lanterns, although there are many other companies making high quality gas-powered lanterns, too. The choice of fuel is liquid or pressured (gas canister). I prefer and recommend the gas canister for convenience and ease of use as well as safety. Gas lanterns are very bright, although they have the drawback of being a tad on the noisy side, rather like camping near a jet engine running at half speed. I always counsel against using a gas lantern inside a tent or camper.

# *Candle lanterns*

Candle lanterns do not throw off a great deal of light, but they are romantic. UCO makes my favorite candle lanterns and, frankly, I think the brand is most reliable. Candle lanterns utilize long-burn candles about two inches in diameter and four to five inches in length. They burn for up to eight hours or more. If you are campground based, you may enjoy the Candelier by UCO, which utilizes three candles in one unit. My wife and I have even used this light at home for emergencies. It burns hot enough that you can put a metal cup full of water on the Candelier's top and the water heats up nicely.

# *LED lights*

LEDs are relatively new to the outdoor recreation market, but you are going to see more and more of them in stores because they are, quite simply, the best alternative to any previous flashlight. LED (light-emitting diode for you engineer types) lights are more durable than any bulb as there is no filament to burn out or fragile glass casing to break. LED lights also burn in excess of 100,000 hours, far more than the traditional 40-hour life most flashlight bulbs now enjoy. Too, LED lights use far less energy yet provide just as bright a light, meaning the two AA-battery power pack might last for 40 hours or more, with no drop-off in light energy. Wow!

# Beware the Invisible Murk

Water-dwelling microcooties such as *giardia* and *cryptosporidium* never cease to hit below the belt. What's worse, they hide even in the most Eden-like waters. These days, you simply have to filter water before you drink. And it's crazy to slurp direct from the source when you regard the current crop of handheld filters. They're compact, light, and easier to use than ever, and some, believe it or not, are dropping in price. A decent filter can be had for as little as $20 — less expensive than a week's supply of Pepto-Bismol and antibiotics.

## What a filter does

The goal of a water filter (see Figure 2-4) is to rid your drinking water of microscopic contaminants, rendering water clear and reasonably pure, depending on the filter's pore size (specifically, what manufacturers call pore-size efficiency). A filter with a rating of one micron or smaller will remove protozoa such as *giardia* and *cryptosporidium*, as well as parasite eggs and larvae. But it takes a pore-size efficiency of less than 0.2 microns to remove harmful bacteria, which all of these filters will do.

K.O.-ing viruses, however, is a another story. Viruses are so tough that experts are now urging recreationists to take virus-prevention measures anywhere in the world, not only in developing countries and other places with undependable water supplies. Until recently, that meant getting a filter that incorporated iodine, or packing a bottle of iodine tablets, such as Potable Aqua. One filter, General Ecology's First Need, claims to meet EPA virus-removal standards by filtration alone — a nice change from the yucky taste (and for some, the health risk) of iodine. Most antiviral filters involve an iodine element followed by a carbon element to rid the water of any face-scrunching aftertaste.

Carbon also reduces the presence of such chemicals as pesticides, herbicides, heavy metals, and chlorine. But take heed: A few recent studies have shown that in certain situations it's best to give the iodine time to do its job. If your water source could possibly be contaminated with sewage, remove the carbon filter and let the iodine sit in the water for 15 to 20 minutes. You can then add ascorbic acid crystals to make the iodine residue more pleasing to the palate. In addition, when a carbon element reaches its limit for what's known as absorbing a particular chemical, the gnarly stuff slips through. Always replace the filter cartridge and the carbon element according to the manufacturer's recommended schedule.

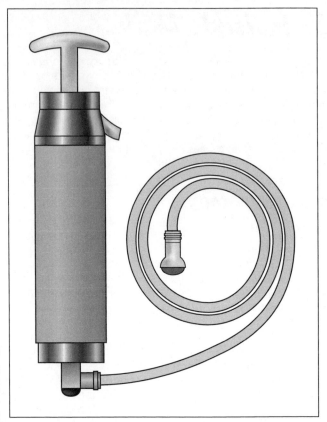

**Figure 2-4:**
A handheld
water filter.

## Features to look for in a filter

A filter worthy of backcountry use weighs less than 20 ounces and is easy to grasp, simple to operate, and a cinch to clean and maintain. Regardless of where you'll be drinking, always buy one that removes protozoa and bacteria. (A number of cheap, pocket-size filters remove only *giardia* and *cryptosporidium* — a risk to your health for the sake of saving a few bucks.) Be sure to check the flow rate of the filter you're considering. If it's slower than a liter per minute, you may be sweating out as much you'd like to filter in.

## Care and feeding of your filter

All filters clog. Clogging means a filter is doing its job. Don't force water through a filter that's becoming difficult to pump; you risk injecting a dose of microscopic skeevies into your bottle. You can backwash or scrub some models to extend their useful lives. And if the filter has a prefilter to screen out the big stuff, use it. A prefilter increases your filter's capacity by as much 100 gallons per disposable element. Finally, each filter has its own idiosyncrasies and care needs, so read the manufacturer's instructions.

I talk more about water in Chapter 6, "Setting Up Camp."

# Axe and Saw

Although wood is becoming increasingly scarce in most areas and campgrounds — to the point that I never recommend gathering wood at any time in any campground — I still advise packing along a folding saw and a small axe on your camping trip if traveling by vehicle. Why? Quite often, the wood you purchase from the campground or nearby areas is too big and needs to be cut down or split to make a good cooking fire. Logs that have simply been split in half or even quartered are still too big to produce good coals.

# Comforts of Home

Though not necessary by any stretch of the imagination, the following items have been known to convince even the most anticamping family members to enjoy a camp outing or two.

## Portable toilet

When traveling to more remote camps where the outhouses are an adventure unto themselves, packing along your own portable toilet often makes the camping experience less stressful. Any RV or large camping supplier carries portable toilets. Avoid the ones with a seat, folding legs, and a simple bag hanging beneath. Opt for more sturdy and reusable units with holding tanks or buckets that can be easily emptied and cleaned. Be sure to also pack along a suitable screen for privacy.

## Solar shower

A hot shower brightens even the grumpiest person's morning. I often pack along a solar shower, which, if placed in the sun's direct rays, heats the water in about two hours. For early morning risers, I add some warm water heated on the stove and then let the sun's early rays do the rest. The 2.5 gallon Solar Shower bags are quite adequate for up to two showers. Add an inflatable screen for privacy.

See Chapters 4 and 6 for more details on bathing in the wilderness.

# Chapter 3

# Dress for Success

*T*he weather is going to change, and that is one of the few promises I can make to you. Whether that change is good or bad honestly depends on your perspective and level of preparedness. Personally, I see rain, snow, sleet, hail, sun, wind — frankly, all types of weather — as simply another adventure outdoors. Some of my most memorable moments have come during or right after significant weather events that I was able to enjoy only because I was prepared and appropriately dressed.

The key to being prepared is to pack along an arsenal of garments that you can put on or take off as the weather conditions dictate. This method of dressing for the outdoors is called *layering* (see Figure 3-1). Layering begins with the *base layer* — the clothing directly against the skin. The next layer, or next few layers, if needed, are the *insulation layers*. And finally, the outermost layer is the *protective layer* — the barrier against moisture and wind.

In putting together your ideal layering system, what you are doing is creating a system that effectively combines elements of breathability, *wicking* (transporting moisture), rapid drying, insulation, durability, wind-resistance, and water-repellence, without adding much weight or impeding freedom of movement. You need to do all this with just a few garments. You don't want to pack so much that you need a mule train. The articles of clothing you choose on a particular day depend on your intended aerobic level and the anticipated weather conditions.

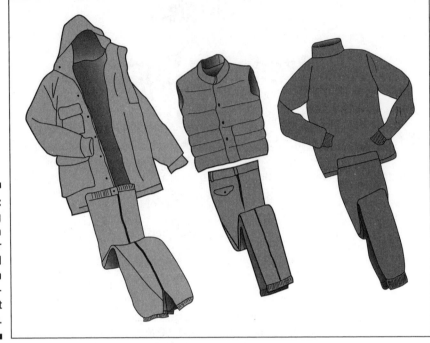

**Figure 3-1:**
Layering
begins with
underwear
(right) and
ends with
weather-
proof jacket
and pants.

# Managing Moisture and Comfort: The Base Layer

The layer against your skin is, essentially, a second skin that keeps you dry, warm, and comfortable. This layer is the workhorse in your moisture management system, moving moisture away from your body all day long. It is the first layer you put on and the last layer you take off. And — um — don't forget that under this layer you're naked.

Thick or thin, special weaves or not, the primary intent of a base layer is to manage moisture (wick or transport perspiration away from your skin) while adding a degree of insulation. How much insulation you want depends on how cold the environment is coupled with your anticipated level of activity.

In general, underwear is offered in three weights:

- ✓ **Lightweight** for high aerobic activity and moderately cool temperatures
- ✓ **Midweight** for optimum versatility, warmth, and wicking when backpacking, fly fishing, skiing, snowshoeing, or hunting on the move in cold temperatures

> ✔ **Heavyweight** (sometimes called expedition weight) for high warmth when activity or movement is limited and the temperatures are quite frigid

# Separating fact from fiction: basic base layering

The way some manufacturers tout their products' amazing fabric properties, and the way some retailers and the media glow on and on about fancy fibers that move and manage moisture away from the body to some mystical location — well, it can be misleading. The bottom line is that your base layer of clothing needs to fit well and be made of the right materials to have any chance at all of helping you stay dry and comfy. Some fabrics work better than others, and none of them work perfectly in all situations. I've tested just about every "miracle" fabric out there and offer the following thoughts and tips to help you cut through the murk and find the best base layer for you.

### Cotton

Cotton does not insulate — never has, never will. If you are still clinging to an old cotton union suit as underwear, do yourself a favor and only wear it to bed, never outdoors. The only time that cotton should become a part of your base layer is when you want to keep cool, not warm.

While underwear can very often be used as outerwear and worn as a second or third layer, the only way it works as a moisture management tool is as a first layer. So, to repeat the caution about cotton: Wearing cotton briefs under your synthetic fabric undies will add an unpleasant chill to the thermal equation.

### Polypropylene

Polypropylene (the original synthetic fiber for underwear) technically does not wick, or transport moisture, by itself, despite what some passionate manufacturers say. Polypro is, you see, water hating, or hydrophobic, and cannot wick or transport moisture without help. With no outer or second clothing layer to absorb moisture, your perspiration can puddle right next to the skin. Yes, it's true that your body heat will force water vapor through polypro, but this is not wicking — no matter who argues the point — it's evaporation; and even under the best of circumstances, evaporation can only dispel so much moisture buildup.

As for solid performance at a very economical price, polypropylene is a superb value and keeps you warm and dry without breaking the bank. But remember to place a wool or fleece sweater or shirt on top of your polypro undies to serve as a wick to pull moisture away from your skin. New antimicrobial (bacteria-hating/smell-eliminating) weaves of polypro are better than ever, so no one can claim you stink, at least not because of your underwear.

### Synthetics

When fitting synthetic underwear, opt for snug and close-fitting, but not constricting. If you fit your tops and bottoms too loosely, they won't be able to efficiently wick or transport moisture (either alone or, as is the case with polypro, with assistance) away from your skin and you'll wonder where you lost the performance you heard you'd be getting. There are exceptions to every rule, so be sure that you understand the manufacturer's individual fit instructions.

### Blends

Blended knits such as polyester/wool or polypropylene/wool work to provide wicking and insulative properties in one layer: The side facing your skin is water-hating while the side away from your skin is water-loving and pulls moisture through. The one drawback to this approach is that because of the wool, the underwear takes longer to dry.

### Polyesters

Chemically treated polyesters such as Capilene, Thermal Dynamics, and MTS are often blended with Lycra for stretch and better fit performance, and nylon for durability. By itself, polyester doesn't manage moisture well at all, but when treated with a water-loving chemical process, it encourages moisture to migrate through the fabric to the outer surface where it can evaporate. The trouble is, the chemical washes out in time. After a year or two of hard use, your underwear can end up feeling flat and clammy.

Another construction approach is to alter polyester structurally, creating weaves and shapes that actually encourage the fabric to absorb water and "pull" the moisture away from your skin. Underwear constructed of Thermax, CoolMax, or Thermastat are all common brand names, dry very quickly, insulate very well, and feel supersoft. But they, too, have their downsides. For one, the process isn't cheap, and it is possible, if your perspiration level is very high, for these fabrics to absorb so much water that they become saturated and stop functioning, leaving you feeling like a damp sponge.

Malden Mills has brought together the best of both chemical and structurally altered polyester and created fabrications dubbed BiPolar 100 (midweight) and BiPolar 200 (expedition weight) with the intent of wicking better and offering more warmth for the weight than comparable underwear. BiPolar also offers a soft, warm, cushy feel against the skin. Many of you may be inclined to wear it both as underwear and as a comfy outer layer.

### Wool

New weaves and precision cutting tools have virtually eliminated the age-old and well-deserved reputation wool had earned as being heavy and scratchy. Today's woolen underwear has a kinder and gentler feel while still performing as an excellent insulator even when wet. Since wool is also made of protein and keratin (sulfur-containing fibrous proteins), sweat neutralizes, which inhibits bacterial growth.

## Meshing performance

Some companies, such as Wiggy's, have opted for a mesh construction for the base layer. The intent is to create a base that enhances moisture transport to outer layers, thereby keeping the skin dryer and, consequently, warmer. While the product does work quite well, the pattern it leaves on your skin after an hour or two of pressure from a backpack makes for interesting conversation.

# Piling on: Insulative layers

To build upon the base layer, you want to have an arsenal of insulative choices. The goal here is a familiar one — provide warmth by creating dead-air space which slows the loss of body heat, as well as continuing to aid in the dissipation of moisture begun by your base layer. Because every person has different insulation requirements depending on body size, weight, and fitness level, there is no pat formula for universal comfort. In general, I find that the more options you have available, the more fine-tuning you can do, and the more comfortable you will be on a daily basis.

You have many options: wool, pile, fleece, down fill, or synthetic fill. I usually choose fleece because it is light, compressible, durable, and versatile, even when used in wet conditions.

For the initial layer or two of outerwear I prefer pullover garments. But for that final, just-in-case, insulative layer, I opt for full-zip every time. You may find that this allows the maximum versatility in ventilation management and makes the last layer much easier to put on and take off. I make sure that all my layers have roomy sleeves so I can push them up or slide them down. I also prefer zip-T necks: They ventilate superbly when open, yet insulate very well when zipped up around the neck. A chest pocket is a worthwhile feature too, as it provides a place to tuck a snack, a notebook, or sunscreen.

# Protecting yourself from wind and rain

To top the camp clothing ensemble, you need a thin, windproof, and water-resistant layer. You want this layer to breathe like crazy, yet not be so porous that rain runs through it like floodwaters through a leaking dike.

When the going gets damp and you want to keep going, you'd best be swathed in a good waterproof/breathable jacket, or, at the very least, a highly water-resistant jacket. Granted, there are many different levels of breathability and waterproofness/water resistance, and the level you choose depends largely on how much moisture is trying to dampen your spirit — and how much spirit you are putting in your pace.

### Three levels of water resistance

The three basic levels of water-shedding/breathable jackets offer a wide range of dryness, depending on the weather and what you're doing.

- **First level:** At the first level of protection are jackets made of microfibers that are highly breathable and adequately water-resistant. This kind of jacket is ideal if you are running, mountain biking, skating, or generally upping your sweat meter while only a little moisture is falling earthward. You want your jacket to offer a good windbreak and prevent you from getting soaked from the inside out, or the outside in. Don't expect jackets in this category to shed much more than drizzle, though, because if Noah comes calling, you'll look and feel like a drowned rat.

- **Second level:** The second level of protection, which adds a water-resistant membrane and often an outer water-repellent chemical treatment to the fabric, moves a notch down on the breathable scale, but also a notch up when it comes to moisture protection. Jackets in this category are intended for use when the aerobic level remains high, but the outer elements are knocking more seriously at the door. They'll still breathe far better than a waterproof/breathable jacket ever will, but unlike the water-resistant jackets, these can and will shed a light sprinkle and even a short downpour or two. If it's dumping cats and dogs, though, head for cover or reach for your scuba gear 'cause you'll soon feel as if you have been walking underwater.

- **Heavy-duty level:** For those times when the weather is really throwing the kitchen sink your way, your only option is to reach for a waterproof/breathable jacket. This level of jacket uses an outer water-repellent treatment on the fabric and a membrane on the inside such as Gore-Tex or any number of proprietary breathable coatings. If your activity level is high (more than a walk for instance) and the rain is pouring down, you still may get a bit damp, but nowhere near as wet as in a water-resistant jacket or a 100-percent waterproof jacket with zero breathability. An added bonus with the breathable jackets is that they dry very quickly if you do get damp — after the rain slackens or your activity level drops.

# Construction and materials

Textiles made of microfibers commonly use a polyester microfilament that is woven so tightly it becomes windproof and somewhat water-repellent by construction. Because typically there are no coatings or finishes, the garment breathes efficiently, making this style perfect for high aerobic level activities when weight and breathability are of prime importance. Occasionally a manufacturer adds a coating or finish to improve water repellency, but this comes with a functional price — less breathability.

The next level of protection comes from membranes that are more breathable than they are waterproof, such as Activent (a Gore company product). Patagonia used Activent long before it was called Activent and continues to use the technology under the name Pneumatic. Highly breathable and water-resistant, Activent is ideal for high aerobic activity and light rain or snow conditions. Jackets manufactured with Activent are not seam-sealed as it makes no sense — breathability is the issue here.

The ultimate level of protection is found in waterproof/breathable outerwear. With waterproof/breathable laminates or coatings designed to repel rain while allowing steamy sweat to pass through, you achieve maximum rain protection but do sacrifice a bit of the breathability. The Gore-Tex laminate (also known as a membrane) is the best-known technology for providing both waterproofness and breathability, and it has an excellent record. All garments using Gore-Tex (including the new and improved Gore-Tex as well as the lighter version, PacLite) must pass Gore's demanding quality standards regarding seam sealing and construction.

The other approach to achieving waterproofness/breathability is through coatings. Jackets that are "WB coated" can also be highly waterproof/breathable — and are usually less expensive than comparable models employing Gore-Tex, though not always. While there used to be a dramatic difference between Gore and "the others," I've found that the performance boundaries have softened with an increasing number of jackets performing as well as, and even better than, Gore-Tex in certain situations.

A few other key jacket-construction terms you should know begin with "DWR," or durable water-repellent finish, applied to the outer fabric. Like the name says, the DWR is what makes water bead up on the shell. Without it, your jacket's performance would be compromised; the shell would feel like a wet dishrag.

Most laminate constructions, certainly those utilizing Gore-Tex, refer to something dubbed "two-layer" or "three-layer" construction. "Two-layer" is actually something of a misnomer: The outer layer is the nylon shell; the inner layer is the laminate. There's also a third element — a free-hanging liner made of nylon mesh, taffeta, or some other material to aid in moisture management. Two-layer jackets are very pliable, and the free-hanging, wicking liner adds a bit of warmth and minimizes any feeling of clamminess. A three-layer construction consists of a nylon shell, the laminate, and an inner layer of wicking material, all sandwiched together. Three-layer jackets are typically lighter but stiffer than their two-layered cousins, and since the sewn lining shields the membrane better than a free-hanging version, the three-layer style is supposedly more durable.

How a jacket is designed to pull apart is just as important as how it's stitched together. Ventilation features, as much as any fabric technology, are key to a jacket's breathability. Mesh-backed pockets and underarm zippers maximize air flow, as do cuffs, waists, and hems that can be adjusted to open wide. I also like storm flaps (the baffle over the zipper) that close with hook-and-loop material or snaps: With these fasteners closed (but with the zipper open), air can still get into the jacket. It's a great way to get some extra ventilation, even with the hatches partially battened down.

### Design and dimensions

A jacket should be roomy enough that you can wear layers of clothing underneath it and pump air through the jacket with your body movements. For general outdoor use, seek a length reaching to about the thigh. The extra inches provide additional protection for your legs and your rear end, and the jacket won't gather at the waist or creep up. Jackets designed for more athletic pursuits are cut hip length because the extra inches would prove restricting. This style often dispenses with a hood, as well, to save weight and eliminate fabric-flapping frustration.

That doesn't mean you should overlook the importance of a hood in the other jackets, however. I like integral hoods because they're easy to reach, generally provide a better fit, and can often be rolled out of the way and held back via a small tab. Hoods stuffed into zippered collars make the collars too stiff and are a pain to access. A properly designed hood moves with your head and has a size-adjustment drawstring or tab, in addition to the drawstrings in front. It should also have an ample bill that shields your face and eyes from sun and rain.

## Finer points

When I go shopping for a jacket, I also run a quick quality check on each garment that says, "Buy me!" The details I look for:

- ✔ Bar tacks (reinforced stitching) at pocket corners and where the zippers attach to the shell

- ✔ Pull tabs on all those zippers to let you get at what's inside your pockets without taking off your gloves

- ✔ Waist pockets lined with a soft, fleecelike fabric, nice for keeping hands warm

- ✔ Waterproof zippers to eliminate the need for bulky storm flaps and maximize the ventilation options

- ✔ A stuff sack — or at least the ability to stuff the shell into one of its own pockets — to make the jacket more packable

- ✔ Reinforced elbow and shoulder patches to protect maximum-wear areas

## Ventilation is the key to happiness

Waterproof/breathable systems only work if the temperature and/or humidity on the inside of the garment is higher than on the outside. Temperature and humidity are the driving mechanisms which serve to encourage water vapor through the coating or laminate/membrane. However, it is important to realize that membranes or coatings will only allow a "physiologically adequate" amount of moisture vapor to escape. How much is physiologically adequate depends on the membrane or coating, but suffice it to say that in no case does this imply 100 percent moisture vapor removal.

Your waterproof/breathable jacket is only as good as its more subtle features, and those that provide for ventilation are the most essential, especially when the jacket is being worn during extreme activity or in warmer temperatures. Ventilation is the key to happiness. If you can't vent your body's heat and moisture to the outside, rather like a chimney, you're going to get damp and disgusted, even in a jacket using the best materials. Ventilation pockets and adequate pit-zips (underarm zipper openings) allow you to maximize airflow, minimize heat retention, and reduce moisture build-up. Storm flaps that close with Velcro or snaps add a wider range of function since you can leave your jacket's zipper undone and still secure the pocket from rain while allowing passage of air. Zippers should be two-way, allowing you to vent from the bottom as well as undo from the top.

When camping and hiking with a child in a child carrier, remember that although you are moving, your child is not, so dress him or her accordingly. But do not overdress a child. I have seen children sitting very unhappily warm in a child carrier, the victim of parents who feel that if one layer of clothes is good, two must be better.

## *Care and feeding of your waterproof/breathable jacket*

Waterproof/breathable jackets won't remain either waterproof or breathable unless you care for them. To help you keep your shells functioning like new, read and adhere to the guidelines printed on the care labels sewn inside every jacket and pant. I offer the following suggestions as additional information to help you get the most out of your jacket:

### *Wash 'em*

✔ Dirt attracts water and can affect how well your jacket's durable water repellency (DWR) works. Wash your jacket periodically in warm water with no detergent.

- ✔ You can wash really dirty jackets in mild powdered detergent or nondetergent-based Nikwax Tech Wash. Rinse the garment twice to thoroughly eliminate soap residue, which can affect DWR.

- ✔ Never use bleach or fabric softeners. Never dry-clean.

### Use heat

- ✔ Use a low dryer heat to restore your jacket's DWR.

- ✔ Periodically ironing the outside of a jacket on a warm/steam setting can work to restore a failing DWR finish.

### Reapply that DWR

- ✔ Washings and wear break down and rub off DWR finishes.

- ✔ Restore the finish by applying a new coating with a spray-on from W. L. Gore called ReviveX.

- ✔ Tectron Fabric Protector or Nikwax TX-Direct Spray are good DWR restoring sprays too.

- ✔ Wash-in applications work, but beware because they will coat your entire jacket inside and out, including the lining that used to wick but now won't.

# A quick guide to layering

I cannot stress ease of use enough. If your layering system is a pain to take on and off, chances are you won't adjust the layers as frequently as you should, and that defeats the purpose of layering. I put together a few sample situations to help guide your layering decisions.

### Is it hot and sunny?

**Challenge:** Temps are in the upper 70s to low 80s and the sun is beating down on you. You have no place to hide from the intensity of the sun's rays. Your primary concern is to protect your skin from the sun (always wear sunscreen) and provide a light layer of fabric next to your body that will aid in the cooling process.

**Solution:** Wear either long- or short-sleeve shirts of loose cotton or cotton/synthetic blend material. Loose-fitting pants or shorts with a built-in mesh brief are best — no cotton briefs as they chafe. Bring along a light-weight fleece jacket and a light-colored windproof/water-resistant shell. Top your noggin in a light-colored hat with a generous bill or brim. Socks should be synthetic or wool — again, not cotton as it chafes.

### Is it warm now, but possibly cooler later? Maybe a hint of rain?

**Challenge:** Temps are in the 60s but you know that as the afternoon sun slips lower in the horizon and you head into the shadows, things are going to get chilly. To make matters more challenging, the clouds gathering above seem to indicate a light drizzle is in the offing. You need to worry about staying cool and dry during the warm hours of the day while having a few garments nearby to hold the heat in when the temperatures start to dip.

**Solution:** Wear a lightweight, synthetic-fiber, long underwear top. If you get cold easily, add the bottoms too. Loose-fitting shorts or long pants cover the lower extremities. A short-sleeve T-shirt of cotton/synthetic blend adorns your upper. **Getting cool?** Toss on a midweight fleece pullover or wool sweater. Light fleece pants will take the chill off your legs. **Wind blowing with a bit of rain sprinkling down?** Slip into a waterproof/breathable shell jacket and add the pants for extra protection. A baseball-style cap tops off the ensemble. Pack along a wool cap just in case.

### Is there a chill to the air, with a bit of damp snow swirling in a breeze that can't make up its mind on strength or direction?

**Challenge:** Brrrr . . . the temperature is hovering around 31 degrees, it's snowing, and a slight breeze is cutting through the air. Call it quits? Not a chance! As long as your layering system works to shed the wind, seal out the damp snow, and move the inevitable sweat storm from inside to outside, you'll be toasty. Remember always the maxim, "cotton kills." The key to happiness is in the judicious donning and doffing of insulative layers that are flexible and light, water-hating undies that whisk moisture away from your skin, and a water-resistant, extremely breathable outer layer. One final tip: Start your winter romp feeling slightly underdressed and chilly. You will soon warm up. Start it warm and you will soon overheat.

**Solution:** Wear lightweight, synthetic fabric, long underwear tops and bottoms. Add a midweight or expedition-weight synthetic underwear top for extra warmth. On top of the underwear put on a light fleece jacket and fleece pants. **Need more insulation?** Add a synthetic or down parka which is large enough to accommodate all the layers underneath. **Is the wind cutting through you?** Slip into a waterproof/breathable mountain parka shell and shell pants with side-zip entry. Add gaiters to keep the snow out of your boots. You will need an insulated hat, either wool or synthetic (I prefer fleece bomber hats). Insulated gloves or mittens are a must. **If it's really cold,** you want to protect your head and face with a synthetic balaclava.

Why do I need all this fancy stuff just to go outdoors in the mud and dirt? Fair question. Like the introduction of Gore-Tex years ago, all this fabric and fiber mumbo jumbo has its skeptics, but they are fast falling by the wayside. You don't have to opt for this high-tech function/fashion statement, but why on earth would you not want to? It works, and it works leagues better than anything that has come before. With an appropriate layering system of advanced materials, weather is no longer a discomfort or nuisance — it's just a pleasurable change of pace. Of course, high-tech preferences aside, the old-school approach of surplus clothing, wool, and silk will work, and if that is all you can afford or want to afford, so be it. You'll still have a much better time being outdoors than sitting in.

# Keeping Your Feet Happy

If your toes could smile, quality socks would make them grin. Nothing ruins a trek through the outdoors faster than wet and hot feet, or cold and clammy feet. And while many folks are quick to run out and purchase a pricey pair of walking, running, or hiking shoes, many of these same folks still don't consider socks an important factor in footwear selection.

## Choosing socks

The best boots are only as good as the socks that go in them. And if you skimp on socks, even the most advanced footwear won't make your feet, socks, or boots comfortable. With that in mind, manufacturers have spent the last few years developing insulating, moisture-managing hosiery that can tread with even the most technical pair of hikers.

Most outdoor-specific socks are built to control the temperature and moisture of the foot by utilizing high-tech fibers that disperse moisture through a given area. But while synthetic fibers have garnered loads of attention for their superior moisture transfer properties, several manufacturers continue to tout the water-absorbing benefits of natural fibers, and are utilizing a blend of hydrophilic fiber (usually natural) and hydrophobic fiber (usually synthetic) for maximum comfort and moisture control.

The natural fiber of choice in hosiery remains wool, long sought for its moisture-loving and thermal-managing qualities. On the synthetic front, performance fibers and fabrics such as CoolMax, Thermax, Thermastat, polypropylene, and acrylic help move moisture away from the feet, keeping them dry and comfortable.

Which brands should you look for? I lean toward Thorlo, Dahlgren, Fox River, Wigwam, and SmartWool as the best socks for the outdoor person's feet.

## *Selecting footwear*

Blistered and aching feet are the vengeful opponents of happy hikers. Sore feet are preventable, however, if you follow a few simple guidelines both before and during a trek on the wilder side. When fitting boots:

- ✔ **Wear hiking socks.** Your hiking footwear must fit well or nothing you can do will save your feet from misery. Wear the socks you will use hiking and use the insole you prefer. All too often, hikers are in a rush and wearing thin socks when they purchase boots. Keep in mind, your feet will swell when hiking.

- ✔ **Do the roll test.** Check the width by lacing the boot firmly and rolling both feet from side to side. If your feet slide or you feel discomfort in the toe area from compression, try another size or boot.

- ✔ **Check toe, heel, and slide.** Correct length can be assured if your toes won't bang the front of the boot when you slide your foot forward (good stores have an incline board for such testing purposes). The heel must be snug to prevent up and down movement, but it should not pinch or bind. If your instep feels uncomfortable pressure, ask the salesperson to show you a boot with more volume.

- ✔ **Break 'em in.** Take the time to adequately break in your new boots. While lightweight boots feel comfortable almost from the moment you put them on, it will take a few days of walking around town to "mold" them to your foot's contours. Heavier boots made of leather require longer to break in adequately. The emergency method of soaking leather boots with warm water and then walking them dry does work, but only in a pinch — it's hellish on your feet.

- ✔ **Bring a second set.** Bring tennis shoes, moccasins, or all-terrain sandals to wear around the camp. Extra shoes such as sandals or tennis shoes also become useful during a stream crossing when footwear should be worn for foot protection and you don't want to get your boots wet.

So, you have a super pair of boots, the perfect fit and well broken in. Is that the end of the boot bit? Not on your tippy toes!

- ✔ **Use gaiters.** When hiking through muck, loose dirt, gravel, water, snow, and other debris that always seems to find its way into your boot, try wearing ankle-high gaiters. Certainly not a fashion statement, but if your feet are happy, who cares.

- ✔ **Reduce friction.** Attend to hot spots on your feet before they turn into fluid-filled monsters. Use molefoam, moleskin, Second Skin, or any other product (some people swear by duct tape — ouch!) that will eliminate friction at its source.

- ✔ **Keep your feet dry.** Use liberal amounts of foot powder while on the trail and take the time during rest breaks to let your toes wiggle in the sun for a while.

- ✔ **Change socks at lunch.** If your feet are prone to perspiring heavily, plan on a complete sock change at lunch or any other time you can enjoy an extended rest break. Dry socks help keep your feet and boots dry, and dry feet are less prone to blistering. The wet socks can be hung from your pack to dry.

Even if your boots fit well, a long hike over several days can swell feet sufficiently so that the toe area becomes tight. If your boots feel cramped in the toe, try trimming a little off the front of the inner soles to loosen up the toe box. You can always replace the inner sole. This won't work if the boots were fitted improperly to begin with.

# Caring for your boot leather

Pssst . . . Hey, you! Those boots of yours are looking a little ragged. Not to worry, mate. We've got just the thing. What's your pleasure? Wax, silicone, grease, oil, creme, lotion, or a blend? Want that in liquid, paste, spray, or squeeze tube? Not sure? Man, just slap some butter on the biscuit, my friend, it's all the same to your boot. Or is it?

Despite what you hear from well-meaning sales folk and knowledgeable friends, leather care tips are often nothing more than age-old myths and common misinformation. Between these poles, there do exist a number of truths about leather conditioning and waterproofing.

I went to the boot manufacturers and leather-care product companies to unearth answers to some questions that seem pretty clear, and eliminate a few of the age-old myths and tidbits of common misinformation.

### How should you care for a Gore-Tex or waterproof/breathable membrane-lined boot?

Forget pastes or waxes that coat the surface of the leather, making it impermeable to water and air, despite what some manufacturers may say to the contrary. According to Gore, you need to treat the leather to keep it water-resistant (rather like using a durable water repellent on a jacket) but the leather must remain breathable. Any treatment that stops the breathability of leather is not recommended by Gore, nor is any treatment that dictates a heavy laydown. Would you coat the outside of a Gore-Tex jacket with a waterproof layer to shed the rain? Not if you still want it to breathe.

Also, according to Gore, salts or dirt do not affect the breathability of Gore-Tex. Neither will oils, polish, silicone, nor any other conditioner or treatment harm the Gore-Tex.

## Adding zip and cush to your stride

Buying a boot without a custom footbed is a bit like purchasing a luxury car that has been outfitted with economy car seats. Why on earth would you want to? It's true enough that every shoe and boot does come with its own insole, or footbed, but those production models are simply designed to inexpensively offer you a "new car feel" and consist more of fillers than functional parts of the shoe.

Why don't the makers of $150-and-up boots put higher-quality footbeds in their boots? Cost is one factor, but fit is the overriding concern. Consider that the foot consists of 26 bones and 109 ligaments, and that the multitude of foot shapes, contours, and curves as well as an individual's body support needs and requirements vary widely. The best a manufacturer can hope for with an insole is to ensure that the boot feels comfortable out of the box and offers a universal fit, within certain parameters.

That is where the custom footbed comes in. A good footbed that meets the needs of the user serves to customize the fit of the boot and give it a more personal feel, and puts the foot in the right places inside the boot and keeps it there. In other words the footbed is an integral part of the boot's fit and performance — essential gear, if you will.

Still think a footbed is unimportant? Then ponder this: According to the Michigan Podiatric Medical Association, the average person will walk 115,000 miles in her lifetime and take between 8,000 and 10,000 steps every day. Each step exerts on the feet a pressure as much as three to four times a person's body weight — more with a backpack on. No wonder your dogs are tired after a long day in the woods!

### Silicone will not destroy a boot's glue or stitching

Silicone comes in both polymer and oil form and is highly compatible with leather and by itself does not hurt a boot's materials. What did hurt boots was the solvent or carrying agent used in the early days — methyl chloroform. That solvent dissolved stitching, glues, and some leather finishes, and is no longer used. Now, the silicone and petroleum solvents used in boot care products carry vital oils into the leather to replenish oils that wear out of leather over time.

### Never use heat to dry a boot

Unless you are planning to cook and eat your boots, heat has no place in the drying process. To properly dry boots, remove the footbeds and laces, open fully, and allow them to dry naturally at room temperature.

### Layer lightly

Too much of a good thing can make your boots droopy or tacky. Properly applied in thin layers, oils and waxes can work well. Improperly applied, waxes gunk up the surface of the leather, attracting dirt and grime, and oils soak into the leather to the point of oversaturation, which can lead to leather breakdown.

### Keep the leather clean

Leather needs to be kept clean to lengthen its life, inside and out. Although a simple washing with ordinary soap and water will suffice, a number of manufacturers offer care kits complete with soap, soft-scrub brushes, and conditioner. Be sure you thoroughly rinse whatever soaps you use out of the leather as many detergents are hydrophilic — not an ideal companion residue for a boot leather.

### Wet leather chills feet

Saturated leather conducts heat away from the foot and can quickly lead to chilling. Worse, it becomes non-breathable. You must treat your boots, even factory-waterproofed leathers, periodically to maintain the water repellency of the outer face of the leather.

### Treatments will darken leather

Most treatments alter the color or look of the leather somewhat. Typically, this means a darkening of the leather. However, in the case of Nubuck, split-grain, rough-out, or suede, waxes and oils will not only darken, they will smooth over the nap.

# Speaking leather

The following are some of the more common terms describing leather:

- **Full-grain or top-grain leather.** Smooth finish and highest-quality leather. Comes from the top layer of hide when split by the knife.

- **Nubuck leather.** A full-grain leather that has been sanded on the surface. Why? To hide possible imperfections, improve penetration of conditioning or waterproofing agents, or simply for cosmetics.

- **Suede or split leather.** Comes from the innermost part of the hide when split. The leather is less dense and more fibrous, also less durable than full-grain.

- **Reversed or rough-out leather.** Full-grain leather where the smooth surface is placed on the inside of the finished boot.

- **Oil-tanned leather.** A softer leather that can be waterproofed or conditioned with nearly all types of topical applications, including silicone, wax, oil, mink oil, grease, or fluoropolymers.

- **Chrome-tanned leather.** A harder leather with low porosity. Oils should not be used as they will soften the leather. Waxes or fluoropolymers or quick-drying silicone applications are best.

- **Waterproofed leather.** While determining the exact formulation is a bit like ferreting out what the specific ingredients are in Coca-Cola, suffice it to say most of these are silicone-based impregnation or tanning. That said, silicone or a water-based wax appears to be the best after-market application and the one most often recommended by boot manufacturers.

# Matching your boot to your activity

I have put together a list of the various kinds of boots and the names of my favorite manufacturers in each category. From there, it is up to you to work with a good salesperson to decide which model, amid the almost mind-boggling array of design choices, feels the best on your foot.

### Light hikers/trekking

Shoes in this category work as well in the mall and out of a travel bag as they do dancing lightly over easy to moderate terrain. The user is seeking freedom of movement and comfort and, unless feeling very adventurous, not seeking to get too wild or carry anything more than a daypack.

Typically an ankle-high or low-top shoe/boot with flexible, well-cushioned soles and reasonably stable laterally — if you can tie them in knots, they should be tossed in the noodle-boot pile. Primarily a fabric/leather construction to keep the boot light and cool, but keep in mind that what you are gaining in flexibility and comfort is traded off for minimal support and only minimal water resistance. Quarter-length steel shanks are common for added support.

Manufacturers of light hikers include Adidas, Asolo, Danner, Fabiano, Five Ten, Hi-Tec, Legends, Lowa, Merrell, New Balance, Nike, Montrail, Raichle, Reebok, Rocky, Salomon, Tecnica, Timberland, and Vasque.

### Backpacking

The category for those who seek to walk on the wilder side while maintaining an air of civility — just the trails and nothing but the trails, thank you. You need more support because the foot must now bear the weight of both the user and his/her 35-plus-pound pack over sometimes variable terrain surfaces.

Although the fabric/leather combinations have dominated this category in the past, the all-leather boot is making a strong comeback because all-leather often offers better fit possibilities, longer lasting footwear, increased waterproofness, and, with improved boot construction technology, lighter weights as well. This category of boot usually features rigid heel cups, solid toe boxes, stiffer midsoles, quarter- to half-length steel shanks for added torsional rigidity, lug soles, and padded uppers, especially around the ankles. Still, despite all the additional features, the boot's flex at the ball of the foot remains relatively supple, a key characteristic when you are walking long trail miles on the beaten path.

Manufacturers of backpacking boots include Adidas, Asolo, Boreal, Coleman, Danner, Fabiano, Five Ten, Hi-Tec, La Sportiva, Lowa, Merrell, New Balance, Nike, Montrail, Raichle, Reebok, Rocky, Salomon, Tecnica, Timberland, and Vasque.

### Off-trail

This is the category for those who venture off the beaten path for days on end, often into rocky, snowy, wet, and trailless terrain. Support, traction, foot protection, waterproofness, and durability are key concerns.

Heavy-duty boots featuring soles with deep, high-traction treads or high-friction rubber combinations and stiff, above-the-ankle support — mostly the domain of the all-leather construction. Fewer seams in the construction and full-grain leather add to the durability and waterproofing capabilities of these boots. Rubber rands around the midsoles add to the durability and weatherproofing capabilities. Soles are stiff enough to smooth out the rough bumps and jumps of off-trail trekking, yet flexible enough to be supportive while remaining comfortable enough to be practical for extended on- and off-trail wandering.

Manufacturers of off-trail boots include Adidas, Alpina, Asolo, Boreal, Danner, Fabiano, Hi-Tec, La Sportiva, Lowa, Merrell, Montrail, Raichle, Salomon, Tecnica, and Vasque.

### Mountaineering

The crampons (climbing irons) are never too far away for those who are looking to wear a mountaineering boot. Boots in this category must protect the user's feet, keep them dry and warm, offer superior traction on a wide variety of terrain including rock and ice, be amazingly durable, and still be reasonably comfortable.

Intended for the world of rock and ice, these boots are heavy and sturdy and need an extended break-in period. Soles are curved or "rockered" for trail comfort, yet stiff enough with a three-quarter to full-length steel shank for rigidity when climbing and wearing crampons. Lug pattern is predominantly Vibram. Full-grain leather with gusseted tongues or plastic shells are the lay-up for the uppers.

Manufacturers of mountaineering footwear include Boreal, Fabiano, Koflach/Atomic, La Sportiva, Lowa, Merrell, Montrail, Raichle, Salomon, Tecnica, and Vasque.

## Fitting tips for hard-to-fit feet

If your foot feels sloppy in the boot (you can't cinch the laces any tighter because the eyelets are already touching) but the length and width appear fine, chances are you have what is called a low-volume foot and you are trying to fit into a high-volume boot. Try these solutions before you toss the boot:

✔ First, try taking the footbed out and replacing it with a better footbed such as one manufactured by SuperFeet.

✔ Second, try a thicker sock.

✔ Third, place a tongue depressor between the laces and the tongue when lacing the boot. If that works, take the boot to a cobbler to open up the tongue and permanently sew the depressor inside the boot's tongue.

✔ Finally, take a piece of five-iron (a one-eighth-inch neoprene rubber midsole material that shoe repair people use) and trace the footbed by angling the pencil inward. Thus, the five-iron cutout will be slightly smaller than the footbed. Place the five-iron cutout under the footbed.

## _Lacing creatively for better fit_

Sure, you learned to tie your shoes when you were a mere tyke, toddling across the earth on uncertain feet. But it's time to add some more lacing options to your shoe-tying repertoire if you wish to guarantee the best fit for your trail-trekking dogs. To maximize your options, be sure that when you purchase your footwear there are no sharp edges on the eyelets, D-rings, or speed hooks that will fray your laces. Also, toss the round laces and install flat nylon laces instead — they hold knots much more securely.

✔ Wrapping the laces three times around each other will allow you to adjust the tension of the lacing both above and below the triple wrap (see Figure 3-2).

**Figure 3-2:**
The triple-wrap lacing technique.

✔ Sometimes, you may encounter a pressure point or hot spot on the top of the foot along the instep. You can alleviate the pain by tying a double or triple wrap below the trouble spot, skipping the eyelets or D-rings at the trouble spot, and then tying another double or triple wrap above the troubled area before resuming your lacing as normal (see Figure 3-3).

**Figure 3-3:**
Lacing to avoid a hot spot.

✔ Are you having trouble maintaining tight laces as you secure your boots? It's a common problem with an easy solution. Tighten your laces up and over speed hooks (see Figure 3-4). By effectively wrapping each hook, you will maintain enough friction to easily tighten your laces.

## P.S.: Lace your gloves, too

Many winter gloves and mittens come without the benefit of security straps or leashes, making it far too easy to lose them should you have to bare your digits to achieve dexterity. It's so easy to create a leash, however, that losing mittens or gloves should become a thing of the past. Cut about 16 to 20 inches of flat lace (available at most specialty outdoor shops) for each glove. You'll also need one cord-lock for each glove. Fold the lace in half and push the folded (closed) end through the cord-lock. Tie a knot at each end of the lace (two ends, two knots). Sew one knotted end of the lace into your glove or mitten. Pull the lace through the cord-lock to make a loop, slide your hand into the loop and then snug the lace around your wrist. Now you can remove your hand from your glove or mitten and it will dangle securely from your wrist, even in a howling wind.

**Figure 3-4:**
The tight-
lace tech-
nique.

## Clothing and more tips for camping with children

Your clothing needs will depend on several basic elements:

- ✔ How young your children are
- ✔ What your definition of dirty is
- ✔ How much you are willing to carry

Babies and toddlers need more clothing because they are more likely to get it dirty. Stretch one-piece suits are ideal for this age as they protect the entire body not only from the elements but from insects as well. The older the child, the less often he or she is likely to require a change. But your standards of cleanliness are a factor, too. The following tips will help you to keep your children comfy and happy:

- Babies should wear a light-colored hat with a shading brim at all times. Some hats for babies come with a darker underside so that they don't reflect the bright sun down into the eyes.

- Never, ever bury diapers in the outdoors. Always carry out what you carry in. While many parents use cloth diapers, the washing and drying can be tiresome.

- Select bright-colored clothing to keep your children visible. Stay away from blue as it does seem to attract mosquitoes and gnats more than other colors. Choose synthetics such as pile, polypropylene, Capilene, fleece, and Thermax, which dry faster than natural fibers.

- Buy clothing with growth in mind. Most younger children tend to grow more in length than width, so do not be afraid to buy clothing a little long: You can always roll up the excess at the ankles or arms. Some manufacturers make clothes with growth adjustments built into their jackets. Look for pants with adjustable or elastic waistbands.

- Washing camp clothes greatly reduces the number of extra outfits you have to carry for your child. But there are some drawbacks. You will be dependent on warm and sunny weather to dry out the clothes — if it is wet and the clothes do not dry, what then? Additionally, I do not find being tied to a wash basin and clothesline my idea of an outdoor recreation escape.

- Most young children seem to prefer tennis shoes to hiking boots. Boots are an appropriate purchase if weather or difficult hiking conditions — snow, loose rocks, wet or muddy terrain — dictate more foot protection. Children should be wearing their hiking socks when you fit them for boots. Do not buy boots with the intention of having the child grow into them — that's only asking for blisters and misery.

# Chapter 4

# Wintering, Paddling, Biking

• • • • • • • • • • • • • • • • • • • • • • • • • • • • • • • • • • • • • • • • • •

• • • • • • • • • • • • • • • • • • • • • • • • • • • • • • • • • • • • • • • • • •

*I*f you've already enjoyed the outdoors by backpack or car-camping expedition, perhaps it's time to ratchet up for new, more demanding adventures. Seeing the wild lands in the winter by snowshoe or ski, or in warm weather from the saddle of a mountain bike or helm of a watercraft, adds a zest to camping that you'll never forget. And with proper planning and a bit of training, these "advanced" camping experiences can be — pleasurable too! My advice in this chapter is not the last word on the topics but, I hope, an inspirational primer to get your juices flowing and guide you in making the best decisions. As always, before you embark on any outdoor adventure, talk to the pros and to campers who've been there, and let common sense be your companion at all times.

# Winter Camping

Just because the mercury has dipped and snow blankets the ground, you don't have to hibernate. Winter camping means escaping crowds, camping without bugs or dirt, and seeing the outdoors in an entirely new light. You can have fun and you can stay warm, if you're well prepared. But winter adventures are very different from warm-weather camping — for lots of reasons besides temperature.

For one thing, how are you going to move around when the woods are heaped with snow? Last time I checked, you couldn't get a trolley in the outback. So — will it be skis or snowshoes? I include advice later in this chapter. And did you say you planned to eat and sleep out there? I cover those topics in this chapter as well. But first, here is some advice on stuff that will warm your heart, and your two thousand other parts.

# Dressing warm

In Chapter 3, I talk about dressing right for any season. The idea is to dress in layers, and it really works, but only if you choose the right textiles and layer properly. Versatility is the key and synthetics are king, although a mix of wool in the outer layers is superb. As for winter attire, I select midweight synthetic long underwear as a base layer with a zip-T top for ventilation. On top of that I place side-zip fleece pants and a full-front zip synthetic sweater. A wool vest, a down parka, and windproof/waterproof shell jacket and pants round out the ensemble. The way to use your layers is to undress and unzip — or dress and zip up — as temperature changes dictate, all with the intent of maintaining a constant and comfortable body temperature with a minimum of sweat output.

Forget cotton — leave those colorful cotton T-shirts and sweats in your "summer" drawer at home. The problem with cotton in the winter is that it holds your sweat like a dishrag and chills you to the bone. That old wilderness saying "Cotton kills" is no cliché but the hard, cold truth!

### Keeping your tootsies warm

Socks should be medium weight and fit well, with no rough or bunchy seams. Thor Lo makes my favorite socks. Wigwam, SmartWool, and Fox River also make super winter socks of wool. Fit your boots with socks in mind. Forget Pac boots, like Sorels, for hiking. They are cumbersome and hot, and your feet will hate them after only a few hours. For performance and warmth, go with well-waterproofed and insulated leather boots or plastic mountaineering boots with removable insulated liners. For added protection on snow and ice, you may want to attach crampons (metal spikes) to your boots. Keep that in mind when you select boots: Are they crampon-adaptable? Gaiters — those leg coverings that reach from instep to ankle or higher — will keep snow from building up on your legs and migrating into your boots. Insulated gaiters add warmth.

### Protecting your head and hands

To keep my hands warm, I wear a thin liner glove inside an insulated outer glove that has reinforced patches to improve grip and protect against rips. This two-part glove works well. As for the head, they say up to 80 percent of your body's heat is lost through the noggin, and who's to argue? It is a simple matter of fact that by wearing a hat, you will feel warmer. I opt for a thin synthetic balaclava — a knit cap covering head and neck — that I can wear under my fleece trapper's hat. So I look like Elmer Fudd?! I'm warm. To complete your headgear, don't forget mountaineering sunglasses with side blocks or goggles to protect your eyes from the burning rays of the sun. I have more to say about eyewear later in this chapter.

# Sleeping warm

Sleeping warm starts with a well-insulated foundation — the sleeping pad. Use a full-length pad. I use a full-length standard ThermaRest. Some people also carry a lightweight closed-cell foam pad in addition to a self-inflating pad, for added insulation and to sit on when taking a break. What you pack depends on how much you're willing to carry. Your sleeping bag should be rated for at least 0°F, although I would take one rated at 10 to 15 degrees below zero on the Fahrenheit scale. You can always unzip a tad if you're too warm. Mummy-style bags are more heat-efficient than the rectangular-shape sleeping bag. And measured by heat-to-weight ratio, down bags are lighter — just be sure to keep your down-filled bag dry 'cause wet feathers don't insulate at all. See Chapter 2 for more on sleeping bags.

# Eating for warmth

You need to eat often on a winter camp-out so that your body can process the food and turn it into heat energy. Winter adventuring demands a lot of fuel — up to 8,000 calories a day. Nuts, cheese, dried fruit, jerky, pasta and vegetable soups, rice, and noodles are super fare. Hot beverages at every opportunity make for a bigger winter camping smile, trust me. Even at a lunch break, I pop out the stove to make a quick cocoa or hot Gatorade. Stay away from caffeine in your tea or coffee as it is a diuretic that causes you to lose vital fluids.

### Thirsty? Hungry? Plan ahead

If you're winter camping in snow, cooking and drinking often means first melting snow, which takes lots of fuel. Think about it: Your body needs four quarts of water per day to stave off dehydration, and you need another two quarts a day for cooking. If your winter water supply is snow, that's a lot of melting! Your stove should be well suited for melting snow and boiling water. Forget a simmer feature; you'll never use it. The old standby MSR XGK is still the best stove for winter camping, bar none. The amount of fuel you need depends on how much cooking you plan to do, but you should plan on taking at least at 4 fluid ounces of fuel per person per day.

### Water

Wide-mouth plastic bottles are super for carrying water as long as you have a pouch or pack pocket to carry them in. But without the pocket, the bottles can become a nuisance — who wants to carry a bottle in the hand all day? However, with a little duct tape and a three- to four-foot section of webbing, you can make a very serviceable carrying strap, turning your bottle into an easy-to-carry canteen. Here's how:

---

## Bathing when it's freezing out

A bandanna and a small pot of warm water is all I use to wash my face and hands — no soap. If you want a little more cleansing and don't relish scrubbing your body with snow (it does work, although there is little pleasure in this method), I suggest using a no-rinse soap or shampoos sold at travel and outdoor specialty stores. You simply apply the product to your hair or body, massage until a lather forms, then towel dry, using something like a PacTowel by Cascade Designs. The towel will get very dirty — the dirt has to go somewhere — but for the one or two cleanings you may desire, one towel should suffice. Atwater Carey/Wisconsin Pharmacal puts together a nifty Camp 'N' Travel kit with towel, scrubber, camp soap (to be used with water), a bottle of No-Rinse Body Bath and a bottle of No-Rinse Shampoo. Another tried and true method of cleaning employs baby wipes in travel packs. Two or three will do to cleanse the face, hands, and other parts of the body. The downside to this routine is that you have to pack out all the used wipes, and the fragrance often used in baby wipes can become a bit much.

---

1. **Using tubular or flat webbing (pick a color and style that matches your personality), create a loop by tying an overhand bend or ring bend knot.**

   Ask your outdoor store to show you how. The loop should be long enough that when draped over your shoulder, each end hangs near your hip.

2. **Using duct tape, secure the loop to the water bottle so that the webbing runs completely down each side and supports the bottom of the bottle.**

3. **Position the knot just above the bottle lid.**

## Practicing "safe sun"

Coming home with a glorious glow of health is one of the many rewards of camping. But getting badly burned is something else. Although the pain of a sunburn fades, the potential lasting damage and even fatal consequences of letting your skin burn are all too real. Does this mean you have to hide indoors and resort to nocturnal explorations? Not at all. Just practice "safe sun" and you should stay happy, healthy, and wise for many years of fun to come.

### Simple truths

You have seen the following "sunspots" a thousand times before. Once more for emphasis:

- **Minimize your exposure to the sun at its strongest times.** It is strongest between 10 a.m. and 2 p.m. (11 a.m. and 3 p.m. during daylight saving time).

✔ **Overcast days are no guarantee of sun protection.** The sun's rays are just as damaging, and sunscreens are still a must.

✔ **The higher you climb, the more intense the sun's rays become.** Less atmosphere exists to diffuse the damaging rays, so pile on the sunscreen.

✔ **Sand, snow, water and even concrete will reflect the sun's rays back to your skin.** Generously coat yourself in sunscreen, even under your earlobes and chin, and just inside your nostrils. The sun reflects unmercifully and can manage to toast some mighty strange places you never thought about tanning.

### Cover up and put on a lid

Select your winter attire with these pointers in mind:

✔ Always wear a hat with a generous bill to shade your face and scalp.

✔ Most clothing is no guarantee of sun protection. Loose weaves and wet clothing still allow dangerous burning rays to get through.

✔ Fair-skinned people should apply sunscreen even under their clothing.

### Seeing clearly

Wear sunglasses or goggles in sunny and slightly overcast conditions. On snow, sunglasses also need to have side-block panels to prevent sun from reflecting into the sides of the glasses. Those kinds of sunglasses are often called glacier glasses.

## Translating those sunscreen numbers

Sunscreening lotions are rated by "SPF" power, which stands for "sun protection factor" — the level of burn protection you can expect over a given period of time. For example, if your unprotected skin turns red in the sun after only 15 minutes of exposure, by applying a sunscreen with an SPF of 10 you can reasonably expect your skin to not burn for 150 minutes. My advice:

✔ **Apply sunscreen with SPF 15 or higher before every exposure to the sun at sea level.** Skiers and mountaineers shouldn't think of heading outdoors without applying a sunscreen with an SPF of 25 or higher.

✔ **Reapply sunscreen frequently and liberally every two hours for as long as you stay in the sun.** Sunscreen should always be reapplied after perspiring heavily or swimming — even if the product claims to be waterproof.

✔ **If you are taking medications, using birth-control pills, or wearing certain cosmetics, you risk an increased sensitivity to the sun and a possible allergic reaction when using sunscreen.** Check with your doctor or dermatologist for advice.

The higher you rise above sea level, the less that the atmosphere filters out radiation. Due to the reflective nature of snow and sand, up to 85 percent of the ultraviolet (UV) radiation may be reflected upward, emphasizing the reason that experienced campers wear mountaineering-style sunglasses or goggles in sunny and slightly overcast conditions.

Long-term exposure to UV radiation has been linked to serious eye disease such as cataracts. Short-term exposure can produce snow blindness. At the very least, goggles or sunglasses should remove 100 percent of UV radiation.

## Winter locomotion: Skis or snowshoes?

What's your choice of transportation — skis or snowshoes? I've seen aficionados come to near blows over which is best. As a user of both, I'll only say that skiing and snowshoeing each has pluses and minuses.

### Snowshoes

For a beginner, snowshoes may be easier because they offer more traction. Snowshoes are also faster when the terrain is steep and there are lots of ups and downs to negotiate; they're much easier to use going uphill. Snowshoes also are easier if the terrain is very rugged with lots of brush and rocks to work through and around. Snowshoes require little skill to master and are typically less expensive than Alpine skis.

---

### Snowshoeing

Many years ago, when I was a young ski instructor (don't ask how young, please) and the head of a cross-country ski center, I attempted to teach my father to ski. He was very patient and — I think to humor me — even went out on his own for a short tour after my lesson. It wasn't long, however, before he showed up back at the lodge and pointed to a pair of old, wooden snowshoes hanging on the wall.

"What are those?" he asked.

"Awww, Dad, those are snowshoes. Skiing is much faster and far more fun. . . ."

My voice trailed off as I recognized the look that said, "Fun for you perhaps, but not fun for me."

I handed Dad the snowshoes and didn't see him again for nearly six hours. But I kept hearing reports from other skiers who passed a "cheerful" man with a marvelous accent (he's British) walking energetically with a big smile and wearing snowshoes and a tweed jacket (like I said, he's British). Because of my father, several others wanted to try snowshoes and returned them hours later telling me it was the most fun on snow they'd had in years.

---

Winter wanderers are finding that snowshoes open up a world of possibility since even a beginning snowshoer or a family with children in tow can often travel over much more territory with much less effort than even an experienced cross-country skier. Why? Because snowshoes are stable and offer superior flotation and grip in even the worst of snow conditions.

What do snowshoes cost? For adult sizes, plan on spending around $150 to $250 for a snowshoe and binding package. For a few dollars here and there, it is possible to add accouterments such as insulated bindings (for those really cold days) and heel cleats (for days when even a surefooted snowshoe wants to act like a runaway bobsled). Snowshoes for children (typically made of molded high-density plastic) cost in the range of $40 to $50. They aren't as streamlined as the adult versions, but frankly, the children won't notice — they're too busy romping and stomping to care.

If you are at all in doubt about how you will use the snowshoe or what size is really best for you, don't buy for awhile — "demo" them. An increasing number of retail stores offer demo rentals, as do many ski resorts. After you have your snowshoes, no other gear is required. Standard hiking boots, or even running shoes if you are seeking a workout, are all the footwear snowshoeing requires. Dress in layers as you would for skiing, but be prepared to peel down to minimum — snowshoeing can work up quite a glow. If balance seems to be a problem, or if you just want an additional security blanket to keep from falling in the white stuff, opt for ski poles. A pole in each hand will offer four-point stability in somewhat awkward conditions.

A few basic technique considerations can make your initial foray a little easier:

- ✔ Always switch off the lead when breaking trail as it can be both tiring and awkward.

- ✔ When climbing uphill, keep your weight over the balls of your feet. Traversing a slope is more difficult, but can be accomplished by either "sawing" or "kicking" your uphill edge of the snowshoe into the snow.

- ✔ Heading downhill means keeping your weight over the balls of the feet and consciously digging the binding cleats into the snow. Lean back and you will "butt-slide" all the way down for sure.

- ✔ As for level terrain, there isn't much more to it than one foot in front of the other.

If you are of the snowshoe persuasion, let me gently remind you and anyone else who elects to hoof it and not ski — ski trails are for skiers only. Foot traffic and snowshoe use should be kept off to the side of any established ski trail.

## Pulka sleds

Pulka sleds are ideal for kids who are too young to ski but want to go skiing anyway. On ski tours, it's not safe to carry infants and toddlers in backpacks or child carriers. Children's legs can get constricted in a pack or carrier, and that can can lead to frostbite and the reduced circulation that promotes hypothermia. The pulka sled is made of wood or fiberglass and is designed to carry one to three children and/or supplies. The sled is towed behind an adult using a padded waist or shoulder harness. A waterproof cover keeps the tykes dry and protected from the wind.

### Skis

On the fun-meter side, snowshoes don't hold a candle to a good pair of backcountry or touring skis on the downhills. Skis are also much quicker and less fatiguing over large tracts of open and flat country.

Cross-country skiing, or Nordic ski touring, is great fun for the family and an excellent add-on to winter camping trips provided the terrain is not too difficult. Basing out of a campground with surrounding meadows laden in snow is good. Even better: basing out of a campground near a resort or a Forest Service area with set tracks, quality teaching areas, warming huts along the trail, certified instructors, and lots of other activities such as skating and sledding.

The skills necessary to stay on your feet and have fun on cross-country skis — Nordic skiing — are quite easily acquired. More and more ski resorts have excellent learn-to-ski programs for families and children. I heartily recommend that everyone in your family who doesn't know how to cross-country ski take a lesson from a professional. (Learning from a family member or close friend can be rewarding but often ends in frustration for all.) What's so good about Nordic skiing is that virtually everyone can join the fun. So teach your tribe this great winter sport — a skill that lasts a lifetime.

## Must-haves for snowy terrain

If you're venturing into heavy snow and rugged terrain, seriously consider adding these items to your gear:

- **An "avalanche shovel."** It's small, compact, lightweight, and durable, and you'll need it to dig tent platforms, create snow walls, or to bury your tent's snow stakes for added security.

- **An avalanche probe.** If an avalanche does descend on your group, the probe will save precious seconds, perhaps someone's life.

- ✔ **First-aid kit with plenty of warming packets, sunblock, lip balm, and moisturizer.**

- ✔ **Mountaineer's headlamp with lithium batteries.** This torch will add brightness to shorter days and longer nights.

- ✔ **Water filter.** Any water you get from a stream is still potentially contaminated, even if the temperature outside is well below zero.

## Quick tips for winter security

Heading out by ski, snowshoe, or foot into a winter wonderland is a mystical, and to some the ultimately satisfying, outdoor experience. But stepping into the world of cold and snow also requires a little more forethought and a different attitude to remain safe, comfortable, and happy. A few tips:

- ✔ **Keep your flashlight, camera, and other battery-powered items warm, unless you are using lithium batteries.** If the batteries appear to be dead, try warming them next to your skin before replacing them. "Dead" batteries sometimes are just cold. Alkaline batteries are especially bad on this score, but rechargeables are the worst.

- ✔ **Keep your water bottles stored upside down in your pack or pack pockets if you are traveling all day.** Why? Because water freezes from the top down, and by storing your bottles upside down you will still have drinkable water near the cap. Forget this tip and you will have to resort to licking ice, assuming you can even remove the bottle top.

- ✔ **Always travel with the following items readily accessible and on your person, not buried in a pack pocket: knife, waterproof matches, sunscreen, map and compass, candy, energy snacks.**

- ✔ **Look like a Ninja.** Black or very dark clothing is more efficient at absorbing solar radiation, keeping you warmer and helping your clothing to dry more quickly should it get damp.

- ✔ **To keep the skin dry, pace yourself.** Overexertion means you will be pumping out sweat to chill the body, and that process burns up energy you need for warmth.

- ✔ **Get in the habit of tucking your mittens/gloves into your coat whenever you take them off.** More pairs of mittens lose their owners at rest stops than you can imagine. And bare fingers are not only uncomfortable in freezing air but susceptible to frostbite if uncovered long enough.

- ✔ **Carry a repair kit.** The items you need in a repair kit depend on the camping gear you are using, but take at least duct tape (wrapped around a ski pole or a water bottle) for miscellaneous repairs, baling wire, an awl (one on your Swiss Army knife or multitool will suffice), sewing needle, extra nylon thread, parts for your stove, and spare parts for your skis or snowshoes if you are using them.

---

## What else to take?

You've heard it before . . . be prepared! You never know what may come in handy when you're outdoors in winter. Here are some additional items to think about tossing in your pack:

- Map/guide book
- Compass
- Ample water and food supply
- Knife
- Flashlight/headlamp (for those unforgettable moonlight jaunts)

- Waterproof matches and lighter
- First-aid kit (including bandages, tape, and ointments)
- Notebook and pencil
- Whistle
- Plastic bags for keeping gear dry
- Camera and film
- Binoculars

---

This tip is a twofer, both parts involving your flashlight. First, a flashlight barrel makes an ideal place to store the duct tape that you will inevitably need for some form of repair — just wrap a few lengths around the barrel. Second, finding your flashlight in the dark can be a challenge. Since they don't make "clap-on" flashlights (thank goodness!), I wrap a length of glow-in-the-dark tape around the lens of my light to make it easier to locate. Sure it looks goofy, but I bet I find my light before yours on any camp-out, any night.

# Paddling Your Way through Wilderness

Exploring the wilderness via raft, canoe, or flat-water kayak may be the ultimate camping experience. Paddle touring presents a virtual smorgasbord of fun and relatively safe trips in extremely beautiful surroundings. Paddling becomes a very comfortable way to transport yourself and your family or friends with a bare minimum of effort. It is especially ideal for the family with young children who can't walk lengthy distances.

## Be safe and learn the skills

Traveling by boat does have its hazards. Heavy winds can whip up waves on a glassy calm lake and overturn a canoe or kayak. A gentle river can surprise the paddler with unannounced rapids around a distant bend. No person should attempt touring on the water without acquiring basic paddling skills and safety knowledge. Classes, clubs, and various demonstration days sponsored by manufacturers are excellent sources of information and instruction.

I recommend that everyone in your group know how to float and tread water comfortably before heading out on a lake or river. Organizations such as the YMCA teach how to drown-proof babies and children as young as 2 years old and teach teens and adults how to swim. Inquire at a local community pool for information.

## Buying supplies and equipment

Purchasing a canoe or kayak, paddles, life preservers, and other necessary gear can be somewhat expensive and a tad confusing. Choosing a boat is a personal and highly individual decision — and no canoe or kayak works well under all circumstances.

Questions, questions. Will you be using the boat on flat water or whitewater? Will you be paddling rivers or lakes? How much weight and gear will the canoe or kayak be holding? How durable does it need to be? How much can you afford to spend? All of these questions need to be explored with a competent salesperson before deciding on your purchase. Although a canoe or kayak purchase is expensive, it is an item that can last a lifetime with proper care.

If buying is beyond your budget this year, that's okay. Many marinas and river and ocean outfitters, and some retailers, provide rental packages at reasonable rates. Most outfitters require you to demonstrate your competency in the craft or take a lesson from them before letting you out on the open water.

## Preserve your life

No safety consideration is more important than wearing a life preserver. Before embarking on a paddle trip, every person in the boat, even the smallest of children, must wear a Coast Guard–approved life preserver. An approved preserver is designed to keep a person floating upright and tilted slightly back with the face supported out of water, even when unconscious.

If you have any doubt about the effectiveness of a life preserver, test it: Have your child or other member of the family don the preserver and hang limp and totally relaxed in a pool. If they are not adequately supported according to the Coast Guard guidelines, the preserver is not safe. Also, be sure to check the fit and buoyancy of a child's preserver every year as the child grows. What may have fit and supported the child's weight last year could flunk the test this year.

# Dressing to paddle

When dressing for a paddle trip, remember that the body chills quite easily when wet, even in a very slight breeze. While a bathing suit or a T-shirt and shorts are appropriate in warm sunny weather, always be sure to pack long pants, a warm sweater, wool socks, and a rain suit just in case. In cooler weather, layer accordingly, just as you would for cross-country skiing or hiking. Beware of cottons and woolens that become extremely heavy when wet and tend to weigh a person down in the water.

### Footwear

You can wear tennis shoes, neoprene booties, sandals, specialized footwear, or go barefoot — the choices all have their pluses and minuses.

- **Tennis shoes:** Tennis shoes work very well in warm water and warm weather, but your feet can chill easily if the water is cold or the weather turns cool. If the shoes are big enough, putting on a pair of wool socks can help. Always pack an extra pair of shoes for everyone to wear when on shore. Hiking around in wet shoes is both uncomfortable and potentially dangerous — wet shoes on slippery rocks are often a bruising combination. Old tennis shoes with holes in them for drainage make great water play shoes. Because of the possibility of sharp rocks or sticks in the water, I think everyone should wear shoes when playing in the water.

- **Neoprene booties:** Some companies do make neoprene booties, rather like the ones divers wear, in smaller sizes with soles for walking. These are super as they keep the feet warm when wet, are lightweight, and easy to slip on. The drawback is that they keep your feet continually wet.

- **Slippers/paddling shoes:** Other types of boating footwear or paddling shoes similar to slippers are on the market and seem to work very well, although some users may think they are bulky and uncomfortable inside a kayak.

- **Sandals:** Sandals like Tevas are also good and can be worn with a pair of wool socks for insulation.

- **Barefoot:** It doesn't cost any extra to go with the footwear you were born with; however, I advise against it. All it takes is one slip on a sharp rock when portaging or getting into or out of your boat and you could end up with a nasty cut that is very uncomfortable, or worse, in a situation requiring immediate medical attention. Always wear footwear!

### Other necessities

Hats, sunglasses, and strong sunblock are absolute necessities when on the water. The sun's rays can be very intense when reflected off the water and will burn your skin very easily, especially if you have sensitive skin. Don't forget to reapply sunscreen after swimming, and don't overlook applying sunscreen under the ears and earlobes, under the chin, and under the nose — in reflected sun, those areas are often overlooked and burn easily.

## Dry bags for dry gear

I've been on many paddling trips where the fun of pounding through waves or running wild rapids quickly turns to discomfort and worry as a chilly night sets in and the sleeping bags are now wringing wet. Do whatever it takes to keep your gear dry! Outfitters and retail stores offer a variety of waterproof bags — called dry bags — made of PVC or heavily waterproofed nylon with a leak-proof seal that won't let water in even if all your gear gets dumped in the river. If you don't have the money for a dry bag, you can make a fairly serviceable one without too much trouble, as I explain in a moment. But remember — it's a poor man's solution and your gear may still get wet.

To make your own dry bag, place a heavy-duty garbage bag inside a nylon stuff sack and fold the top of the garbage bag back over the stuff sack. Place your sleeping bag or other items you need to keep dry inside the bag. Now, roll the bag shut, squeezing the air out of the garbage bag as you roll. Tuck the rolled top down inside the stuff sack and secure the stuff sack's drawstring.

For watertight packing of smaller items such as cameras and books, a military surplus ammunition can works well. I have several that have been painted orange for visibility (easier to spot floating in a river than olive drab) and lined with foam plastic to pad my camera gear. The ammunition cans have been subjected to many a whitewater rapid rafting, and my cameras and notebooks have never suffered from a drop of water.

## Boating with children

Because children seem to enjoy boating, and because you can pack along a large camp stove, kitchen, and lots of fresh food in a cooler, canoeing does seem to be a perfect opportunity to go camping with children. It is not without its drawbacks, however, if certain considerations are not taken into account.

### Prepare for squirming

Children are naturally active. The younger the child, the shorter the attention span and the less amount of time they will be able to sit anywhere quietly. Don't plan on driving for a long period of time to go boating, and then expect the child to sit quietly in the boat for several more hours while you paddle around. A certain amount of activity and entertainment is necessary to keep them happy while on the water and not squirming around — potentially dumping the boat.

Try, if at all possible, to keep the driving distance to and from the boating destination to a minimum. About 2 to 3 hours is about the most any parent can expect of a child without a break. After you get to the boat launch site, take some time to throw a Frisbee, toss a ball, or do something that is fun and active for the children. Don't just unload the car, load the boat, and head out.

### Providing entertainment

After you are on the water, keeping a child entertained and interested is not too difficult. Just as with backpacking or hiking, activity ideas need to be creative and varied — nothing will work forever or all the time. With smaller children, it is a great idea to give them a tiny paddle that they can dip in and out of the water. Although their paddling will be ineffective, it doesn't hamper the adult's paddling efforts and makes the children feel like an important and active part of the excursion.

Many youngsters like to fish. Although this activity will usually only work if the parent likes to fish as well, giving a child a fishing pole to use as you float along is great fun for them. Who knows, they may even catch the evening's dinner! Whether they catch anything isn't the point, however. As any learned fisherman will tell you, "It's the fishin' that's important, not the catchin'."

### Stay close to shore

Staying as close to shore as is safely allowed is a super way to keep a child interested. This way, there will be lots of sandbars, undercut banks, and marshy areas for them to look at as you glide by. You also increase the possibility of spotting wildlife. Imagine the amazement in the eyes of your child as you quietly slip by a large moose chewing river grasses, water dripping from its muzzle and weeds hanging from its antlers.

Be sure to plan on plenty of shore breaks; one every 30 minutes is perfect. Children will not benefit from all-day paddling grinds to reach the ideal campsite. Just as you spent time playing on shore between the car and loading the boat, you will need similar time during a day-long paddle trip.

## Paddling overnight: Choosing an outfitter

Given the pressure of time and the limits of space, many folks never get the chance to enjoy paddling overnights simply because they don't have the time or equipment necessary. That is where outfitters come in. However, with hundreds of rafting outfitters to choose from, finding the right whitewater trip for you and your group that is memorable for pleasure and not pain can seem somewhat like a crapshoot. In actual fact, finding the right outfitter means nothing more than asking the right questions.

Here are some questions you should ask yourself:

- ✔ **What is your motivation for a trip?** Before picking up the phone, ask yourself what your motivation for taking a river trip is. Are you looking for relaxation or are you looking for a physical or mental challenge? Are you looking for a family-type trip, a trip for singles, or something else?

- ✔ **How fit are you?** You also need to honestly determine how physically fit you are. No sense in trying to kid yourself because it will only come back to haunt you later. Most river guides feel that if you are reasonably fit (exercise three or more times a week) then you should have no trouble with rivers up to Class IV (see "Rating the rapids," later in this chapter).

After you have perused the catalogues and advertisement offerings and honed your list of outfitters down to a manageable few, give them a call and be prepared to ask a lot of questions. Don't hesitate to grill the outfitter. It is your money and your camping trip. If a reservation person is uncomfortable answering your every query, or unable to refer you to someone in the company who can, then hang up the phone and call someone else. Those outfitters willing to patiently spend time answering questions in a detailed and organized manner provide a good indicator of how smoothly the actual trip will run.

You need to include the following points when asking questions of the outfitter:

- ✔ **Safety:** Address points of safety first! How long has the river company been in business and how experienced are the guides? You don't want to experience your dream week on the river with a gang of novice guides working for a company that just blossomed out of some maverick's garage.

- ✔ **Children:** If you are planning on bringing your children, find out if the outfitter is experienced in dealing with children and if they provide child-sized lifejackets. I recommend that families only go rafting with those companies that have demonstrated skill with children, which in itself is a safety factor, especially since children are unpredictable.

- ✔ **Guide-to-client ratio:** Don't overlook questions regarding the guide-to-ratio (6 guides to 24 guests is an absolute minimum) and the quality of the guides' wilderness rescue and first-aid experience.

- ✔ **Paddling difficulty:** Inquire about the range of paddling difficulty offered and which trips the outfitter would recommend for someone with your particular skill (be brutally honest here) and personal goals (relaxation, excitement, or meeting someone, for example).

- ✔ **Client mix:** You don't want to be the only single on a family trip nor do you want to be the only family on a river full of singles.

✔ **Equipment quality:** Take the time to ask about the condition of equipment, what types of rafts will be used (oar or paddle), what kind of transportation is provided and how many other people will be on the trip. You may also want to inquire about the wilderness qualities of each trip. There is a vast difference between the virtual river carnival experienced during weekends on the South Fork of the American River in California and the wilderness sanctity of a trip in the Yukon Territory.

✔ **Activity options:** Because there is much more to an enjoyable rafting adventure than rafts and water, take the time to investigate all the options available to you on a particular voyage. Natural history walks, historical walks, wildflower hikes, and more are often added bonuses on many whitewater trips.

✔ **Paddling options:** Find out, too, what the paddling options are: paddle (you paddle), oar (the guide rows while you sit), or a combination. Check to see if the outfitter packs along inflatable kayaks for added fun and adventure.

✔ **Dietary needs:** If you have special dietary needs, then now is the time to air those concerns to be sure the outfitter can adequately meet your requirements. On the river is too late to find out that a no-salt menu isn't available.

✔ **Activities for children:** Families will want to pay special attention to child-oriented activities. Does the guide provide bug cages, identification books, storytellers, special activities for children? Additionally, some outfitters, but not all, offer planned time-alone opportunities for parents to sneak away while their children are being entertained.

✔ **References:** If you're planning to embark on an extended rafting adventure, request a list of references. If the outfitter is unwilling or unable to provide them, take your business elsewhere.

## Rating the rapids

Rapids are divided into six classes, Class I being the easiest and Class VI considered downright unthinkable except by experts. Use the following to best match your needs and ability to the appropriate whitewater conditions:

✔ **Class I:** Moving water with small riffles, small waves, and limited obstructions. Too easy for most river rats.

✔ **Class II:** Gentle rapids with waves up to three feet. While some boat maneuvering is required, the channels are wide, clear, and easily negotiated. Great for float trips, ideal for family groups.

✔ **Class III:** Rapids with irregular waves capable of swamping an open canoe. Narrow channels that often require a coordinated sequence of navigational moves. Suitable for adventurous and experienced family groups and beginning adults.

✔ **Class IV:** Long, very turbulent rapids requiring precise maneuvering skills in extremely narrow channels. People do get tossed from the paddle rafts with regularity and rafts sometimes flip, so if you don't like to get wet, Class IV is not for you. This paddle craft is suitable only for individuals with previous rafting experience. Beginners are okay on an oar boat.

✔ **Class V:** Highly technical maneuvering required through extremely difficult, long, and very violent rapids. Class V rapids are considered hazardous. Depth of experience on Class IV rivers a mandatory prerequisite. Advanced rafters only. *No children!*

✔ **Class VI:** If you fancy Class VI, make sure your life insurance policy is up to date. Highly dangerous and technical rapids requiring precision teamwork by experts only. Children? Are you kidding?

# Touring by Mountain or Road Bike

Bicycle touring on a road bike is an option for almost any age. Mountain biking, on the other hand, presents problems that are best solved by folks over 16. Mountain biking requires a strong sense of balance, agility, concentration, and a certain amount of stamina. Bicycling in general is a very adaptable sport, however. Paved bike paths, smooth dirt fire roads, and bike lanes on certain roads all provide plenty of access.

## Gearing up

For the last word on biking, you must consult *Bicycling For Dummies*. But if you're interested in combining biking with camping, I want to pass along some suggestions and tips from my personal experience for you to use as a primer.

### Wear a helmet!

Helmets are mandatory for everyone! Under no circumstances should you allow anyone to ride without a helmet. A helmet must fit properly to work properly. Many helmets include special fit pads that can be installed in the helmet to achieve proper fit. Helmets are generally constructed of lightweight, air-filled foam covered with an impact-resistant plastic shell. Vent holes help keep you cool as you ride. All helmets have a lifespan because the foam padding dries out. I recommend purchasing a new helmet every three to four years to ensure maximum protection.

### Wear gloves

Whether you're riding on road or trail, padded cycling gloves help prevent hand, wrist, arm, and shoulder fatigue by absorbing shock. They also provide a better grip on the handlebars and help prevent blisters. Some people like fingerless gloves. If you want more protection from wind and cold, select full-coverage gloves.

### Protect your eyes

Eye protection is essential cycling gear — almost as important as a helmet. Sport shields keep dust, dirt, and other debris out of your eyes. They also provide better visibility in low-light conditions and help keep the wind from making your eyes tear up when you're traveling at high speeds.

### Dress smart

For tops, think synthetic fibers and think wicking performance. Your shirt should keep you dry in the saddle. If you get wet, you will chill.

The same high-performance fabrics that make cycling shirts more comfortable also add comfort to cycling shorts. I look for a looser fitting short that doubles as a casual short when I am not riding. All styles of cycling shorts have a seat pad built in for extra comfort in the saddle. Finally, add a good cycling rain suit to your arsenal — jacket and pants. Look for waterproof/breathable construction with venting features to help dissipate moisture buildup. Store your rainwear in a handlebar bag so you can get to it quickly and easily.

### Choose the right shoes

Cycling shoes are constructed with a hard sole that prevents the aching arches often caused by soft-soled athletic shoes. If you plan to do any touring, get your feet shod appropriately. Road cyclists generally prefer lightweight, low-cut cycling shoes. Mountain bikers prefer shoes with an over-the-ankle design for added stability and protection on the trail.

## Things to take along

A "loaded" car has add-ons for safety, convenience, and comfort. Bikes are the same.

### Think a drink

Unless you plan to pass out or collapse on the ride, you must always drink fluids while you are riding. Most bikes have multiple fittings designed to accept water-bottle cages, making bottles easy to reach. I also carry a hydration pack on my back with a hose looped over my shoulder for easy sipping access. CamelBak, Cascade Designs, and Ultimate Direction make super models for this purpose. See Chapter 2 for more on hydration systems.

### Pick a pack o' panniers (bags for bikes)

All your stuff can be stowed securely:

- A handlebar bag holds often-needed gear — maps, snacks, a waterproof jacket, and so on.

- An under-the-seat "wedge bag" is a compact case for carrying tools.

- Bike panniers are designed to work in concert with a rear rack. This bag will contain much of your clothing and gear for the trip. Panniers hang on both sides of a tire for the best balance as you ride.

- A rack trunk also works in conjunction with a rear rack. Rack trunks are hard sided to offer extra protection for cameras and other fragile gear.

### Take a tire iron and patch kit

I can promise you one thing: You *will* get a flat tire at some point. My daughter and I once got three flats, each with multiple punctures, on one afternoon. The best way to avoid a flat is with preventative maintenance. Check your tires regularly for tread wear and keep them properly inflated at all times. Make sure your tool kit includes several tire irons and a patch kit for repairing holes in the inner tube. Familiarize yourself with the procedure for changing a flat. I also include a few strips of duct tape and some pocket change in case I need to make a phone call. Why duct tape? If your tire tears, you can effect an emergency repair by lining the inside of the tire with the tape, thus giving you a ride to the nearest shop — beats having to bike-walk the whole way!

### Carry a tool kit and pump

The kit should include various wrenches and bike tools in one compact package. My favorite is the Alien, which is constructed like a jack-knife and contains several essential tools in one unit. Your kit should always include a few $CO_2$ cartridges or a bike pump. Some pumps attach along the bike frame. A compact size fits in the bike bag and is designed only to get you to a bike shop, gas station, or other location where you can fill the tire to proper inflation levels.

## Other biking tips

Mirrors? Lights? Bright clothing? Visibility is a key concern. So is security.

- **See and be seen:** Installing a mirror will keep you looking forward, reducing having to turn around in the saddle to check for traffic. Add headlights and taillights — essential safety gear for any cyclist. Wear brightly colored clothing — and reflective clothing if cycling at night or in the early dawn or late evening hours.

✔ **Lock your bike:** Protect your bike from casual thieves by locking it either with a cable lock or a U-lock. Your bike should remain locked anytime you are not with it — including while you are transporting it on your vehicle.

## Rules of the road for bikers

If bikers were licensed, they'd be tested on matters like these:

✔ **Ride on open trails only.** Please respect and abide by all trail closures, private property notices, and fences, and all requirements for permits and authorization. Mountain bikes are never ever permitted within wilderness areas, on any section of the Pacific Crest Trail, on most National Park trails, or on many state park trails. Don't assume a trail is legal for mountain bikes just because it is not signed — inquire before pedaling is the motto.

✔ **Leave no trace.** Do not skid your tires or ride on ground that is rain-soaked and easily scarred. Stick to established trails.

✔ **Control your bicycle.** Save the "need for speed" for a race. Stay alert at all times. The combination of speed and an out-of-control biker leads to trouble and often injury to other trail users. Expect that other bikers may be just around every blind corner.

✔ **Always yield right-of-way.** Mountain bikes are low man on the totem pole and must always yield trail to horses and hikers. When encountering other trail users (hikers, equestrians, or fellow bikers) a friendly greeting to announce your presence is considerate and appreciated. One unfriendly or negative encounter with a mountain biker leaves a lasting impression on all other trail users. Slow to a walk or stop your bike, especially when encountering horses.

✔ **Never spook animals.** Leave ranch and farm gates as you find them. Running livestock and disturbing wild animals can cause serious harm and in many places is against the law. Give animals plenty of room.

✔ **Plan ahead.** Know your equipment, know your ability, and know the requirements of the area you are riding in, and then plan accordingly. Be self-sufficient at all times.

# Part II
# Getting There Is Half the Fun

The 5th Wave                    By Rich Tennant

"Well, that was one angry bear! And obviously not too happy
we hung our food from this tree branch."

# In this part. . .

In Chapter 5, I offer advice on properly packing your vehicle, suggest games to play whilst driving, and remind you of things to do to be sure your vehicle gets you to where you want to go. Chapter 6 helps you select a campsite, set it up in the safest and most efficient manner, and pack it up, too.

# Chapter 5

# Hitting the Road

In This Chapter

▶ Bringing your vehicle up to speed before you depart

▶ Fitting all that stuff in your vehicle

▶ Choosing a car rack so you can pack even more stuff

▶ Making sure that home sweet home stays that way while you're gone

▶ Making sure that everyone's still a happy camper at the end of the drive

*Y*ou've spent weeks planning your camping trip — or perhaps not. Two hours into the adventure, jammed into a car and surrounded by piles of gear with some piece of something jabbing you in the ribs, the engine starts to shake, rattle, and roll, and the left turn you just made onto an unlit road is, quite clearly, not the right one. Your stomach is grumbling almost as loudly as your friends in the back seat are, and — as if all this is not enough — it has just started to pour, and your rain jacket is somewhere in the trunk. If only you'd had the car serviced before leaving. If only you'd spent more time packing the car. If only you'd studied the maps. If only you'd packed a small cooler with snacks for the road. If only....

# Preparing Your Vehicle for the Trip

While it seems logical to most people that it takes a certain amount of preparation to pack and plan for a trip, the vehicle often qualifies for only a last-minute afterthought or no thought at all. Wrong planning approach! In this section, I give you a few key things to consider and check off to be sure that your vehicle is going to get you to where you want to go, and back again.

## Summer pretrip care

Before you hit the road for a summertime camping trip, check the following (or have your friendly mechanic take a look if you're not mechanically inclined):

- **Radiator and coolant recovery tank.** To protect your car's engine from oppressive summer heat, regularly check both the coolant level and the antifreeze/water mixture in the radiator. Visually check the coolant level when the engine is cool. If the coolant is rust-colored, flush the system.

- **Tires.** Improper tire pressure causes premature wear and makes the car more difficult to handle. Keep a tire gauge in the glove compartment and regularly check the pressure (see your owner's manual for recommendations). Make sure that your spare tire is properly inflated as well. Tires should be rotated every 15,000 miles to ensure even wear. Slippery winter weather and spring potholes are tough on front-end alignment. Uneven tire wear is a telltale sign of suspension problems.

- **Hoses.** Check radiator and heater hoses for signs of deterioration and replace those that are cracked or leaking. A worn hose can burst anytime, especially during hot-weather driving. Replacing a worn hose with a new hose that costs $25 can save as much as $1,000 in repairs on an overheated engine.

- **Belts.** Check the belts driving your alternator, air conditioner, water pump, air pump, and power steering. Loose belts reduce the efficiency of the devices they operate. Worn belts can fail unexpectedly and leave you stranded.

- **Battery.** Check the battery to ensure that it's held securely in place. Clean any corroded connections. If your battery is not maintenance-free, check the water.

- **Oil.** Change the oil every three months or 3,000 miles, whichever comes first. Make sure the oil level is always in the safe zone on the dipstick. This basic and extremely important rule of auto maintenance helps prevent premature engine wear.

- **Jack.** Make sure that your car jack is in the car and that all parts are in working order.

- **Emergency kit.** Pack flares, a flashlight, jumper cables, flat fixer, windshield washer fluid, and a blanket.

## Winterizing your vehicle

When I worked at a ski resort back east many years ago, we had a standard Sunday afternoon routine: head to the parking lot to help unprepared city slickers start their cars and unfreeze their engines. Armed with powerful heater/blowers, jumper cables, deicing liquids, and cold-weather starting fluid, we would work our way through dozens of bewildered drivers who couldn't understand why the car they drove just yesterday from sea level and 40 degrees was not working now at 5,000 feet and 0 degrees.

Had the unfortunates thought to prepare themselves and their cars for the environment they were heading to, our parking lot patrol wouldn't have been needed, and I could have spent more time skiing the mountain.

Before you head out to ski, wander, or whatever next winter, take the time to get your vehicle in good working order. The following tips should help:

- ✔ **Change your oil.** In the winter, thinner oil is better. Drain off your summer 10W40 and replace it with 5W30, which is what most experts recommend for optimum engine performance in the cold. Hey, you needed an oil change anyway.

- ✔ **Keep your tires pressurized.** As the temperature drops, so does your tire pressure. Each 10-degree drop accounts for an approximate 1-pound pressure reduction in your tire.

- ✔ **Check your antifreeze.** Worn-out antifreeze or coolant loses its heat-transfer ability, which means the heater won't blow as hot as it should and your radiator actually might freeze up. Replace your antifreeze every 24,000 miles — if in doubt, drain and replace it anyway.

- ✔ **Keep your locks lubricated as a freeze preventative.** Should they freeze, heat the key with a match or lighter then work it gently around and into the lock. Be gentle, or you could break your key — or worse, the lock.

- ✔ **Check your battery.** Is it charged? Make sure that all its reservoirs are filled to their correct levels. Keep your alternator belt tight and your battery terminals corrosion-free.

- ✔ **Keep your gas tank full.** That's right. Water in the tank can freeze the gas line and foul the fuel-injection system. Don't ever let your tank drop below one-quarter full, and always tank up before parking for the night. That way, you minimize the chances of allowing condensation to form in your gas tank.

- ✔ **Replace your windshield wiper blades and check your windshield wiper fluid level.** Squinting through smears and haze on a slushy road is no time to find out your windshield wipers need replacing. Also, be sure your windshield wiper fluid is filled with solution that resists freezing.

- ✔ **Be prepared for emergencies.** The American Automobile Association recommends that anyone driving in cold or winter conditions carry the following items: windshield washer fluid, flashlight, flares, ice scraper, flat fixer (pressurized can that will fill a flat and seal the leak), shovel, jumper cables, blanket, gloves (leather gloves are best), tire chains, traction mats, and rags.

## Renting an RV

Although personally I don't typically consider cruising in recreational vehicles to be "camping," an RV might be a suitable vehicle alternative for families or groups traveling together who would like to travel with some of the conveniences of home.

With a little practice and preflight inspection, an RV is not all that difficult to drive. (And you don't need a special license to drive an RV, either.) Most RVs come with automatic transmission, power brakes, and power steering. I recommend the Class C RV (using a van-based chassis) for most folks. It offers sleeping space for four or six people with an over-the-cab bed design. Class C RVs are also within the 30-foot range, which is the maximum allowable at many public campgrounds.

A number of resources can help you research the RV world prior to renting your beast. These two are good starting points:

- **The Recreation Vehicle Rental Association (RVRA)** offers a 32-page "Rental Ventures" brochure, which also comes with a copy of "Who's Who in RV Rentals?" — gripping reading, to be sure. Write to RVRA at 3251 Old Lee Highway, Suite 500, Fairfax, VA 22030 or call the association at 800-336-0355.

- **The Recreation Vehicle Industry Association (RVIA)** offers literature on RV safety and renting RVs. Write to RVIA at 1896 Preston White Drive, Reston, VA 20191 or call the association at 703-620-6003.

# Packing According to Plan

Your trip essentially begins as soon as you leave the driveway, so it makes sense to take the time to carefully plan your trip, beginning with how you'll pack the vehicle. Keep in mind the following tips as you try to find a place for everything (and check out "Car Rack 101," later in this chapter, for tips on choosing and using a car rack if you need more room for your gear):

- **Use a car rack to handle gear overflow from the trunk.** Never — and I do mean never — pack the inside of the vehicle with gear. If you can't travel comfortably, then either rent a bigger car or acquire a car top case to handle the overflow for you.

- **Pack blankets and pillows for comfortable napping along the route.**

- **Place all maps, carefully marked with the travel route from the driveway to the campground, within easy reach of the driver and/or navigator.**

- **Keep a small cooler loaded with cold drinks, candy bars, sliced fruit, vegetable sticks, cubed cheese, sandwiches, and so on, inside the car.**

- **Place removable sun screens on the rear side windows to shield your passengers from the sun.**

- Make sure that you have cash handy for tolls, a meal along the way, and campground entry fees.

- Place a litter bag within easy reach of everyone inside the car. Dump the bag every time you pull over to refuel.

- Put soft and light items in a case above the car.

- Load boats on a rack above the car.

- Stow bikes on a trailer hitch–mounted rack if the car-top rack is full. Trailer hitch–mounted racks can be rented if necessary.

- Load coolers, food, and fuel items in the trunk. Stow liquids carefully so they don't tip and spill. (Cooking oil all over a sleeping bag is funny for everyone but the person who must sleep in the bag. It also ceases to be funny for everyone when a bear decides cooking oil is now on the menu.)

- Keep extra clothes handy inside the car. If you are traveling to the mountains, realize that temperatures will likely get cooler as you climb in elevation. Keeping warm jackets available for everyone to slip into will make arrivals at fuel stops, campground, or trailhead more pleasurable experiences.

- Toss a few old towels into the car. They make super rags for mopping up the inevitable spills, and they make great covers for hot seats in unbearably sticky weather.

- If you bring kids along, pack a goodie bag full of activities and games that they don't ordinarily play: pads of paper, crayons, washable felt pens, car games, stickers, magnetic puzzles or games, story books, a small chalkboard and chalk, workbooks, an Etch-A-Sketch, coloring books, comics, or Play Dough — use your imagination.

# Getting Ready to Head Out

I have always found it helpful to lay out all equipment in plain view on the living room floor. While this does tend to make the room appear as if it has been the victim of a small nuclear explosion, it does serve to keep all items in plain view, making it easy to visually determine if we have everything necessary for the trip. As one or more of the people in our camping group call out the planned items on the checklist, one of us puts that item to one side in the room ready to be packed and checked.

All equipment does get checked: pots for cleanliness, stoves for fuel and function (a stove that will not light is more easily repaired at home than in the field), flashlights for power, knives for sharpness, tent for tears and dirt, sleeping bags for loft and cleanliness and tears, sleeping pads for air leaks, packs for tears and frame cracks, first-aid kit for contents. The first-aid kit requires very careful checking to be sure that all medications are current and not expired, that all materials are clean and stocked, and that any items last used have either been replaced or sterilized.

# A backpack packing primer

This isn't as hard as it sounds. With all the gear still laid out on the living room floor, and the food arranged by meals and days, begin loading the packs. The rough rule of thumb is to keep heavier items close to your center of gravity, your back, and not too high or too low in the pack. For men this is usually higher on the back next to the shoulders. Women will tend to be more comfortable by packing heavier weight lower and more towards the middle of the pack — just above the small of the back and next to the frame. Work your way out with medium weight items and then, finally, the lightest items should find their way into the most distant corners of your pack.

## Young children

Children should be carefully supervised when loading up their packs. Smaller, younger children want to be involved, but should not be allowed to carry much more two or three small and fairly lightweight items. Older children will be able to carry more, but beware of allowing them to become pack mules, restricting their freedom to play and romp — the reason you are heading into the wilderness with them in the first place.

## Teenagers

Teenagers should be allowed to carry more, but be careful of egos here. Some children will attempt to carry too much in order to impress and only end up exhausting or injuring themselves. Other children may begin to feel very self-conscious about not being able to carry what they perceive as their fair share. This is a very vulnerable age and emotions must be handled tenderly. I have found it most effective to play down the importance of carrying larger loads and play up particular wilderness skills that anyone can acquire. Campfire building, map reading, weather reading, and food preparation are the more important of the skills, not who can carry the heaviest load. When I worked as a camp counselor, I found that if a teenager was that gung ho to carry a large load, I was the first to begin unloading my pack on them, suggesting that carrying a heavy load is not such a desirable plan.

## Carrying children and a load

The younger the children, the more of a carrying burden the parents must endure. It is quite conceivable that one parent will end up carrying the bulk of the family gear and food while the other parent carries a child and whatever other equipment is left over. If one parent is left carrying a ridiculously heavy and awkward load, I would recommend hiking a short way to a wilderness base camp. After you are at the base camp, your family can continue to enjoy a wide and varied wilderness experience by day-hiking. If necessary, you can still hike to the vehicles to pick up cached gear or food.

For more thoughts about packing a pack, see Chapter 2.

Finally, with all planned items except food spread out in an orderly fashion on the floor we go through the list to determine if we are leaving anything out or if we are packing too much. Always operate under the KISS principle — Keep It Simple, Stupid! No insult intended. Pack and carry as little as necessary to be comfortable and safe. If in doubt, leave it behind. If one item will do a similar job, choose the one that suits the purpose best and leave the other home — for example, a spoon works as well as a fork, but not vice versa, so leave the fork at home.

Missing gear and not sure what to buy? Then read Chapters 2, 4, and 6.

# Car Camping Survival Kit

The beauty of car camping trips, or any camping trip for that matter, lies in spontaneity, although it is almost impossible to be spontaneous unless you are sure you have all the necessary gear on hand. I learned long ago, from a Scoutmaster friend who had to manage not only his own family of five but his troop of 15, that you can give the illusion of spontaneous camping decisions as long as you subscribe to the car-camping-prepacked-box method. If you have all the necessities already packed and ready to go at a moment's notice, all you need to do is determine the destination and find the kids. I keep all the items in a large plastic cargo box, next to the large cooler in the garage. Here are my box-contents suggestions (but feel free to modify this list to meet your own needs):

No-stick skillet, large pot, small pot, two-burner stove, spatula, pot grips, plastic cutting board, 9-inch slice 'n' chop knife, multitool knife, small paring knife, plastic plates, plastic cups, plastic knife/fork/spoon sets, camping hammock, oven mitts, water filter, first aid kit, spice kit, roll of paper towels, can opener, barbecue tongs and fork, wooden matches, resealable plastic bags, large garbage bags, water filter, 5-gallon water jug, aluminum foil, tablecloth, sponge, camp soap, dishwashing basin, dish towel, lantern, flashlight, extra batteries, folding chairs, duct tape, 50-foot nylon cord, bungee cord assortment, 12-x-12 heavyweight blue plastic tarp, sleeping pads, camp tent, Frisbee, Nerf balls, football, playing cards, travel games set.

# Car Rack 101

When our forefathers went camping, they did so with all their gear loaded in a covered wagon, on a sled, on their backs, or on one of several other primitive carrying devices. Today, we have cars, trucks, SUVs, and RVs. Although the mode of transportation has changed, the need to tote along essential gear has not. Of course, toting along mountain bikes, canoes, tents, inflatable mattresses, and the like is not something any pioneer I've read about had to deal with — or even wanted to deal with. Still, it is darn hard to fit all your toys into a vehicle along with yourself and your other necessary gear. Enter the roof rack, car rack, sports rack, or whatever other name you want to tag this utilitarian item with. If you're serious about camping, then you had best get serious about your rack because you need a good one to safely carry your toys to and from your camping adventures.

## Things to consider when buying a car rack

What should you consider before plunking down the green and walking out with a new rack? The Sports Rack (www.sportsrack.com), a nationally known retail and mail order outfit based in Sacramento, California, that specializes only in rack systems for vehicles, offers the following hints to "picking the right rack for whatever you pack":

- ✔ **Think about the loads that you will be carrying, well beyond your immediate carrying needs.** What about utility loads, luggage, and skis, and long loads such as kayaks, sailboards, or even lumber?

- ✔ **What type of vehicle are you outfitting?** Is it a tall vehicle (van or sport utility vehicle), short vehicle, old vehicle, new vehicle, or leased vehicle? Does it have (or not have) rain gutters, a receiver hitch, an externally mounted spare tire, or a factory roof rack? Do you want this rack to fit more than one vehicle?

- ✔ **Will load-carrying space be a problem in the future?** Are children on the way or will friends or relatives travel with you in the near future? Should you think about a cargo box?

- ✔ **How often will you use the rack?** Once or twice a year (in that case, it may make more sense to rent a rack), or on a monthly or weekly basis?

- ✔ **Will your vehicle be garaged?** Find out if roofline clearance will be a problem with your vehicle or if the length of the vehicle with an added rear rack creates difficulties. If your rack will need to come off, is it easily removable and just as easy to reinstall?

- ✔ **Think about security.** Will you leave your vehicle unattended for long periods of time with your recreational gear stowed? How expensive is your gear? People do steal racks, too, so how important is it to secure the rack itself to your vehicle?

- ✔ **Think about quality and warranty coverage.** Are name brands important to you? Ensure that the rack will not damage your car in any way. Find out how long the warranty period is.

# Loading your car rack

Watching in your rearview mirror as your $1,000 canoe bounces down the highway or hearing a crunch as an audible reminder that your $750 mountain bike is still on top of your car as you pull into a low-clearance gas station is a preventable occurrence that happens all too frequently. In this section, I offer some tips for carrying some popular outdoor items.

 Multisport racks work well as utility racks, carrying anything from large boxes to construction materials and are an ideal choice for outdoorsfolk who participate in a wide variety of outdoor activities. Never, however, exceed 150 pounds (100 pounds with Yakima SST racks). Secure the load properly with adequate tie-down strapping. Disperse weight over the entire rack system, keeping the heaviest loads nearest the towers and away from the middle of the rack where the load may bend the crossbars. Long loads must always be tied with additional strapping to the front and rear bumpers. Also, always follow a manufacturer's specific attaching and loading instructions. Failing to do so can result in an untimely unloading of your valuables, damaging them and, probably, your vehicle too.

### Loading bikes

When carrying bikes above, find some way to remind yourself to be aware of low clearances. Liston Concepts in Salt Lake City, Utah, manufactures a bright yellow arrow attached to a suction cup that you place on your window or rear view mirror anytime you have a bike on the rack. It's a neat idea, but you have to remember to use it.

 Bike child seats and panniers can create extreme wind resistance that places unnecessary stress on a roof rack. Remove them when transporting bikes on a roof rack. Always load bikes with the chains to the inside. That prevents grease from getting all over you when you lift the bikes on and off.

### Loading skis

Skis should always be mounted with tips facing to the rear. Sandwich skis bottom to bottom to prevent shifting within a ski mount. Worried about someone stealing your skis set? While no rack is theft-proof, you can minimize quick snatches of equipment by making sure that the crossbars are close enough together so that the skis cannot be slid forward enough to remove the tails and then back to slip out the tips.

### Loading sailboards and surfboards

 Never load sailboards or surfboards with the nose facing forward and in the up position. The upward wind force placed on the rack in this situation may be enough to literally tear the rack from your car. The recommended way to mount boards is with the nose forward and the bottom up, or the nose to the rear and bottom down.

### Loading canoes and kayaks

Canoes and kayaks should always be secured by the bow and stern to the front and rear bumpers of the vehicle. This is in addition to the tie-down straps across the body of the craft.

## Caring for your car rack

Like your car, roof rack systems require maintenance and a certain amount of attention if you expect them to remain in safe working order. Periodically lubricate all locks, hubs, fastening bolts, and knobs. Always remove your roof rack before running your car through a car wash. Dirt can collect under the pads of a rack and abrade your car's paint, so clean the pads and the roof of your car monthly. Inspect your roof rack regularly for signs of wear. The plastic parts of a rack may fade over time, but color can be restored somewhat with a little Armor-All.

Does your rack whistle or whine in the wind when you drive? Try moving the rack forward or back. Next, try rearranging the load configuration. If none of those solutions work, you may be able to purchase a fairing that minimizes wind resistance and noise. (Check with your car rack's manufacturer.)

It's a great idea to pack along a number of bungee cords to tighten a load that has become a tad wobbly enroute, or to simply add additional security to a valuable load. To prevent the load wobbles, you will want to know how to tie some key knots — check out my suggestions in Chapter 7.

## What about hitch-mounted racks?

With continuing improvements in aerodynamics, it doesn't make much sense to put a lot of equipment on SUV roofs, and besides, it's far too difficult for the average person to lift a bike onto the roof of an SUV. Enter the hitch-mounted rack. Hitch mounts allow people to take the tallest items (bikes, for example) off the roof and put them in an easier and more manageable loading zone at the back of the vehicle, freeing up the roof for luggage boxes and boats.

Today's hitch-mounted rack designs are stable, secure, and far easier to lock down. They either tilt down (keep in mind that with bikes on board, you will be lifting upwards of 60 pounds using this feature) or swing out of the way.

Still, while hitch-mounted racks are great for bikes, remember that skis, boats, and luggage are still best stowed on top of the vehicle.

# Safeguarding Your Home While You're Away

Although there is no way to guarantee that your home is completely protected from crime, there are ways to minimize the risk. Follow these tips to take a proactive approach to securing your property when leaving home on a camping vacation:

- ✔ **Ask a trusted friend or neighbor to watch your house while you're away.** Give her the phone number where you'll be staying and other pertinent information.

- ✔ **Have someone pick up your mail, newspapers, and so on.** *Do not* stop delivery.

- ✔ **Hire someone to clear the driveway and sidewalks of snow in the winter and mow the lawn in the summer.**

- ✔ **If you don't have a second car you can leave in the driveway, have a neighbor park his car in your driveway to give the house a "lived-in" appearance.**

- ✔ **Make sure that all doors and windows are secured before you leave your home.** Arm your security system if you have one.

- ✔ **Set household lights (inside and out) on variable timers.**

- ✔ **Leave spare keys with a neighbor or relative rather than hiding them outside the house.** A burglar knows where to look!

- ✔ **Compile an inventory of your household items for insurance purposes.** This will help speed replacement of lost or stolen items.

# Surviving the Drive

Getting to your destination does not need to become a speed or endurance event. Watch the movie *National Lampoon's Vacation* with Chevy Chase if you need a refresher in vacation disaster. Take the time to enjoy the sites along the way, and please, take the time to take time. Get out and stretch your legs frequently.

For starters, don't eat and drive at the same time, and stay the heck away from fast food stops simply to make fast escapes faster. Plan a picnic and make it an organized stop along the way. Use a travel guide (if you are a AAA member, you're in luck) to help you find quaint roadside stops along streams, in city parks, and so on. The extra 30 minutes or so the stop will take can be just the thing a cramped carload of passengers and the aggravated driver need. Remember, the point is to arrive at your destination in a good mood and not wondering why you decided to go camping with a group of savages and morons — who are, incidentally, probably thinking the same of you. (See "Entertaining the Troops . . ." later in this chapter, for more tips on keeping everyone sane.)

Perhaps more important than keeping your passengers content is keeping them safe. Careless moments, distractions, and trying to rush to a destination in hazardous driving conditions can all put a dark cloud over an otherwise bright trip. In this section, I offer driving tips that can help you get to the campsite safely.

## Driving in wet conditions

When the road becomes wet, it becomes slick. Seems obvious enough, and yet each year too many folks get injured or killed simply because either they or someone else failed to drive safely. If a drizzle begins to fall or the rain to cascade down, take the following tips to heart for a safer driving experience:

- **Slow down.** Your car needs three times more space to stop on slick roads. Roads become slick and dangerous after a rainfall, especially early in the winter season.

- **Maintain a distance of six to eight seconds between your vehicle and the vehicle in front of you.**

- **Be deliberate in maneuvering your vehicle.** Most skidding is caused by sudden stops and turns.

- **If your vehicle skids, don't hit the brakes.** Ease off of the accelerator and steer into the direction of the skid.

- **If you drive through standing water, lightly apply the brakes to dry them.**

- **Don't speed up when navigating through standing water.** Doing so may cause tires to lose contact with the road (a scary phenomenon known as *hydroplaning*). If this occurs, hold the steering wheel steady and lightly apply the brakes. After your wheels regain contact with the road, slow down until you have full control of the car.

- **Turn on your lights even in the daytime.** If your car doesn't have daytime running lamps, turn on your headlights, even during the day. It improves the visibility of your vehicle and your margin of safety.

## Don't be a victim of crime on your next trip

Criminals can be pretty creative. In 1999, a wave of crime hit cars left at several trailheads near Lake Tahoe in California. The crooks apparently watched who was coming and going from the parking lot, carefully broke into cars, removed only credit cards, and then carefully locked the cars back up. Several victims were unaware that they had been the burglarized until several days after returning home when credit card companies called to question large cash withdrawals at ATM casinos.

Keeping in mind the following tips can help you stay safe on your next trip:

- Be aware of your surroundings. Watch who is watching you.

- Flashing wads of cash can make a camper or traveler an easy theft target. Consider a variety of payment methods to ensure maximum convenience and security. Traveler's checks are a good option because, if lost or stolen, they can be replaced. Keep serial numbers separate from the checks.

- Use credit cards to cover unexpected or very large expenses incurred while traveling. Credit charges are the easiest to challenge if services or merchandise purchased are unsatisfactory or incorrectly charged.

- Split up cash among family members so funds are still available, should one person experience a loss. Carry enough cash to cover campground fees, shuttle fares, telephone calls, and other miscellaneous small expenses. Carry money separately from credit cards or use a "fanny pack."

- Carry your purse close to your body and your wallet in an inside coat or front trouser pocket. Consider bringing an automatic teller machine (ATM) card on vacation. Withdraw only small amounts of cash as needed. When possible, do all ATM banking during daylight and business hours. After hours, only frequent ATM machines located in grocery stores, malls, or other busy areas.

- If your car is bumped from behind or if someone says there is something wrong with your car, don't stop. Go to a service station or a well-lit area and call for help.

- Don't pull over for flashing headlights. Police vehicles have red or blue lights.

- Never leave video cameras, car phones, or other expensive equipment visible in your car. Also, never leave a wallet lying in plain view. Lock them in the trunk.

- Remove any items you might have stowed on a car rack and store them safely inside the trunk or inside your car if possible. Don't leave a vehicle for extended periods with valuable bikes or boats stowed on top. It is likely they will be gone when you return.

## *Driving in foggy conditions*

Visibility in fog can deteriorate at any moment to as little as ⅛ mile (660 feet) or less. This rapid loss of visibility creates a serious road hazard. If you haven't left for your trip yet, consider postponing your outing until the fog clears. If fog suddenly appears while you're driving, stay calm and remember the following tips:

✔ **Drive with your lights on low beam.** High beams only bounce back in the milk of a fog and reduce your ability to safely see.

✔ **Reduce your speed.** It stands to reason that since you can't see as far ahead as when it is clear, you need to slow down to give yourself plenty of time to react should an obstacle suddenly appear in your way — like a stopped truck.

✔ **Avoid crossing traffic unless doing so is absolutely necessary.**

✔ **Listen for traffic you cannot see.** If you do have to cross intersections, use your ears. Since you can't see, you might be able to hear oncoming trucks and traffic keeping you and your passengers out of harm's way.

✔ **Use your windshield wipers and defroster as necessary for maximum visibility.** If it is cold, it is very likely that your windows will begin to steam up. Crank that defroster to improve your vision.

✔ **Be patient!** Don't pass lines of traffic. If traffic is going slowly, it is going slowly for a reason. Passing the line of traffic simply to get where you are going faster may put you in danger of not getting there at all.

✔ **Unless it's absolutely necessary, don't stop on any freeway or other heavily traveled road.** If you must stop because you feel it is unsafe to drive, pull as far off the shoulder of the road as possible, without putting your vehicle in jeopardy of becoming stuck. Stopping on or near the edge of a heavily traveled road could place you at risk of being rear-ended.

# Entertaining the Troops for Sanity's Sake

Even in the best scenario, getting to a destination can be a battle of nerves and boredom — especially if children are in the car. Enter the world of car games. In this section, I list a few that are very effective and have stood the test of time under the grateful eyes of millions of parents and camp counselors.

## Games to play with children

If you are into store-bought, prepackaged kits for entertaining kids, I can think of none better than *Kids Travel: A Backseat Survival Kit*, by the editors of Klutz Press. Otherwise, read on for some kid-tested classics.

### The alphabet game

This is a classic game that can be played anywhere, and, best of all, it will help to develop a child's vocabulary. Start the game by naming something that you packed in the car or your pack, or use your imagination. The key is that the first item named must begin with "A." The second item named must begin with "B," and so forth. You can also use words on road signs to complete the alphabet — but good luck with Q, X, and Z!

### I spy

If your kids are older, this is one game that stands a chance of keeping the natives alert and engaged during long rides. The game also helps to encourage thinking and observation skills. The first player picks out an object that everyone can see — something common and easy to spot. The player says, "I spy with my little eye something . . ." and gives a clue to what the object is. Each object starts out with a value of 5 points. For each additional clue given, deduct 1 point. An object that is guessed with just the first clue is worth 5 points; if 2 clues are needed, it's worth 4 points, and so forth. You'll need to establish a scorekeeper, preferably an adult, to tally the points and help keep the peace.

### License plate bingo

Write the alphabet on cards and give one to each person in the car. The idea is for everyone to look out the window and see which letters of the alphabet they can find on the license plates of nearby cars. As you see letters, you can then check off the letters on your card. Once all the letters on a card are marked off, the winner shouts "Bingo!" If you want the game to last a little longer — or if you want to make it more challenging — announce that the letters must be found in sequence — for example, you can't cross off "C" until you find "A" and "B."

### License plate tag

Choose a number between 1 and 20. The other players look for license plates that have numbers on them adding up to the chosen number. The first person to find that license plate gets a point and gets to be "it." Whoever is "it" chooses the next number. The game can be made infinitely more difficult by playing the same game with multiplication — specify that players must multiply two of the numbers on a license plate to get the desired value.

## Games to play with adults

Not one to leave adults who are young at heart out of all the fun, in this section I share a few popular games that grown-ups can play to pass the time on a long drive.

### Theme songs

One person hums the tune to a favorite TV show such as *Get Smart, Hawaii Five-O, Gilligan's Island, Flipper, Lassie, Friends, Frazier,* and so on. The person who guesses correctly hums the next song.

### Guess what I am

One person states that he is a person, place, or thing, and the others then ask questions (Are you an animal? Are you a movie star? Are you alive? Can you be eaten? and so on) until they guess what the chosen item is. Whoever guesses the person, place, or thing correctly is the next person to choose an item.

### Animals, cities, geography

One version of this game is naming animals. Moving around the car clockwise, each person must name an animal (no repeating!) that starts with the last letter of the last animal named — or the first letter of the last animal named. You can play the same game with cities, geographical locations, or whatever you choose. If you want to raise the level of difficulty (feeling cocky, are we?), you can name geographical regions that start and end with a particular letter — "A," for example (Asia, Aegean Sea, America, Atlanta . . . you get the idea).

# Chapter 6

# Setting Up Camp

· · · · · · · · · · · · · · · · · · · · · · · · · · · · · · · · · · · · · · · ·

## In This Chapter

▶ Discovering the perfect campsite

▶ Pitching tent

▶ Creating your designer kitchen in the wild

▶ Siting the "bathroom"

▶ Assigning chores — especially to kids

▶ Tucking into bed and sleeping tight

▶ Moving on the next day — without leaving a trace

· · · · · · · · · · · · · · · · · · · · · · · · · · · · · · · · · · · · · · · ·

After you arrive at the site, either by car, foot, bike, paddle, or some other means, it is important to stay focused on setting up camp before commencing fun and games or going off on a personal adventure. As you set up your home away from home, focus on the "big three," in this order:

1. Shelter
2. Fire
3. Food

Start by putting up your tent and getting your gear inside it. Then collect firewood. Then set up the kitchen. Those are the three things you want to complete before darkness falls, rain starts, or any other interruption occurs. Organization is the key to successfully setting up the camp area. In addition to the sleeping area designated by your tent, be sure to establish a well-defined kitchen area, toilet area, and waste disposal. Food and cooking equipment should be in one clearly designated area, personal gear and washing/cleaning stuff in another. Personal camping gear such as backpacks and duffels should be emptied of any food and sheltered from possible inclement weather near the tent.

After you complete camp setup, you can kick back and enjoy the surroundings.

# Finding Camp

The perfect campsite is never made, it is discovered. So, stow that bush-whacker: Trenching, cutting branches, leveling, and removing vegetation are inappropriate camping techniques. Use your eyes, instead. Look for level sites that have naturally adequate drainage and are not sensitive areas that will be irreparably damaged by your presence.

As in real estate, there are three things to consider when choosing the best campsite: location, location, and location. The ideal site is level, with a relatively rock- and root-free spot to pitch your tent. In hot weather, an open site located on top of a hill or ridge may offer a cooling breeze — which can also help to minimize bugs. (In cool or windy weather, it's wise, of course, to avoid such sites.) Campsites surrounded by trees offer privacy and protection from the sun. Keep in mind that the closer you are to a stream or body of water in a valley bottom, the colder the night will be.

## Car camping

When camping at a public campground, take the time to walk or drive around the campground before you choose a site so that you can see and evaluate all the options. Plan to arrive early in the day, the earlier the better, to find the widest choice of sites, especially at popular destinations and during the peak months of July and August. Popular destinations can fill up during midsummer. Make reservations when possible. Also, try camping off-season. June and September offer great camping weather in many parts of the country. Even popular destinations are less crowded during these months because many kids are in school.

Consider whether the site has plenty of room for everyone to walk around without bumping into one another. Well-positioned or movable stumps or cut logs are key site furnishings if you haven't brought chairs. Decide how close you want to be to toilets, showers, or drinking- and cooking-water spigots. Toilets and showers are definitely convenient to have nearby, but you may pay a price in traffic and noise — at all hours of the day and night. The same can be said about a nearby water spigot.

## Wilderness camping

When wilderness camping, you are limited by either your permit designation or your sense of adventure, coupled with Leave No Trace guidelines. Few spots are perfect, so be prepared to make compromises that suit your tastes, the season, and the weather. You should be aware of poisonous plants, steep banks by a river edge, loose rocks near a cliff edge, dead trees that may topple, and similar hazards. Be sure everyone in your group is aware of any dangers that they should avoid. And, of course, avoid camping nearby or directly under any of the aforementioned hazards. I also advise that you position your camp as far away as possible from any stagnant water, which is often home to biting insects. Also, be sure you are very familiar with your camping permit regulations and obey all rules about how close to trails, water sources, and tree lines you are permitted to camp.

## *Stay warm*

I put this reminder here under choosing a campsite because you also need to take into account your personal well-being whilst seeking the site. If you have been sitting in a warm vehicle a long time before hopping out at camp, your body can quickly chill if the temperatures are cooler — often before you realize it. If you have been hiking or backpacking, your damp clothing can chill you further. Be sure you are wearing dry and warm clothing, and you will be that much happier for the few minutes it took to change.

# Campsite hazards to watch out for

Safe campsites far outnumber the risky kind. You can sort the bad places out of the mix by paying close attention to the terrain — and using your eyes.

✔ **Wind:** Check out the "flag" trees around you. If the branches all grow on one side or all the trees lean in the same direction, this is a good indication that the prevailing winds are strong and constant much of the day or night, even if they are calm when you arrive.

✔ **Rockfall or avalanche:** If you camp at the base of a slope or the end of a gully or ravine, or near a cliff, look around you. If there is a lot of rock rubble, chances are these souvenirs rained from above and you are possibly in the path of more missiles. If you are camping in the winter, be especially cautious if you camp in a gully or on a slope on the side of a mountain.

✔ **Flash flood:** The best advice is not to camp in ravines or gullies, period. However, sometimes this is not possible. But if you see clear signs of flash flooding in the area, such as a large log lodged in the rocks above you or debris wrapped around the trunks of trees above your head, chances are the area you are in is susceptible to flash flooding. GET OUT!

✔ **Lightning:** Seems silly to have to remind folks of this, but if a thunderstorm is approaching, setting up camp on an exposed ridge or exposed mountainside is not a very bright idea.

✔ **Cold-air sink:** Warm air rises; cold air sinks. So, in a valley, the warmer campsites are up the slope, and the coldest will be on the valley floor. Add water to the mix and you have evaporative cooling, which lowers temperatures even further.

*(continued)*

*(continued)*

- ✔ **Bear habitat:** "Bear-bag" your food if you are wilderness camping. Store your food in bear-proof containers if at a campground. Never take food into a tent or leave around the camp the clothing you have been wearing while fishing.

- ✔ **Insects:** Wasps, ants, ticks, mosquitoes, black flies, and the like can ruin a peaceful camping experience. If you pitch camp near a marsh or standing water, expect to be visited as the dinner hour arrives. If insects appear to be a problem, try to move camp into a higher elevation. Sometimes a simple 200-yard move further up the side of a valley and off the floor can make all the difference.

- ✔ **Scorpions:** If you are camping in the desert, you are going to be camping with scorpions at one time or another. It is no problem, really. Simply use caution. Scorpions like to crawl under tent floors (so don't reach blindly under the floor when taking down the tent) or under sleeping bags if you are sleeping under the stars (get up carefully in the morning) or in boots (shake out footwear before slipping toes inside).

# Pitching the Tent

After you are in your camping location, survey the area to choose the best tent site. In the grand scheme of campsite setup, erecting the tent should be the first order of business. Find the smoothest, most level surface for your tent site. Lay down a protective ground cloth as a barrier against moisture and rain. I cut my ground cover out of heavyweight plastic from a hardware store. The ground cover mirrors the shape of the tent floor, less one inch on every side. That way, the tent floor overhangs the ground cloth, letting moisture drain into the ground instead of creeping back between the tent floor and the ground cloth. After the ground cloth is in place and the tent spread out on top, follow the instructions for pitching your tent. Steps taken out of sequence can come back to haunt you later.

Face the tent in any direction you want. A scenic view is always a good choice. Facing the downhill side of any natural slope is another good idea — if it should rain, water won't run in the door. If it's windy, face the tent door downwind to help keep dust or rain from blowing in as you enter and exit. Facing — or not facing — east, into the rising sun, is another option. Consider your surroundings and do what seems best. Because a tent is a mobile domicile, you can always change your mind and rotate the tent or move it to one side or another.

Even if your tent is of the freestanding variety, I recommend securing it to the ground with tent pegs or stakes. I once witnessed a $500 dome tent turn into a very expensive kite — not the way you want to begin what you hoped would be a restful evening. Finally, as I note earlier, take the time to tuck any exposed edges of your ground cover an inch or so under your tent so it won't collect rainwater or dew. Roll edges down toward the ground, not up toward the tent, for greater moisture protection.

## Tent rules and regulations

There are a few things you should never do in or around your tent. Here is a handy list to remind you:

**Don't ever . . .**

- **. . . wear shoes or boots inside the tent.** Shoes bring in dirt that will turn to mud if it begins to rain and wet people begin climbing in and out of the tent. Dirt also acts as sandpaper on the floor of the tent, wearing the coating away and speeding up wear points.

- **. . . bring food into the tent.** Food inside a tent is a ready invitation to bugs — red ants — and animals. While rodents chewing or climbing into a tent are merely an irritation, bears chewing or climbing into a tent invite disaster.

- **. . . light matches, stoves, lanterns, or any flame inside a tent.** Even if the tent is of the nonflammable variety, which most are these days, a fire out of control inside a tent is not only serious, it can be deadly.

- **. . . bring a heater into a tent.** The possibility of carbon monoxide poisoning should say it all. No camper should be a victim, yet some are every year. Even if it is cold outside, the introduction of a heater to a sealed environment is a recipe for disaster.

- **. . . use the tent for a springboard.** Think I'm kidding? I've witnessed hundreds of children over the years, including my own daughter when she was little, finding great joy in flinging themselves against the side of a tent. If all goes well, the tent flexes, bends, and then flings them back out again. If all does not go well, the tent flexes, bends, and breaks — and Dad flings the kids out again.

- **. . . run around the tent area.** Tent stakes and guy lines are very easy to trip over. At best, the person takes a flier and dusts himself off embarrassed and none the worse for wear. At worst, the tent gets damaged and the person adds a painful face-plant to the list.

## Fluffing your pads and bags

After you set up the tent, immediately unpack your sleeping pads and sleeping bags. If the sleeping pads are of the self-inflating variety, open the valves and allow the mattresses to begin inflating. At the same time, unpack your sleeping bags, give them a few good shakes, and allow them to fluff up.

## Venting the tenting

If your tent is well-designed, and I am assuming it is (you bought the tent from a specialty outdoor store or online retailer, I hope), then it is designed with high/low venting in mind. Essentially, warm air rises. If you open up the windows at the top of the tent and just below the rain fly window and door awnings, warm air escapes. As the warm air leaves the tent, more air must be brought in to replace it. So, if your tent also has window or vent openings near the bottom of the rain fly and nearer the tent floor, by opening these vents you create airflow, with cooler air coming in the lower vents and warm air leaving via the high vents. In essence, the warm, humid air filled with the smells of dirty socks and camp grime gets flushed out, keeping the inside tent environment more comfortable.

## Set up a tarp

I carry an extra 9-by-9-foot nylon tarp with grommets on the sides and at the corners and 50 feet of extra cord. In the event of a wet trip, I set up the tarp as quickly as possible near the fire (taking care that sparks and flame won't destroy the tarp) or over the stove for all to sit under while eating, reading, or playing quiet games. Several companies make tarp shelters (see Figure 6-1) that are ideal for this purpose, and the package includes poles, stakes, and guy lines for tying out the tarp. The Moss Parawing is perhaps my favorite, although Mountain Hardwear and Walrus also make several versions.

**Figure 6-1:**
You can set
up a tarp
very quickly.

*Photo by Michael Hodgson.*

# Establishing the Kitchen Area

In a public campground, establishing a kitchen area is not an issue: Where the picnic table and the food storage area (if there is one) reside is where your kitchen will be. For wilderness campers, though, there are choices.

Locate your kitchen area carefully because this is probably where you will spend most of your time when not in your tent or out exploring. Look for a wind-sheltered spot, if possible, and as far away from your tent area as seems reasonable — 100 feet is about right. Why? Think bears. Also look for a spot that is warm and sunny, especially in the morning and late afternoon hours.

## Using a fire or stove

The fire or stove is the center of attention in every camp kitchen. And the surrounding space is sacred — clear space of five feet or more on all sides around the cooking area. This space is off-limits to running and playing, and free of stray pieces of equipment, unneeded food, and wood. Always keep pots and kitchen utensils in one place and nearby so that the cook has easy access. Organize food, spices, and kitchen utensils nearby — everything required for meal preparation should be readily at hand.

Open fires fueled by wood gathered around the campsite are becoming less and less acceptable as a means of cooking. Stoves are more environmentally sound and, frankly, easier to cook over. Still, it is hard to beat the romance of dancing firelight and snapping flames while camped under a star-flecked sky on a crisp, clear night. Let your conscience be your guide.

If you choose to have a fire, keep some guidelines in mind. Never break branches or twigs from a tree, even if they appear to be dead. To do so may cause irreparable damage to the tree. If you are car camping or on a paddling trip, bring your own wood or charcoal briquettes, or both. If you have to gather wood for the fire, choose smaller branches and wood that will burn easily and completely in the fire. Go beyond the immediate area of the campsite to collect wood. Never, ever, burn the last deadfall in the area. If wood seems sparse, use your stove.

### Rules seared in flame

For maximum pleasure and minimum unpleasant surprises at the campfire, abide by the following rules:

- ✔ **Always wear shoes.** Stray embers will burn and can cause a serious foot injury.
- ✔ **To minimize the risk of burning skin or wasting food, always remove pots from a fire when adding ingredients.**
- ✔ **Use pot grabbers with work gloves to remove pots.**
- ✔ **Keep nylon clothing, tents, and sleeping gear away from the fire.** Nylon melts easily under a stray ember.

- ✔ **Keep polypropylene and other synthetic fiber away from the fire.** These types of fiber used in underwear and clothing melt at very low temperatures. Getting too close to a fire while wearing polypropylene could create a painful situation with liner gloves or underwear melting on the skin. I have melted a pair of gloves myself, and it hurt!

- ✔ **Never, ever, leave a fire unattended.** If you leave for any reason, put it out.

- ✔ **Remember that having a fire is a privilege and not a right.** If the area appears overcamped and wood is scarce, or if building a fire will permanently scar the land (such as near or above timberline), use a stove.

### Children and fire

Although you must be very careful with children around an open flame, it is important to allow them to become involved with the building and maintaining of the campfire. It is crucially important that they realize fire building is serious business and not something for play. If they cannot take fire building seriously and are apt to play with flaming sticks, take away their fire-helping privileges.

Children of all ages are excellent wood *gatherers*, but not until they are 10 or 11 do they typically become patient and responsible enough to take on the task of fire *building*. After they reach 10 or 11, however, they can carefully build a fire using kindling and smaller twigs, gradually adding larger sticks to feed the growing flame. If parents set the proper example, the kids will develop a proper respect for the power of fire. (Find more on campfire skills in Chapter 7.)

## Whip up hot drinks to warm spirits

If it has been raining or the air is cold, you will want to get a fire or stove going for hot drinks — almost at the same time you are pitching your shelter. If there are several people in your group, assign one person to kitchen setup detail while the others put up the tent. There is nothing like a mug of hot chocolate, tea, coffee, or even hot flavored gelatin to put the sparkle back in even the coldest camper's eye.

## Get into camp shoes

If you have been wearing hiking boots all day, your dogs deserve a rest. Tennis shoes, all-terrain sandals, leather moccasins, insulated camp booties, and water shoes all make suitable camp footwear. I lean toward the water shoes for children around public campgrounds as they can also be used as bathroom/shower shoes. My personal preference? I slip into a pair of leather moccasins, even though they get very slippery when damp — and I have gone inverted on a number of occasions when I wasn't paying attention. But moccasins get my nod because they are very light and compact.

## Purify the water

Don't assume that water at a campground is safe to drink, even if it comes from a spigot. The water in lakes, rivers, and springs may look crystal clear but often contains various bacteria that can cause illness. Unless it is posted or an official from the campground has told you that the water is safe to drink, you must use one of three purification methods: filter, chemical tablets, or boiling.

- ✔ **Filters:** With a filter, you simply pump water from the source into a container. The filter mechanically removes protozoa and bacteria and you are good to go. If the filter also has an iodine system built-in, it will kill viruses too.

- ✔ **Chemical tablets:** Water purification tablets, such as Potable Aqua, are a second option. They employ chemicals, usually iodine, to kill harmful bacteria. Tablets are easy, inexpensive, and quick, but can affect the taste of the water. Tablets also have a limited shelf life — six months once the bottle is opened. Another concern is that chemicals are ineffective against some protozoa, such as *cryptosporidium,* and require much longer to work if the water is full of sediment or is very cold.

- ✔ **Boiling:** Bringing water to a rolling boil is a third option. Boiling has no effect on taste. But it has drawbacks as well. Boiling water is time-consuming, must be done in small batches, requires pouring hot water into containers and then waiting for it to cool, and uses up fuel.

# Locating the "Bathroom"

If your campsite includes toilets and showers, you can skip this part. If you have to create your own "bathroom," however, the following guidelines apply. Locate your toilet at least 200 feet from water, trails, and camp. You don't have to use a tape measure to get the distance right — simply pace off 70 to 80 steps. For an adult, that translates closely to the recommended distance. Always look for a site where other folks are not likely to camp or travel. Imagine the joy of the camper who follows you, pitching his tent on your toilet!

Other than packing your own portable toilet, which is the most responsible though certainly not always the most practical means of dealing with human waste, you have two choices in creating a backcountry toilet:

- **Cathole.** With a small trowel, dig a hole 6 to 8 inches deep and 4 to 6 inches in diameter. When you are finished using the cathole, cover with loose soil and disguise the area with natural materials.

- **Latrine.** Figure 6-2 shows the dimensions of a latrine. Latrines are the least desirable method of dealing with human waste, but they are appropriate when camping with younger children or if you are staying in one place for longer than two or three nights. Always dig a latrine wider than it is deep, but always at least 12 inches in depth. After each use, cover with a layer of soil and then compress with your boot or a shovel to encourage decomposition. Once the latrine fills to within 4 inches of the surface, fill it in and disguise the area with natural materials.

## Toilet paper, sanitary napkins, tampons, diapers

Toilet paper, sanitary napkins, tampons, and disposable diapers must always be packed out and never buried. If you are camping in an area that allows campfires, you can burn this "paper" waste in a very hot fire — I'd recommend this not be done while cooking, of course. As for diapers, no fire is going to be hot enough to adequately burn a diaper. And besides, burning plastic is bad for the environment. That said, if you opt to use disposable diapers, you can empty the solid human waste into a cathole or a latrine, but you must pack out all the used diapers themselves and dispose of them properly when you get home. *Don't even think* of rinsing them out in streams or lakes.

What haven't we covered? Oh, yes — it's okay to pee in the woods. Aside from odor, urine causes few problems for the environment or for human health.

## Portable potty

Some parks and wilderness areas require human waste to be hauled out and disposed of in approved sewage treatment facilities. In that case, you need a portable potty of some kind. Ask your outdoor outfitter for suggestions, or give a call to Emergency Essentials, Inc., in Orem, Utah, 800-999-1863 or 801-222-9596.

## Bathing

Bathing is the simpler part of your "bathroom" setup — I talk about backwoods bathing in Chapter 4 in a section on winter camping. In warm weather, you may want to pack a nifty little camp shower, which is basically a bag and a hose (see Figure 6-3, for example).

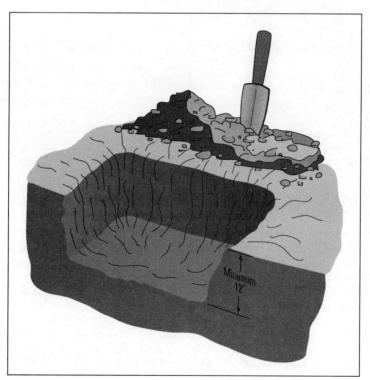

**Figure 6-2:**
Latrine.

**Figure 6-3:**
Water bag
with shower
hose.

Photo courtesy of Stearns Outdoor.

# Keeping Your Site Clean

Cleanliness is important at a campsite. Clutter takes up valuable space. Garbage, food, and dirty dishes attract animals and insects. Keeping your site neat and tidy is always worth the very small effort it takes. Keep a trash bag set up and handy for all litter to go into. When eating in a campground, eat over a tarp, then use a whisk broom to sweep up the crumbs and food debris so these morsels do not attract insects.

# Chores for Everybody, Kids Included

Every camping trip has its own set of chores and demands. Setting up camp, breaking down camp, laying out sleeping bags, stuffing sleeping bags, cooking, cleaning, and hanging food ensure that there's no shortage of chores. Though it may seem easier at the moment to do everything yourself, everyone on the trip, including children, should lend a hand.

Oh, the many ways kids can help! And the best part is, having regular chores adds to their fun, though they may grumble a little (mild protests really mean, "I'm a trusted member of this expedition!").

- ✔ **Setting up:** Use the extra set of little hands to help you roll out the tent, separate the stakes, assemble the poles, even hold up an end of the tent while you secure the other. Give your child the task of unpacking everyone's sleeping pad and bags and laying them out neatly in the tent. It may take them an incredibly long time, but children seem to universally enjoy this activity and it is well within their capabilities.

- ✔ **Cooking:** During cooking time, young children should not be playing around the fire or stove. However, children love to help with cooking by adding water and mixing ingredients. You can easily accomplish this by setting up a place away from the fire and main food preparation area to minimize dirt kicked in food and knocked-over pots. It is important for your children to realize that when they are given a cooking task, they need to sit at a designated location under adult supervision until the task is done, and then clear out until you serve the food.

- ✔ **Dishes:** Younger children often enjoy playing in warm dishwater. This desire can be capitalized upon by giving them cups and utensils to clean (no knives) after most of the other pots and pans are clean. Chances are they will enjoy playing and cleaning in the water for quite some time.

As your children grow older they can assume more difficult chores and become more active participants in day-to-day activities of the camp. In all situations, try to create a positive atmosphere. The only time I have seen a really negative response to chores by children was when a parent sat on his duff and assigned chores like a dictator, never once lifting a finger to help. All aspects of wilderness travel, to be successful, involve teamwork.

# Shutting Down for the Night

As yawns begin to prevail, thoughts of slumber push tired campers toward the sleeping bags and a night of rest. But hold on! If you don't secure the camp, you may be inviting problems during the night or in the morning, not the least of which is clothing and gear that has disappeared by claw or wind. Your bedtime checklist follows:

- ✔ **Gather water.** It is far easier to do your filling and filtering in the evening hours than in the early and often chilly morning hours. Fill a kettle or pot for hot water in the morning now, too. That way, the first one up simply ignites the fire and begins heating water.

- ✔ **Clean the dishes and hang or store the food properly.** Any food scraps or food left lying around camp is an invitation to foraging by wildlife, raising toothier issues than mere mice — say, a bear?

f the Fun _____

items around the camp. If you leave it loose, it will disap-
ts have been known to become collectors of all sorts of
oo, has Mother Nature simply by kicking up a strong wind
rs anything loose, like clothing or papers.

mportant personal gear. Place these within easy reach of your
ag: water bottle, flashlight/headlamp, personal items such as
s, clothing for the morning, and your boots.

emergency items within easy reach of your sleeping bag. My
ddes pocketknife, whistle, and bear spray, for example. Why a
t knife? Because it is a lot easier to cut your way out of a tent — in
an avalanche, if a bear is coming in the front door and you need to get
out the back — than it is to chew your way through a nylon wall.

✔ **Check out all the tents.** Recheck the tent to be sure it is secure and
staked out properly. Chances are your tent has loosened up slightly from
the time you initially pitched it. Now is the time to discover that guy
lines need tightening or stakes need repositioning. Much better now
than in the middle of a midnight storm you didn't expect.

✔ **Food stowed?** This is really a double-check to the second bullet: Be sure
no food items are stored in or around your tent.

✔ **Check the tarp.** If you have a tarp over the kitchen area, either tighten
the lines or lower the tarp in anticipation of winds or an incoming storm.

# Answering Nature's Call at Night

When nature calls after the lights are out and everyone is tucked in (and I
promise you, she will call), ignore the urge to stay snug in your sleeping bag.
If you have to use the toilet, then go. I advise slipping into your camp shoes
for safety's sake. I remember several times when friends — and when I was
guiding, clients — slipped out to relieve themselves and ended up stepping
on a sharp thorn, rock, or stick, and injuring their foot. Special advice to men
and boys: Make certain you know where you are standing in the dark. It is not
unknown for nighttime relievers to rudely awaken other campers who have
chosen to sleep under the stars.

Be sure to zip up the tent door immediately after exiting to protect tentmates
from an invasion of moisture or insects.

If the weather is very stormy or the bugs too thick to tolerate, you can always
attempt the mountaineer's trick by relieving yourself in a clearly designated
wide-mouth bottle — yes, men and women can use a wide mouth, though

women have a decidedly more difficult time. Keep in mind that when such a maneuver is attempted, mishaps do occur and include missing the bottle (makes you very unpopular with your tentmates), overflowing the bottle (also makes you very unpopular), or reaching for what you thought was your water bottle for a drink and — well, you get the disgusting picture (makes you hugely popular with your tentmates simply for the humor you have provided them).

Don't use your flashlight at night unless you have to. Using your flashlight does two things: It limits your peripheral vision and restricts what you see to only the illuminated area, and it makes the darkness appear even darker after you turn off the light. On moonlit nights, and even those nights when there is little moonlight, you will be surprised how much your eyes can actually see if you give them enough time to adjust without flashing them with light. If you have to use a flashlight to view a map, try using a red transparent filter over the lens. This preserves your night vision significantly.

# Taking Down Camp

When breaking camp, be sure to restore the site as close to its natural appearance as possible. Taking down camp should be done according to the following guide to ensure everything goes smoothly:

- ✔ **Begin by stuffing your sleeping bag and stowing your sleeping gear.** If you really want to speed things up, open the valve on your air mattress or self-inflating sleeping pad while you are still lying on it, just before you get up.

- ✔ **Top off your water bottles for the day's journey, if needed.**

- ✔ **Put items you will need quickly during the day in an accessible area of your backpack (if backpacking), front handlebar bag (if biking), or nearby small waterproof bag (if paddling).** These include snacks, maps, compass, binoculars, sunscreen, sunglasses, and so on.

- ✔ **If it is raining, take down your tent and the tarp last.** If it's not raining, take tent and tarp down first. Shake off any excess moisture by holding the rain fly vertically and then shaking it wildly from side to side. Stuff your tent into its stuff sack. Wipe off the poles and stakes and place them carefully inside their stuff sacks if they're separate pieces, or inside the main stuff sack if not.

- ✔ **If you cleared sticks and twigs from an area under your tent, return them.**

ECO ETIQUETTE

✔ **After your stove is cool to the touch, pack it away along with your pots and pans.**

✔ **Completely douse any fire with water and stir the mixture so that the coals become cold to the touch.** If there was an established fire ring before you got to the campsite, leave it. If not, bury the coals, scatter the rocks, blackened side down, and smooth over the area.

✔ **Walk through the camp with every member of the camping party to be sure that all signs of your presence are removed and all litter, yours or not, is carried out.**

# Part III
# Camping Skills, Food, and Fun

## In this part...

From coping with wildlife to repairing gear and tying knots, I teach you enough campcraft skills in Chapter 7 to have you dreaming of living off the land — almost. And because camping doesn't mean eating burnt food, in Chapter 8, I show you how to plan a menu, prepare a meal, and even clean and serve fresh fish, whether you cook over a camp stove or on open flames. In Chapter 9, I get you ready for a hike on the wild side — a round-trip ticket. Chapter 10 is packed with my suggestions for campsite activities such as stargazing, storytelling, and doing nothing — you know, stuff to do once you get to where you're going if you really feel you have to do something. You can also find practical tips about using your camera and binoculars.

# Chapter 7

# Skilling Up at Camp

*Y*ou can buy all the gear in the world to make you look good outdoors, but there's no way to buy skill and experience. In the outdoors, skills derived from experience mean the difference between planning and luck, success and possible emergency. In this chapter, I show you how to tie some basic knots, build a fire, repair your gear, and build an emergency shelter — simple skills that will make you a more confident and safer outdoorsperson.

## Tying Knots

Ropes and knots are as much a part of any skilled outdoor adventurer's arsenal as a knife, compass, and waterproof matches. With just a little rope-tying know-how, you can modify and even secure your world. You can tie trucker's hitches to attach a boat to your car rack, tie taut line hitches to take up the slack in a sagging tent line, tie a bowline to secure a person to a rope in a rescue situation — the list is endless.

Which knots are best? There are literally thousands of different knots (some obsessed knot-tiers with entirely too much time on their hands claim that there are over 4,000), each with its own purpose and use. Be thankful that I limit your skill-set requirements to a few basic knots that should see you through almost any situation you may encounter outdoors.

The accompanying illustrations are the best means for learning to tie the knots. Study them along with the descriptions and then practice, practice, practice.

To make things easier — I hope — I routinely use a few simple terms you will need to keep in mind. The *running end* of the rope is the shorter or active end of the rope that you weave in and out of the knot. The *standing part* of the rope is the longest and least active end of the rope and is the opposite end of the rope from the running end (a rope only has two ends, gang!). I also refer to a *bight* on the rope, which means, simply, a bend in the rope. (I don't just say *bend* because *bight* is a technical term you need to come to grips with if you are to understand even the basics of ropes and knots, and I say it time and again.) Finally, I refer to something called a *stopper knot*. Like the name implies, this is designed to stop a rope from sliding through a loop, hole or, in the case of climbing, a descending device — rappelling off the end of a rope is not impossible and is no laughing matter. The basic overhand knot is most typically used as a *stopper*. Now, on to Knot Tying 101.

## Bowline

The bowline is best known to sailors and climbers. As a climber's knot, the bowline has its roots in the days when climbers tied directly into a rope with a loop around their waist. As such, it is still a very useful knot to know for rescue situations or any time you may need to tie a secure loop in the end of a rope — a secure knot that won't come undone. (See Figure 7-1.) "The rabbit comes out of the hole, around the tree, and back down the hole again," is the chant often used by folks remembering how to tie this knot. The hole is a small loop formed by crossing one end of the rope over the other. The rabbit is the running end of the rope.

## Clove hitch

Used most often to secure tent lines to poles or stakes and sometimes as a temporary mooring line for a canoe or kayak, the clove hitch is a classic outdoor knot. (See Figure 7-2.) Take the running end of the rope and wrap it once around the pole, fence post, or stake, passing the running end under the standing end before completing the wrap. Continue around the post, pole, or stake once more, this time above the standing end with the running end. As you complete the second wrap, feed the running end back through itself and above the standing end wrapped around the pole and then pull tight. You can add security to the line by adding a stopper knot at the end of the rope's running end so that it cannot pull through on itself.

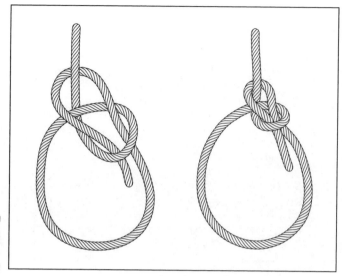

**Figure 7-1:**
Bowline.

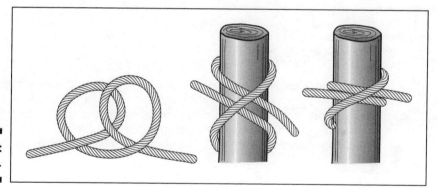

**Figure 7-2:**
Clove hitch.

# Fisherman's knot

This knot has been called many names over the centuries, including a waterman's, but it is still best known as a fisherman's and is designed to attach two lengths of rope of equal diameter securely together to form a longer length of rope (see Figure 7-3). Begin by placing two ends of two ropes next to each other. Pass the running end of rope one under the running end of rope two, pass it back over the top of both ropes, and then push the running end of rope one up through the loop just formed. Pull tight. Now, take the running end of rope two and pass it under the running end (behind the knot just formed) of rope one and over the top of both ropes, and then push the running end up through the loop just formed. Pull the two knots together by pulling in opposite directions on the standing ends of each rope.

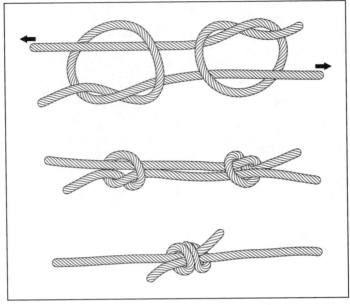

**Figure 7-3:**
Fisherman's
knot.

## Figure eight

Like the name implies, this knot forms a figure eight in the rope. (See Figure 7-4.) A figure eight is used as a stopper knot at the end of a rope or as a means to prevent a rope from unraveling. To form the knot in the rope, cross the running end of the rope over the standing part. Wrap the running end around the standing part and then feed that end back through the loop just formed.

**Figure 7-4:**
Figure eight.

# Figure eight threaded

As its name implies, this knot forms a figure eight in the rope with a loop below the knot. (See Figure 7-5.) You can use this knot to tie into a climbing harness or to form a secure loop for pulling or hauling items. The figure eight threaded also forms part of the trucker's hitch described later in this section. To form the knot, cross the running end of the rope over the standing part. Wrap the running end around the standing part and then feed that end back through the loop just formed. Now, form a bight in the running end below the eight and begin threading the running end back through the loop, retracing the rope as it winds and twists through the original eight. Be careful to follow the path exactly so that the running end parallels and pairs up with itself on the original knot and exits back toward the standing end. Add a stopper knot to prevent the running end from slipping.

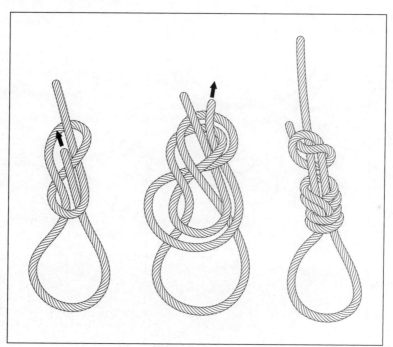

**Figure 7-5:**
Figure eight
threaded.

## Two half hitches and two half hitches slipped

One of the most widely used knots for hanging objects from branches, posts, poles, and so on, the half hitch is easy to tie and easy to learn. Wrap the running end of the rope around the object you are securing the rope to. Feed the running end around the standing part and then back up or through the loop formed between the pole, post, or branch and the rope. That completes one half hitch. For two half hitches (a more secure knot), wrap another loop around the standing end of the rope below the first hitch. (See Figure 7-6.) To create a quick-to-untie knot, slip the knot. To do this, create a bight in the running end of the rope and feed the bight through the loop, leaving the last inch or so of the running end sticking out (see Figure 7-7). A quick tug on the running end of the rope releases the knot.

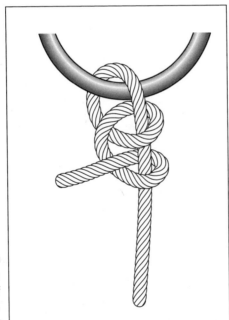

**Figure 7-6:**
Two half hitches.

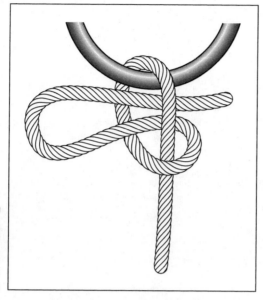

**Figure 7-7:**
Two half
hitches
slipped.

# Round turn and two half hitches

This knot is best used to fasten large items to a roof rack (you can also use
the trucker's hitch, described later in this chapter, for that purpose, although
that knot isn't as versatile), to secure a boat to a mooring overnight, or to
fasten a line to a beam, post, or branch when you want the line to be able to
support a heavy load. Wrap the running end of the rope around the beam,
post, or branch twice. Now secure the running end to the standing end with
two half hitches as described in the previous section. (See Figure 7-8.)

# Constrictor knot

I've used the constrictor knot (see Figure 7-9) many times to close stuff sacks
and bags whose draw-cords have worn out or disappeared. It also works
great on the end of a rope to prevent it from unraveling or as a rope clamp to
hold two items firmly together. Wrap the running end around the object once,
passing the running end under the standing end to form one wrap (leave the
first wrap loose enough to form a slight loop). Now complete a second wrap,
this time above the first wrap so the running end crosses over the standing
end. Feed the running end back under itself as you complete the second wrap
and then pass the running end up through the loop formed by the first loose
wrap. Pull both ends of the rope snug. If you want to be able to easily untie
the knot, slip the knot by putting a bight in the running end and then pass
this bight through the loop formed by the first wrap.

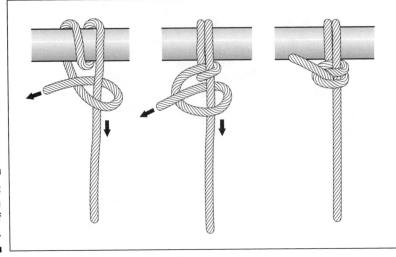

**Figure 7-8:**
Round turn
and two half
hitches.

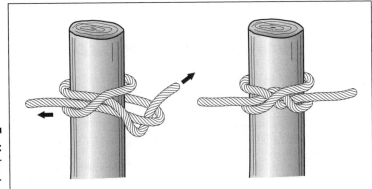

**Figure 7-9:**
Constrictor
knot.

## Taut line hitch

Probably the most important knot to know for securing lines that tend to loosen or sag over time, such as tent guy lines and clotheslines, the taut line (see Figure 7-10) can hold securely in one direction but can be easily slid in the other — it's a kind of rope-ratchet. Begin by wrapping the running end of the rope around a tent stake, post, pole, or branch. Wrap the running end of the rope around the standing end twice, toward the post, branch, pole, or stake. After completing the second wrap, feed the running end of the rope under the standing rope above the wraps, around the standing rope, and then back through the loop you just formed. The running end should now point away from the stake, pole, branch, or post and toward the standing end. Pull tightly.

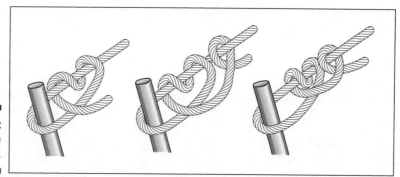

**Figure 7-10:**
Taut line
hitch.

# Trucker's hitch

What person hasn't tied the nightmare knot on a luggage rack or truck bed? You know the one — all twists, tucks, bends, and overlaps with no logic or hope of ever actually untying the thing once you need to release the load. Well, my friends, help is at hand. You need to know how to tie the trucker's hitch, which is really three knots in one. (See Figure 7-11.)

Start with the bowline or figure eight. Tighten, leaving about a 5-inch-diameter loop below the knot.

Now, toss the end of the rope without the bowline or figure eight in it over the item you want to secure and bring it back around. Pull the slack out of the rope by holding onto the bowline or figure eight loop. Twist the free end of the rope as illustrated, forming a loop. Bend the free end of the rope above the loop to form a bight, and push the bight through. A quick tug will tighten the first loop around the bend, forming a new loop. Now pass the free end through the bowline loop and then back down through the loop and pull. As you pull the rope through and it tightens, the loop will bind on the rope, securing it under tension. You can secure any load under extreme tension this way. As a final precaution, tie off the end of the rope using two half hitches slipped.

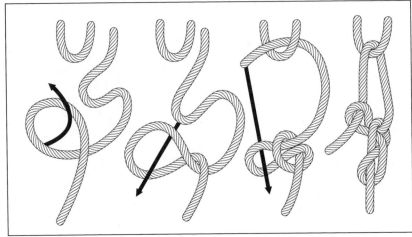

**Figure 7-11:**
The trucker's hitch.

# Dealing with Wildlife

*Snuffle, snuffle, slurp* is a nocturnal sound that, when heard outside your tent flap, means one of two things: Either your camping partner has developed a case of the sniffles while trying to gorge secretly on your highly prized personal stash of sweets, or Ursus americanus is rototilling his way through your pack in search of anything remotely edible.

Before going hiking and/or camping, find out which animals may or may not frequent the area you are trekking in. From kangaroo rats to bears, animals are an inquisitive lot that are likely to take advantage of each and every opportunity for free food. A kangaroo rat gnawing through a pack to reach some nuts inside is not an immediate threat to nearby humans, but the damage to the pack could create real problems.

A bear, on the other hand, rummaging through camp and smelling food in or around a tent is going to be very surprised when it encounters humans as well as chocolate or fish. The surprise and resulting screaming and growling can lead, and has led, to very unfortunate consequences. In a conflict between bears and unarmed humans, bears usually cause the most immediate damage.

Whether you're sharing your outdoor home with a creature as small as a rat or as intimidating as a bear, you should respect the animals and take the proper precautions to protect yourself and them.

# Bearproofing yourself and your campsite

The first step to take to avoid unpleasant encounters is to bearproof your camp. Bear-bag your food well away from camp (see Figure 7-12), or place your food in special bearproof containers such as the Backpackers' Cache (209-732-3785), leaving no food in packs, and never take food or clothing that smells of food into tents. In general, if you keep your camp clean, you should experience no serious bear problems. A bear may still periodically attempt to wander through just because you are on his selected route for the evening.

Effective bear-bagging takes a bit of practice, but once you get the technique down, you'll be slinging rope and hauling bags with the most experienced outdoorsperson. I carry two 50-foot lengths of parachute cord, although sometimes a heavier cord or rope would make tossing through dense foliage easier. If you can find a branch large enough so you can toss the rope up and over it, and then haul up the food bag so it is 4 feet away from the trunk and 8 to 10 feet off the ground, you're set. If not, then you'll need to string one line up between two trees, about 10 to 12 feet apart. Before you tighten and secure the line, tie a carabiner or pulley in the middle of the cord between the two trees. Feed the second line through the pulley or carabiner. Now, tighten the cord between the two trees and secure it. Attach the bear bag (stuff sack full of food) to the second cord and haul it up. Tie off the end of the cord and you're set.

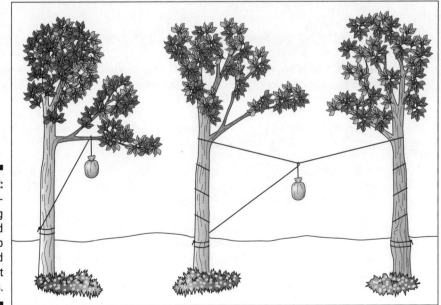

**Figure 7-12:** Bear-bagging your food can help you avoid unpleasant encounters.

If a bear should approach you in camp, yell, wave your arms, bang pots — anything to alert the bear to your presence, which should encourage it to retreat. If the bear chooses not to retreat (and this technique is also the one to use if you encounter a bear while on a trail), you should! Move away from the bear slowly and methodically with your eyes to the ground and making no outward appearance of being aggressive. Speak to the bear in calm but firm tones to help it recognize that you are human and not a threat. If the bear attacks, don't run! Ball up and protect your vitals and lie still.

When traveling through bear country, your best defense is good ears and alert senses. Some people wear bells or clap their hands to alert bears to their presence. In theory, this approach sounds good. If the bear knows you are there, you are less likely to surprise it, and it's more likely to move out of the way. On the other hand — aside from the fact that some areas of our wilderness are beginning to sound like a bad rendition of "Jingle Bells" — there is evidence to support the idea that bears are learning to identify bells and other human noises like clapping as meaning "Dinner's on!" Not exactly the approach we want.

A better idea is to travel quietly and learn to anticipate bear country. Look for signs such as fresh tracks, fresh scat (animal poop, silly), and so on — if you see the bear, that would be a sign, too. Listen frequently for noises. Try to see a bear before it sees you. If you are traveling in bear country, realize that each district has its own rules and guidelines for you to follow. Be sure to check in and find out what they are.

## Beware the wayward rodent

If you choose not to hang your food because there's no bear hazard where you're camping, leave your pack pockets open anytime you leave your pack for a period of time. An eager rodent will just as soon gnaw through fabric to get to food, but it will usually take the easy route if an invitation is left via an open zipper or flap. To ensure that you receive no unwanted visitors in your tent, leave all food outside your sleeping area.

When sleeping in shelters and in some canyon areas or high desert environments, you'll encounter some very ingenious mice who seem to have nothing better to do with their time than divine ways to get around animal-proofing attempts and reach your delectables. You can easily make the antirodent/mouse food storage system shown in Figure 7-13. (I have yet to meet a rodent who has figured it out.) Take three feet of parachute cord. Tie a knot one foot from the end of your choice. Save the lid from a tin can, file the edges smooth so they won't slice and dice your equipment or your skin, and drill a hole in the middle of the lid. Feed the one-foot length of cord through the hole and slide the lid down the rope until it rests on the knot you tied. Tie a loop in the end just above the lid. At the end of the two-foot section of rope below the lid, attach a hook or a section of stick. To use this contraption, attach the looped end to a nail or a secure branch. Hang your stuff sacks of food from the hook or stick and several feet above the ground. The rodents will be able to shimmy down the cord to the tin can lid, but they won't be able to figure out a way around it.

**Figure 7-13:**
Safeguard
your food by
constructing
a simple
antirodent
food storage
system.

# Knife Sharpening 101

Numerous guidebooks, articles, and how-to instruction manuals address the importance of knives as tools for outdoorspeople, yet I am amazed at how few also speak about knife sharpening. Why? Doesn't anyone use knives anymore? It is a fact that as a knife blade gets used, it grows dull and less efficient. Perhaps people use their knives until they dull and then buy new ones, although I doubt it. It stands to reason, then, that if you own a knife, you should also own a sharpening tool such as a simple Arkansas stone.

## Using a sharpening stone

An Arkansas stone is a relatively thin, 3-inch-long rectangular block of stone that is typically coarse to the touch on one side and fine on the other. A stone is perfectly flat on each side and rough enough — like sandpaper — so that you can work out the burrs, knicks, and dull areas of a knife's blade easily. The fine side of the stone is for finishing your work and putting a nice, smooth edge on the knife. To sharpen a blade, you choose the angle you wish to achieve — most pocket knives should be sharpened at a 20- to 25-degree angle — and then smoothly and with even pressure begin moving the blade in an even, circular motion without lifting the blade from the stone. A circular motion produces the most consistent edge. The closer you maintain a consistent angle throughout the sharpening process, the better the edge you will achieve. With a little practice, you'll find it's easy. Complete several full rotations in a counterclockwise direction first. Count the number! Turn the blade over and make the same number of smooth, circular motions in a clockwise direction. Repeat this process on both sides until you have the edge you want.

## Getting a good angle

Contrary to myth, the angle of a blade's cutting edge has nothing to do with sharpness — larger- and smaller-angled cutting edges are equally sharp. The angle at which you choose to sharpen a blade, and consequently the angle to which the cutting edge gets ground, affects the durability and drag of the cutting edge. In other words, the smaller the angle, the less drag but the more delicate the cutting edge will be. A larger angle means more blade drag, but more durability — less frequent sharpening is required. (See Figure 7-14.)

Knife experts recommend the following sharpening angles as a guide:

✔ **11 to 15 degrees:** Highly delicate edge for hobby knives, woodcarving tools, and specialty blades. This type of blade requires frequent sharpening.

- ✔ **15 to 17 degrees:** A moderately delicate edge used in fillet, boning, and other thin specialty blades. This type of blade requires frequent sharpening.

- ✔ **17 to 20 degrees:** Common angle for kitchen knives. The frequency of sharpening depends on what you're cutting.

- ✔ **20 to 25 degrees:** Wider bevel and more durable edge intended for pocket knives, folding hunting knives, fixed-blade field knives, and serrated knife blades. These types have a durable and long-lasting cutting edge.

- ✔ **25 to 30 degrees:** Widest bevel and longest lasting of the edges. These types are only intended for heavy-duty use such as with utility knives for cutting cardboard, carpet, wire, and linoleum.

**Figure 7-14:**
Choose a
sharpening
angle based
on how
you'll use
the blade
and how
frequently
you want to
sharpen it.

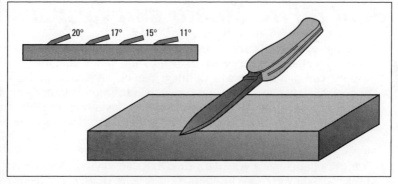

# *What are the oil and water for?*

On stones intended for hand sharpening, oil or water's sole purpose, in theory, is to keep the metal shavings and bits of stone in suspension so that they do not clog the sharpening stone and affect its honing efficiency. On power sharpeners, water is primarily used to cool the stone so that the knife's blade does not overheat with the friction and become damaged. All that aside, an increasing number of knife experts — and I agree with them — recommend that you do not use oil or water on your hand stone. Sharpen your blades dry, and you achieve maximum performance from both the stone and the knife.

# *When should you replace your stone?*

A stone should be flat for effective sharpening. Over time, the grinding process will wear a noticeable belly or curvature in the stone. You can tune your stones from time to time by rubbing them back and forth on 100 grit silicon carbide sandpaper placed on an absolutely flat surface. If, after performing this stone first aid you still notice a curvature, it's time to toss the stone and buy a new one.

## Easier sharpening

Is it possible to maintain an exact angle with only a sharpening stone? Yes, but only with lots of practice. A far better solution is to outfit yourself with a knife sharpening system. With a specially engineered clamp and angle guide, anyone — even a youngster — can precisely sharpen a knife blade to a desired angle. Gatco and Lansky Sharpeners are two of a number of companies offering specialty knife sharpening systems. Suggested retail prices range from $19 to $50.

# Building a Fire Safely and Responsibly

Although fires were once necessary for survival, for the most part this is no longer true today. We cook with stoves, shed light with lanterns, and provide warmth through shelter and clothing. Man may never shake the romantic appeal, however, of a crackling fire deep in the woods under a star-flecked sky. For those intoxicated with the thrills of adventure, the fire serves as an after-dark elixir — warmly coaxing forward camaraderie, tall tales, and quiet reflections.

But campfires have a very dark side, more subtle than the scarring forest fires caused by careless builders. Charred fire rings, rocks smudged black from use, scattered coals evident from half-hearted attempts at a wilderness ethic, broken or cut trees and branches, and half-burned logs too large for consumption and left strewn around an abandoned camp are a few of the more noticeable impacts. More detrimental than any of these obviously visual scars, though, is the irreversible depletion of natural resources vital for the maintenance of an ecological balance.

Downed and dead timber is often collected to the point of complete eradication, with campers venturing further and further afield, depleting an ever-widening circle in the process. The result is a loss of food and habitat for animals and the elimination of a source of vital nutrients necessary for the continued growth of plants and trees.

Not all campfires are bad! Certainly, if you are camping beside a high alpine lake in the Sierra Nevada of California or at tree line along the Appalachian Trail in the White Mountains of New England — both locations where firewood is in limited supply — a fire is not a suitable choice. However, move the camp location to deep within the pine forests of the Wind River Range of Wyoming or the Cascades of Washington with abundant quantities of downed wood, and a properly built fire is a fine addition to the overall experience. Let your common sense guide you.

TIP

## How young is too young to build a fire?

Keep in mind that although your fire is a vital source of warmth and heat for cooking, it is a very dangerous tool capable of destroying vast amounts of land and many animals if it is left to burn out of control. Not all children should be allowed to build fires, and there is no hard and fast rule about what age is appropriate. I was building outstanding fires from scratch at age 8, and yet I had several friends who should not have been trusted with a match until 18.

Keep in mind that what a fire does add in terms of romantic warmth to the scene it takes away in equal parts the potential for you and anyone sitting around the campfire to enjoy a complete nocturnal experience. There is firewood to collect and the knowledge that you will have a fire to clean up. And then there is the dancing light that all but destroys your night vision, obscuring everything that may exist to you outside the limited boundaries of the flame.

In this section, I explain how to build a safe, efficient fire and then clean it up when you're ready to move on.

## Choosing a site for the fire

Select an area that is free from ground debris, roots, and other vegetation that may catch fire and spread the flame to surrounding trees. Don't build a fire under overhanging tree limbs or within 10 to 15 feet of any shelter. Building a fire in a cave or next to wet or damp rocks is dangerous because water or moisture in the rocks can be brought to boiling point, causing steam to expand and explode the rock, much like a bomb. When I was ten, a member of our campfire group tossed a wet sandstone rock into the fire. It exploded and sent embers showering over all of us. Fortunately, no one was hurt, but the potential for serious injury was very high.

Try to pick an area that has natural wind breaks, and clear the area of all loose debris. If your campsite has a pre-existing fire ring or area, then use that. Don't build a fire in a new site when a fire ring already exists, even if it is not in the most ideal location aesthetically.

## Selecting firewood

Select the right kind of wood, and I guarantee that the fire will not only burn brightly and warmly, but with less smoke and greater cooking efficiency. Remember that every fire starts with patience and kindling — not necessarily in that order. Kindling should be made up of very small, dry twigs that, when lit using a firestarter, will catch fire quickly and help to start the flame eating into the larger wood.

### Choosing the right type of wood

Each type of wood has its own special characteristics that lend themselves to particular types of fires. If you learn to identify various trees and the dead-wood lying around, then you will build fires that are the envy of everyone. Keep in mind the following characteristics when choosing your firewood:

- **Aspen:** This wood is moderately difficult to ignite, has fair cooking characteristics, throws off a moderate number of sparks, produces very little smoke, and adds nice flavor to fish and meat.

- **Birch:** This wood is very easy to ignite, has fair cooking characteristics, throws off a moderate number of sparks, produces moderate amounts of smoke, and adds nice flavor to fish and meat.

- **Fir:** This wood is very easy to ignite, has poor cooking characteristics, throws off large quantities of sparks, produces heavy smoke, and is not advised for cooking.

- **Maple:** This wood is difficult to ignite, has excellent cooking characteristics, throws off very few sparks, produces very little smoke, and adds a very nice flavor to fish and meat.

- **Oak:** This wood is difficult to start, has excellent cooking characteristics, throws off very few sparks, produces very little smoke, and adds a nice, subtle flavor to fish and meat.

- **Pine:** This wood is very easy to ignite, has poor cooking characteristics, throws off large quantities of sparks, produces heavy smoke, and is not advised for cooking.

- **Spruce:** This wood is very easy to start, has poor cooking characteristics, throws off large quantities of sparks, produces heavy smoke, and is not advised for cooking.

### Gathering firewood responsibly

Let the following tips guide you as you choose firewood:

- **Never cut down trees or branches, living or apparently dead.** To do so can cause irreparable harm to the tree, disrupting an available habitat for animals — and it's illegal in most regions anyway.

- **Select only wood that is one to two inches in diameter and lying broken on the ground.** (Figure 7-15 gives you an idea about sizes.) This wood is more readily consumed by the flames and results in hotter coals and a better fire for cooking and heating.

- **Always gather your wood away from camp.** This helps to prevent immediate depletion of vital wood resources lying around the camp area.

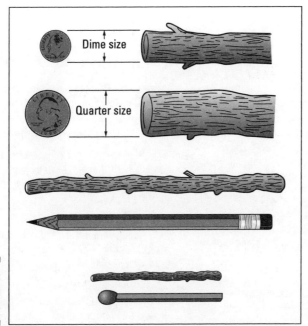

Figure 7-15:
Twig size
guide.

## Constructing the fire

Every fire must be constructed in some way. In the case of campgrounds, both drive-in and backcountry, where fire rings (circles of rocks that enclose fire sites to prevent embers and coals from scattering) or designated fire pits already exist, your fire-building tasks are limited to constructing a fire that provides hot coals for cooking or flames for warming.

If a fire site or location does not exist and the area you are camping in permits the building of fires, then you need to construct a place to start your fire. You can see descriptions for building mound fires or pit fires and also using a fire pan later in this chapter. In all cases, it is essential that you build a fire that is small enough to be easily scattered once the coals are cool and then covered over or removed before you leave. Why? So the next person who follows in your steps can experience the joy of discovering a wild place without finding evidence of your passing.

Using a small cooking grate with folding legs (available from any good camping supply store, mail order catalog, or Internet outlet) eliminates the need to utilize rocks for securing and supporting cook pots, thereby preventing the scarring of rocks.

## Creative fire-starting materials

Sure, you can light a fire with one match, but pack along some home-remedy kindling and some waterproof matches anyway. Why? Because they'll light the fire when things don't go exactly according to plan — like when Mother Nature opens the fire hose on your camp and douses your fire-building plans.

I always carry a lighter with me and an old plastic film canister filled with wooden strike-any-where matches. As for starting materials, here are a few ideas that should get the flames roaring in no time:

✔ Commercial firestarters such as fire ribbon or petroleum-based tablets (Esbit by MPI Outdoors, for example) work very well.

✔ Fill each hole of an old egg carton with shredded newspaper and several spoonfuls of sawdust. Pour in melted paraffin (wax) to bind the sawdust and newspaper into a solid lump. Once the wax hardens, you have one dozen wax-based firestarters.

✔ Fill a film canister with lint from your drier. (Make sure that the lint comes from wool, cotton, and fleece and not fire-retardant fabrics.)

✔ Look to nature. Even in the worst storm, you can find dry tinder around the base of tree trunks, under rock ledges, in tree hollows, and next to downed logs.

✔ Make your own kindling from a larger log that is soaked on the outside but dry on the inside by whittling down to the dry center. Whittle dry shavings from this piece.

### Teepee fire

The teepee fire is the very best fire for quick lighting, even in severe weather (see Figure 7-16). It puts out a tremendous amount of heat, even with a relatively small fire, and is quite easy to maintain.

Follow these steps to build a teepee fire:

1. **Bunch up a ball of frayed bark, dried grasses, and tiny twigs from a pine tree, evergreen, or other available tree along with your fire-starting materials if you have them.**

2. **Lay very small twigs and sticks — not much larger than the kindling — against one another and over the ball to form a teepee shape.**

   Leave a small opening through which you can place the match to ignite the fire.

3. **Continue adding more wood, gradually longer and thicker (up to the width of two fingers).**

   Maintain the shape of a teepee at all times.

4. **Once the teepee is built to your satisfaction, carefully strike a match, shield it from the wind, and place it next to the waiting ball of kindling to ignite it.**

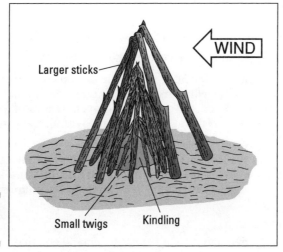

**Figure 7-16:**
Teepee fire.

When adding wood, lay each piece carefully into the flame and always keep the shape of the teepee intact. Do not toss or arbitrarily throw wood on a fire as at best it sends up a shower of sparks, creating a fire and safety hazard, and it could destroy the fire.

### Pit fire

Pit fires should be used only in situations where ground vegetation will not be damaged or where there are only a few inches of underlying duff (the dead layer of leaves, plants, and needles covering the forest floor). A pit fire is created by digging a shallow hole where the mineral soil is exposed and the duff is cleared away, making cleanup easier and dramatically reducing the chance of starting a forest fire. (See Figure 7-17.)

**Figure 7-17:**
Pit fire.

Follow these steps to build a pit fire:

1. **Scrape away all the duff, exposing the mineral soil underneath.**

   Clear an area larger than the fire you intend to build.

2. **Create a shallow pit that is wider than your fire and several inches deep. Use a small backpacking trowel or your hands to create the pit, and be sure to save the earth you have removed because when the fire is out, you want to return the earth and cover up the evidence of your passing.**

3. **Build your fire in the pit, keeping it small and efficient and never allowing it to grow larger than the pit you have built. To build a fire, follow the directions for the teepee fire earlier in the chapter.**

### Mound fire

Mound fires are ideal when you can find suitable mineral soil that can be dug without disturbing the natural area (see Figure 7-18). Streambeds and sandy areas around boulders are ideal mineral soil sources.

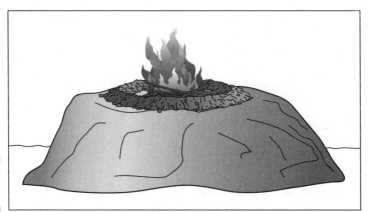

**Figure 7-18:**
Mound fire.

Follow these steps to build a mound fire:

1. **Choose a large flat rock that is either portable or immobile, or create a rock base by placing two or more relatively flat rocks side by side.**

2. **Using a trowel and one of your cook pots, gather soil and spread it at least three inches deep on top of the rock base.**

   Create a wide platform that is larger than the area the fire will utilize — 2 to 2.5 feet wide is usually sufficient.

3.  **Build a small and efficient fire directly on top of the mineral soil, making sure that your fire never grows larger than the base of soil on top of the rocks. To build a fire, follow the directions for the teepee fire earlier in this chapter.**

### Fire pan

Although common with river runners, fire pans are gaining popularity with other wilderness users (see Figure 7-19). Certainly, the prospect of lugging an iron fire pan in a backpack is not an inviting thought; however, there are many lighter alternatives.

**Figure 7-19:**
Fire pan.

The following steps explain how to build a fire in a fire pan:

1.  **Place the fire pan, such as a pie-sized aluminum pan or a store-bought manufactured pan, on a layer of small rocks or line it with mineral soil so the heat will not scorch the earth.**

    **Alternatively, you can lay several 3-foot-long strips of heavy-gauge aluminum foil side by side with a one-inch overlap.**

    You can also retire an old aluminum space blanket and fold it into a 3-foot-by-3-foot square.

2.  **Cover the aluminum with several inches of mineral soil so the heat will not damage the fire pan or scorch the earth beneath.**

3. **Build a small and efficient fire directly on top of the soil, never allowing it to grow beyond the boundaries of the fire pan or foil barrier. To build a fire, follow the directions for the teepee fire earlier in the chapter.**

## Cleaning up your fire

Since it is infinitely more difficult to clean up a fire immediately after you have doused the flames, it is recommended that you do not build a campfire in the morning. That way, no water is needed to douse the fire, and cleanup is cleaner and faster.

Nothing should be left in the fire ring but ashes. Refrain from adding additional wood to the flames approximately one hour before finishing the fire. Keep pushing the partially burned pieces of larger wood into the center or hottest coals of the fire. You may find that you need to add very small pieces of wood, twigs, and such, to keep the fire hot enough to consume any larger sections of wood.

If you need to add water to douse any embers, do so slowly, and sprinkle it on rather than soaking the fire and surrounding soil. Stirring the coals while sprinkling additional water until the embers are out and the fire is cold will speed the process. Check the fire for live embers by carefully placing your palm near, then on, the fire site. (If the fire is still smoking, don't touch it. Sizzling flesh is not a good indicator of an extinguished fire.) If, as you place your hand near and then on the ashes, you do not sense heat, stir the ashes carefully and look for hot embers again. If you still see none, then carefully sift through the ashes with your fingers. Again, if you do not feel any warmth, the fire may be declared dead.

After the fire is cold, crush any large lumps of charcoal. Spread the ashes and crushed charcoal away from the site, leaving no sign of your campfire. Pick out any food or other trash remnants and pack those out. It is not appropriate to bury or scatter fire-blackened or charred trash with the ashes.

If you had to build the fire site, then be sure to fill in the pit, scatter the mound, or fold up the fire pan. Rinse off the rock from the mound fire before placing it back in its natural setting. Camouflage evidence of your fire with duff.

If the fire ring already existed when you arrived, leave it assembled after cleaning up the ashes and trash. When multiple fire rings are discovered at a single campsite, do the land a favor and dismantle all but one — pick the one in the safest location and in an area that appears to have the least impact upon the ground or surrounding area. When dismantling rings, place any fire-blackened rocks blackened side down and camouflage them. Take the time to carefully scatter the ashes from the dismantled rings, pack out the trash, and camouflage the sites.

# Repairing Your Gear

Murphy's Law has an uncanny way of cropping up when you're traveling in the wilds. Leave your raincoat at home and presto, a downpour. Forget your stove repair kit and, you guessed it, your stove decides to take an untimely vacation from work. Of course, the best cure for the Murphy syndrome is good planning and a good field repair kit.

If you are really into learning how to maintain and repair all of your outdoor gear, get *The Essential Outdoor Gear Manual*, written by Annie Getchell and published by Ragged Mountain Press/McGraw Hill. It is *the* gear-repair bible.

## Assembling your repair kit

Through years of working as a professional mountain guide and in search and rescue, I have put together a basic repair kit of the following essential items:

- Duct tape for hole patching, tent pole splinting, boot repairing — the list goes on and on
- A multitool that combines a knife, pliers, and other necessary tools for repair purposes in one compact kit
- Sandpaper for roughing up surfaces I may have to glue together
- Seam Grip, a waterproof urethane rubber compound that works as a seam sealer and patching compound
- Spare flashlight batteries and bulb
- Miscellaneous stove repair parts
- Waxed thread, like dental floss
- One medium and one leather needle for leather and webbing repairs
- One spare one-inch nylon strap with buckle
- One tent pole sleeve (a standard three-inch, heavy-gauge aluminum tube that fits over broken tent poles and serves as an effective splint)

Because each trip demands repair items specific to that trip (a backcountry ski trip requires ski binding parts, pole splint material, and a spare ski tip, for example), I evaluate the basic kit and make necessary adjustments. As for the weight of the kit, I try to keep it around one to one and a half pounds — not light by any means, but I'll take a pound of prevention over a ton of misery any day.

Mark Jenkins, a former editor for *Backpacker* magazine, an author, and now a columnist for *Outside,* suggests some additional items that, from his extensive experience, may come in useful on any prolonged trip into the hinterlands:

- ✔ One 5-x-5-inch patch of mosquito netting for the one time a hole appears in your tent screening
- ✔ Five inches of one-inch-wide Velcro with adhesive coating on the back sides of both the hook and loop for jacket or sleeping bag repair, should the zippers give out
- ✔ Several hose clamps for splinting a broken pack frame

Many repair kit lists include rubber bands for securing things. I used to pack several heavyweight ones myself. Pat McHugh of MPI Outdoor Safety Products suggests substituting a large-size 25-cent balloon for a rubber band, and he makes a good case.

The elasticity of a large balloon allows you to lash poles together to make an emergency shelter or repair; you can also use the balloon as a tent tie-down line or to secure gear to a pack or in a canoe. Partially inflate the balloon and use it as a makeshift outdoor pillow. For hunters, a balloon stretched over the barrel of a gun or scope protects the weapon from debris and moisture. Inflate several balloons to provide cushioning during transport of fragile gear over rocky terrain or rapids. The list goes on in almost as unlimited a manner as Pat's imagination.

The bottom line is that you should assemble a repair kit to meet your needs. Use your imagination and the basic guidelines I offer, and plan for the unexpected, because you can bet that the one time you aren't ready for the unexpected is the one time the unexpected will happen to you. In the wilderness, after all, you can't call a repairperson. You have to make do yourself.

## Repairing zippers

Zippers are the most underappreciated workhorse-fastener on today's outdoor equipment. They are used and abused to such a level that it's a wonder they last as long as they do. The most important thing you can do is treat your zippers with care. Keep them clean by flushing them with water after each trip. (I don't recommend using a silicon lubricant on the zipper's teeth since that only serves to attract more dirt.) Pull your zipper sides together when closing your pack or tent door. Slow your zipping pace when closing a zipper, especially around tight corners.

The most common reason coiled zippers (the ones found on most gear these days) won't close is that the slider (the bit of hardware with the tab on it that you pull on to close or open the zipper's teeth) is worn. If the teeth of your zipper stay open after a pass by the slider, reach for your pliers. Work the slider back up to the top of the zipper or to the point where the zipper would be open if it was working. Take your time — this can be a challenge. Now, gently squeeze one side of the slider and then the other, using equal pressure (don't oversqueeze — you can jam the slider or even crush the zipper coils). Try the zipper again. Do this several more times until the coils remain closed after a pass by the slider. If this fails to work, you need a new slider and should consult your nearest specialty outdoor store for advice.

## Repairing tent poles

Tent poles can break, whether they're aluminum or fiberglass. For replacement poles or aluminum pole repair by a professional — assuming your tent is a name brand and not some discount throwaway — try contacting TA Enterprises in Vancouver, Washington at 206-260-9527. They specialize in repairing and replacing aluminum tent poles. If your poles are fiberglass, you have a hit-or-miss chance of getting replacement sections from Ralph's Tent and Tarp in Coon Rapids, Minnesota. Call Ralph's at 612-421-7053.

## Repairing air mattresses

There is something truly disconcerting about hearing "Pffsssssss" while lying comfortably on your self-inflating mattress, because unless you packed a repair kit, you can count on spending a cold and lumpy night wishing for sun.

Self-inflating mattresses have become luxuriant necessities for many outdoor travelers, replacing the reliable yet cheap ensolite pad and the unreliable yet cheap air mattress. Because these self-inflating mattresses are relatively expensive — $45 and up — a patch kit is usually the last thing a buyer wants to think about, so it's often forgotten in the rush for the woods.

While it is true that you can prevent most leaks by carefully protecting your pad from sharp objects such as cactus spines or broken branch ends, a slow leak is something most wilderness denizens experience at one time or another. Duct tape works in a pinch but invariably leaks after only several days and usually leaves a sticky residue that will thwart any attempt at a more permanent repair. Self-adhesive ripstop nylon or packcloth repair tape, available at most outdoor shops, is a good repair choice and can also be used to repair rips and tears that may occur in your tent fly or sleeping bag.

Should you find yourself in the campground without any nylon tape, try rousting up some urethane-based sealant, such as AquaSeal, Seam Grip, or Urebond and glue a small piece of nylon (cut from a ground cloth) over the offending hole. If you're only dealing with a pinhole, a small amount of seam-sealer, especially a sealer designed for use on Gore-Tex garments, often works.

Of course, the very best alternative for repairing leaks is to have a patch kit supplied by the manufacturer. Whatever your method of repair, adhere to the following steps to guarantee success.

1. **To find the offending leak, inflate the pad to its maximum and listen for hissing air. If no leak can be audibly detected, submerge the pad in water (a quiet pool in a nearby stream works well) and look for a telltale stream of bubbles.**

   If you can't find a leak, check the valve. A few slow bubbles are not abnormal, but a steady stream is. If you still can't find a leak, try saying your mantras before you go to sleep.

2. **Mark the spot for later identification once the pad is dry.**

   If the leak is located at a seam, return the pad to the manufacturer for replacement or repair.

3. **Clean the pad around the leak.**

4. **After the pad is dry, wipe the area around the leak thoroughly with an alcohol wipe from your first aid kit to get the pad really clean.**

   Oils and dirt prevent the patch from adhering properly.

5. **Cut the patch larger than the hole.**

   While a pinhole can be satisfactorily repaired with just a dab of glue and no patch, larger holes require fabric to hold the air back. Cut a patch that extends ¼ inch around all the edges of the hole. Center the patch over the hole and mark the edges.

   Gashes or holes larger than 2 inches or deep burn holes usually call for a proper burial of the mattress.

6. **Apply adhesive.**

   Work a small amount of adhesive in a circular motion outward from the hole toward the marked edges of your patch. Keep the layer of adhesive thin and let it dry until tacky.

7. **Apply the patch.**

   Center the patch carefully and press it firmly onto the adhesive. You won't have an opportunity to reposition the patch because the adhesive will grab it quickly, so be sure of your placement.

8. **Place a pot full of rocks over the patched area to secure the patch until it is cured — approximately one hour, longer in cold weather.**

# Chapter 8

# Cooking and Eating in the Wild

● ● ● ● ● ● ● ● ● ● ● ● ● ● ● ● ● ● ● ● ● ● ● ● ● ● ● ● ● ● ● ● ● ● ● ● ● ● ● ● ● ●

## In This Chapter

▶ Planning menus, stocking supplies

▶ Outfitting your camp kitchen

▶ Cooking, baking, snack-making

▶ Cleaning and preparing fresh-caught fish

● ● ● ● ● ● ● ● ● ● ● ● ● ● ● ● ● ● ● ● ● ● ● ● ● ● ● ● ● ● ● ● ● ● ● ● ● ● ● ● ● ●

*T*he phrase "camp kitchen" evokes a kind of nostalgic feeling — warm sunsets, crackling fires, the tawny smell of smoke wafting through the pines while dinner sizzles away. And that recollection is absolutely true! A well-outfitted and productive camp kitchen is to wilderness camping what the galley is to a luxury cruise ship: the source of much pleasure for everyone aboard.

Satisfying, memorable camp meals don't just happen, of course. You have to plan for them. This chapter covers the details, beginning with menus and shopping lists, then turning to kitchen setup and cooking routines.

## Planning Menus, Making Lists

Planning the perfect menu for any outing involves a careful balance of taste, nutrition, and energy content. While your diet shouldn't become one of sugar and fat during a camping adventure, simple, high-energy carbohydrates are an essential element. Weight, ease of packaging and handling, as well as an appropriate variety — no one wants to eat your favorite "Chili Surprise" three nights running, no matter how tasty — are also necessary considerations.

### Water is essential to health

Water is a critically important part of menu planning. It is vital that each person drink two to four quarts of water per day. Just as important is the need to maintain the body's balance of water and salt. The normal diet typically includes an adequate provision of salt in meals without your having to be concerned about adding more. If the trip is extremely difficult or the weather unusually hot, then an electrolyte additive to the water is appropriate. Be careful not to overdo the salt intake, as too much salt is more harmful than too little.

Proper hydration helps to prevent hypothermia, heat stroke, heat cramps, frostbite, and altitude sickness. If water is not going to be available at the campsite or while traveling, be sure to pack it with you.

## Planning light when camp is mobile

You can reduce weight by combining dried, dehydrated, and freeze-dried foods along with any fresh selections in your menu. You can further lighten your load by repackaging everything into zip-lock plastic bags. Choose sturdy, freezer-quality, resealable bags and not flimsy sandwich bags. Stay away from canned goods.

I have found that it is more convenient and more efficient to prepackage meals together into a freezer-size zip-lock bag. If possible, I premeasure and premix all the dry ingredients in the same bag. Don't forget to label the bag as to its contents, and unless you have an incredible memory, drop in brief instructions with each meal.

## What, no cooler?

Spoilage is a problem when camping without the benefit of a cooler. Stay away from real butter, cooked meats, eggs, and noncanned bacon. Real cheese is fine outdoors and does not spoil; however, processed cheeses and spreads such as cheddar and Muenster do spoil and you should avoid them. The softer the cheese or the greater the oil content, the more likely it will turn gooey and oily. Try to get a child to eat oily-looking cheese and you'll see what I mean about avoiding the softer cheeses. I prefer hard cheeses like Jarlsberg or Gouda.

## Stocking up for meals and snacks

The basic rule is to plan your meals and snacks so that they are easy and fun to prepare, visually appealing, and tasty. As you think of specific ingredients, try to combine textures (crunchy/chewy) and tastes (salt/sweet) in each meal so that hungry campers don't get bored. Use the following breakfast-lunch-dinner suggestions as a backstop to your own shopping lists. And if the camping party includes kids, remember to include their favorite foods.

## Breakfast suggestions

✔ **Drinks:** Cocoa, orange juice crystals, Tang, tea, coffee, and low-fat dried milk.

✔ **Cereal:** Cheerios, shredded wheat, oatmeal, cream of wheat, Malto Meal, cream of rice, granola, seven-grain, and muesli.

✔ **Main dishes:** Pancake mix (Bisquick works great), western omelet (freeze-dried), eggs (fresh if in a campground, freeze-dried when on the trail).

✔ **Mixed fruit:** Freeze-dried for weight concerns, canned if campground-based.

✔ **Dried fruit:** Apricots, papaya, prunes, raisins, apples, pineapples, plums, cherries, pears, peaches.

## Trail-lunch suggestions

✔ **Meat:** Jerky (beef or turkey), salami, pemmican, beef stick.

✔ **Cheese:** Gouda, Jarlsberg, German Swiss, or the like (any unpasteurized, unprocessed cheese that does not require refrigeration).

✔ **Nuts:** Peanuts, pecans, cashews, pine nuts, walnuts, hazelnuts, and almonds.

✔ **Seeds:** Pumpkin, sunflower, soya, and sesame.

✔ **Fresh vegetables:** Carrots, radishes, cauliflower, jicama, celery, turnips, and broccoli.

✔ **Fresh fruits:** Apples, oranges, and tangerines.

✔ **Dried or freeze-dried fruits:** Dates, apples, pineapple, bananas, peaches, prunes, apricots, raisins.

✔ **Breads/crackers/pastries:** Lebanese flat bread, sourdough, rye, Pilot Biscuits, Ritz, Waverly, Triscuits, Rye-Crisps, Japanese rice crackers, Cheese Nips, Melba toast, trail biscuits, Pop-Tarts, Danish Go-Rounds.

✔ **Sweets:** Licorice, Tootsie Rolls, lemon drops, candy orange slices, tropical chocolate, malted milk tablets, Life Savers, fruit bars or rollups, sesame seed bars, pudding (various flavors in small aluminum cans — pack out the cans), cookies.

✔ **Drinks:** Kool-Aid, Wyler's, juice crystals, Tang, hot cocoa (nothing better for a cold day), individual serving size boxes of juice, Gatorade instant mix.

## *Dinner suggestions*

- ✔ **Drinks:** Wyler's, Kool-Aid, tea, coffee, hot cocoa, Tang.

- ✔ **Soups:** Lipton Instant, Knorr Instant, and Top Ramen.

- ✔ **Prepared dinners (freeze-dried):** Richmoor, Natural High, Backpacker Pantry, AlpineAire, and Mountain House. (If you have never tried freeze-dried dinners before, buy several to sample at home. I prefer Backpacker Pantry desserts and side dishes and AlpineAire and Natural High main courses, but everyone's taste is different.)

## *Prepare your own meal staples and mixes*

- ✔ **Textured vegetable protein:** Made of soybean and good added to soups or casseroles.

- ✔ **Uncle Ben's Quick Brown Rice:** For stir-fry, curries, and casseroles

- ✔ **Bisquick:** For dumplings, breads, and biscuits.

- ✔ **Pastas:** Homemade macaroni and cheese, for example.

- ✔ **Lentils, pinto beans, and lima beans:** All make great bases and additives for soups and stews.

- ✔ **Corn bread mixes:** Alternative to Bisquick.

- ✔ **Instant potatoes:** To thicken soups, bases, make potato pancakes.

- ✔ **Miso, tomato base, chicken base, beef base, and instant gravy or sauce packets:** Flavoring and bases for soups, stir-fry, casseroles, curries.

- ✔ **Freeze-dried chicken, beef, or fish:** Meat additives to soups or casseroles.

- ✔ **Freeze-dried vegetables:** Additives for soups, meals, casseroles, and stir-fry.

## *Spices and additives*

- ✔ **Cinnamon sugar:** Sprinkle on cereal, hot biscuits, pancakes, etc.

- ✔ **Margarine.**

- ✔ **Crisco:** In small container. Better than oils and butter for cooking and frying, and it doesn't burn or break down as easily on a hot flame. After each use, pour back into container and reuse.

- ✔ **Honey:** Healthier than white sugar for sweetening. Package in a squeeze tube or 8-ounce Nalgene bottle.

- ✔ **Peanut butter and honey mix:** Premix 2 parts peanut butter to 1 part honey and package in squeeze tube. Add more honey to soften consistency.

- ✔ **Brown sugar:** Alternative to honey and not as messy.

- **Dry milk:** Milkman low-fat for flavoring and mixes. Make into a paste before adding all the water required to prevent lumping.

- **Spices:** Cinnamon, nutmeg, curry, oregano, chili powder, garlic, black pepper, salt, dry mustard — package each in one-ounce Nalgene bottles and label.

- **Soy sauce:** The backpacker's ketchup.

- **Worcestershire sauce and Tabasco sauce:** Package in flip-top bottles for spicing up otherwise somewhat bland freeze-dried meals.

- **Bouillon cubes or powder.**

## Repackaging food

Leave cardboard packaging, non-resealing containers, and wax paper packaging at home. Self-sealing plastic bags are a camper's best friend. Much of the food you take to camp, with the exception of fresh produce, should be repackaged into resealable plastic.

It's best if you carry fresh produce in a breathable mesh bag near the top or to the outside of a pack — produce tends to spoil in plastic unless you refrigerate it.

Bulk and frequently used foods will get packaged either in double freezer zip-lock baggies or one-quart Nalgene bottles with a wide mouth.

For beverages, sugar, milk, and coffee, I prefer wide-mouth Nalgene bottles. They are easy to open and close, and they won't tear or break.

Food items like Bisquick, flour, pasta, and dried fruits, for example, pack and carry nicely in a double-bag zip-lock system. I recommend double-bagging to prevent accidental bursting and puncturing.

Be sure to label all your food, take any preparation instructions that exist on original packaging, and place them inside the resealable plastic bag you have placed the food in. I can tell you from experience that cooking up ingredients for which you "sort of" remember how much water and cooking time is required leads to adventurous cooking experiences you can live without.

## Fresh greens in a pack

A fun thing to try, if you wish a little fresh food on your outing, is to grow sprouts. You can obtain seeds from a health food store as well as specific instructions on how to grow them. The basic idea is to take some alfalfa seeds, place them in a smaller zip-lock baggie, keep the seeds moist, and rinse with fresh water every day. This is especially fun when camping with children as each child can be put in charge of cultivating his or her own plastic bag garden for mealtime. They will enjoy watching the seeds sprout in their packs while on the trip.

# Baking

Yes you can! Using a stove-top oven — for example, the Outback Oven, by Backerpacker's Pantry (see Figure 8-1) — baking becomes simple. Ready-made mixes are available for brownies, quiches, coffee cakes, and pizza, to name a few. The only drawback to this oven-cooking system is that the gear is heavy. Still, the flavors are phenomenal, and I don't know of any camper who won't be thrilled at the thought of brownies while outdoors.

**Figure 8-1:**
Stove-top
oven.

Photo courtesy of Backpacker's Pantry

If you don't want to buy a stove-top oven, you can rig something like it with a frying pan and lid, with the stove on low flame below and a small fire built of twigs burning on the lid. I have had more consistent success, however, using a fire. When using a fire, the temperature is critical. If your hand, held about six inches from the bed of embers, feels hot but not uncomfortable, the fire is ready. Be sure you have a very good supply of hot coals. Place the frying pan on a level bed of embers and shovel a generous layer on top of the lid. You will need to check the baking goods periodically. Brush off the top coals and quickly peek inside without letting in cold air. Always keep flames away from the baking site.

# Cast-iron cooking

Sure, there are lighter ways to cook, and no, we're not debating calories here. What we're focusing on is good ol', home-on-the-range, slap-the-butter-on-a-biscuit-and-toss-a-rasher-of-bacon-onto-the-skillet cast iron cookery. From Dutch ovens to skillets, you won't find a more effective and efficient way to cook over a fire than cast iron — as long as you're not backpacking, that is. Ten pounds for a four-quart pot is not shaving ounces!

*Photo courtesy of Lodge Manufacturing Co.*

**Figure 8-2:**
Cast-iron
cookware.

The beauty of iron is that it retains heat extremely well and distributes it more evenly than almost any other cooking vessel. Aluminum, glass-lined, and steel versions of the Dutch oven are poor imitations at best, primarily because food scorches in them.

Look for cast-iron cookware from companies such as Tennessee-based Lodge Manufacturing (see Figure 8-2), the largest producer of cast-iron cookware in the U.S. They don't make engine blocks or anything else but cookware in their machines, which means they dedicate their entire process to making the best product possible for cooking. I won't cook on anything else.

# Outfitting Your Camp Kitchen

The way you outfit your camp kitchen depends a lot on the way you are traveling. That's why, in the lists that follow, I state the kind of camping in parentheses. I list several suggestions of items for you to use in planning your next well-outfitted camp kitchen. (And see Figures 8-3, 8-4, and 8-5 for standard equipment.)

**Kitchen furniture:**

- ✔ Roll-A-Table (car camping, paddling)
- ✔ Padded folding chairs (car camping, paddling)

**Kitchen organizers:**

- ✔ Beaver Tree Kitchen (car camping, paddling)
- ✔ Coleman Kitchen (car camping)
- ✔ Large dry bag or duffel (car camping, paddling, horseback)
- ✔ Smaller kitchen organizer (backpacking, bike touring, kayak touring)

**Shelter from the elements:**

- ✔ Cook Tarp, 10 by 12 feet, with plenty of alternate tie-out points for a variety of sheltering configurations (car camping, bike touring, paddling, backpacking with groups)

**Coolers and food storage:**

- ✔ Hard coolers
- ✔ Soft coolers — Outdoor Research and Seattle Sports are two of my favorite brands for those campers who need to keep food fresh and cool on a trip where space is at a premium (paddling, car camping)

**Personal commissary:**

- ✔ Insulated stainless steel mug
- ✔ Knife/fork/spoon set
- ✔ Plastic bowl and plate

**Stove and fuel:**

- ✔ Backpacking stove (car camping, paddling, kayak touring, bike touring)
- ✔ Fuel bottles with pour spout — MSR, Sigg, Peak 1, and vauDe all offer excellent fuel bottles.
- ✔ Lighter
- ✔ Two-burner stove (car camping, paddling)
- ✔ Waterproof matches

**Figure 8-3:**
Two-burner
stove.

**Figure 8-4:**
Two-mantle
lantern.

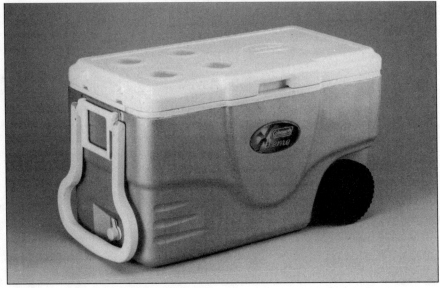

**Figure 8-5:**
50-quart
cooler.

*Photos courtesy of The Coleman Company, Inc.*

**Pots, pans, and ovens:**

- Cast-aluminum griddle with lip (car camping, paddling).

- Cast-iron Dutch oven 10 to 12 inches in diameter (car camping, paddling).

- Coffee filter that does not require paper inserts. Why? Because as any tea or coffee aficionado knows, brewed drinks are simply better with a filter, and if you don't need paper, you can brew many drinks with the same filter.

- Dutch oven lid lifter.

- Euro coffee grinder. There is nothing like grinding fresh roast whilst on the trail.

- Folding grill (car camping, paddling, bike touring, kayak touring).

- Fry pan with lid.

- GSI espresso makers.

- Lexan Coffee Press by GSI. Cowboy coffee? Who are you kidding!

- One-gallon cook pot (car camping, paddling).

- Outback Oven by Backerpacker's Pantry.

- Pot lifter (backpacking, car camping, paddling, bike touring).

- Stainless steel cookset with 1.5-, 2-, and 2.5-quart cookpots; 7.25-inch fry pan; two large bowls/lids; pot gripper; and a storage bag (backpacking, paddling, bike touring).

✔ Stuff sacks for pots and pans.

✔ Two-quart pot.

**Food preparation and serving:**

✔ Fillet knife

✔ Kitchen knife

✔ Lightweight plastic cutting board

✔ Small spatula

✔ Small whisk

✔ Wooden spoon

**Water needs:**

✔ 2.5-gallon collapsible water containers

✔ Water filter

**Hygiene:**

✔ Soap and scrubbies

✔ Wash and rinse buckets (car camping, paddling)

**Specialty tools:**

✔ Folding saw or hatchet (car camping, paddling)

✔ Lantern, gas or battery (car camping, paddling)

✔ Multitool knives

✔ Pocket knife with cord (group leader on paddling, backpacking or camping trip)

✔ Small trowel

## Packing your gear

If any of your cookware is Teflon-coated, take care to avoid scratching the cooking surface. Place a paper towel, a soft cleaning towel, or other soft and thin fabric or paper between pot surfaces to prevent scratching. Also, keep in mind that storing a stove inside of cookware can indirectly transfer fuel tastes to food. A far better idea is to pack foodstuffs inside cookware. If you are backpacking, I recommend that you pack the cookware midway up the pack and as close to the back as possible to minimize damage from denting or crushing. Most people tend to drop their packs on their bottoms or fronts.

# Stove Repair and Maintenance

A chilly, damp evening turned perceptibly colder as the hiss from our stove faded away with the last warming rays of sunlight. My backpacking partner on this trip, Marcus Woolf, and I stared first at the stove, then at each other, then back to the bubbling concoction that promised to be delicious brownies if the flame stayed hot. I shook the fuel bottle — still full. Apparently, our stove had decided it liked brownies poured, not baked. Upon further inspection, we discovered a manufacturer's flaw with the fuel canister — the plastic resealing nipple that prevents fuel from leaking when the canister is disconnected had become hot enough to melt and inject itself into the stove's jet, clogging it completely. Sadly, we had failed to pack along a spare jet. What followed was an epic evening of stove repair using a multitool, a cleaning needle, and solvents and heat from a lighter. I finally restored a flame to our world, albeit a sputtering, pathetic semblance of its former self barely able to heat water. And, no, eating half-baked brownie mix with a spoon is not appetizing.

Note to self: Always pack a spare jet no matter how short the journey.

## Repair tips for common stove problems

What's the most common stove problem? Clogged jet, of course. That's why most stoves come with a needle and jet-removal tool for performing this simple task. MSR backpacking stoves have a built-in pin that "self-cleans" the jet simply by shaking or turning the stove upside down.

If a jet is really clogged, you'll need to remove it from the stove with the jet tool and soak the jet in a container of white gas. White gas is a solvent and eats away most carbon buildup and other residues.

If a stove does not seem to be generating any pressure even with continued pumping, chances are the leather pump cup may need lubricating. Apply mineral oil to both sides of the cup and mold it back into a slightly conical shape if it has gone flat. If the stove still does not pressurize, the fuel bottle O-ring may be cracked (look for fuel leaks).

Each manufacturer has a specific set of remedies for its various stove designs — whether backpacking stoves or two-burner camp models. Reading the instructions is not enough. Spend some time taking your stove apart and putting it back together again so you are familiar with how everything goes together. But do this well in advance of the trip, never right before a trip.

A cleaning needle and jet-removal tool plus an extra jet should be all you need to keep your camp stove working well.

If your camp stove sits idle a long time between trips — a year or more — count on taking it apart and lubricating the O-rings and leather pump cup (if the stove has a pump). Never store a fuel bottle with the pump still in it. Instead, remove the pump and store the bottle in an upright position. And don't store opened fuel longer than a year. The older the fuel, the more likely it is to contaminate a stove with soot and other lacquer-type residue. Don't burn any fuel in a stove other than white gas, and only use the highest grade of white gas.

# Fuel Traveling Tips

What do the rules and regulations say about transporting camp fuel aboard a commercial plane, bus, train, or boat? They say you can't do it, that's what. Commercial carriers prohibit the carrying of any type of fuel, whether liquid or pressurized. You can carry the stove without fuel as long as the fuel lines are completely clear of any residue. A friend of mine recently received the third degree from baggage inspectors who wanted to know what his Coleman Xpedition stove was, and then he had to prove the fuel lines were empty.

If your stove has a permanently attached fuel tank, as is the case with some of the Optimus and older Coleman stoves, you may be prohibited from taking the stove on board any plane even if the tank is clearly empty, depending on how strict the air carrier is. From my experience talking with major airlines about their policy regarding stoves and fuel bottles, they are somewhat arbitrary.

My recommendation? If you are planning to travel by commercial carrier to your vacation destination, check with your carrier first. If you intend to take your old fuel bottles, they must be so clean they're practically odorless with absolutely no evidence of any fuel residue. I suggest buying new fuel bottles that have never seen a drop of fuel inside, understanding you may have to part with them for the return trip. Only one fuel is currently permitted for shipment by the U.S. Postal Service, and that is the three-pack of 170-gram Coleman Max fuel. Under USPS regulations, you can mail and have that fuel delivered to any address or post office in the 50 states and Puerto Rico.

# Chow Down!

Four years as a camp counselor and camp trip director, 5 years as a mountain guide and outings program director, 14 years as a parent taking my daughter and her friends on outings, and 7 years taking my daughter to summer camp and swapping ideas with other parents have shown me what kids like and don't like to eat. While no two sets of taste buds react quite the same way to the wide world of flavors, you and your family may find some favorites to make and munch on in this chapter — from my files of favorite recipes and snacks. Enjoy!

## Favorite meal suggestions for the trail

My vast experience and unscientific poll suggest you can't go wrong fixing the following, at least once:

✔ **Breakfast:** Pancakes and wild berry syrup, hot cocoa or orange juice crystals, and dried fruit.

✔ **Lunch:** Gorp (your house blend of M&Ms, raisins, nuts), peanut butter & honey mix on Ritz crackers or party rye bread, beef jerky, lemonade mix or water, and a candy bar.

✔ **Dinner:** Freeze-dried spaghetti mix, instant vegetable soup, instant chocolate pudding using instant milk, and Tang, Wyler's, or water.

## Trail food: It's so much more than gorp

Gorp is forever. But if you are hunting for the best trail mix, I suggest looking in a health food store or a specialty food store. Typically, these kinds of stores have large bins full of delectable trail mixes alongside other bins of dried fruits, nuts, seeds, and more. Begin with a basic mix, such as a tropical blend with premixed bits of nuts, papaya, coconut, raisins, and add other ingredients to your heart's content. I never pass up adding butterscotch chips and bittersweet chocolate chips to my mix. As for estimating how much you will need, I have found that about one-half pound of trail mix per person per eight-hour hiking day does the trick quite nicely. If you want to try something truly exotic, taste-test the following:

Blend together two cups of cereal (containing flakes, bits of fruit, and nuts) with one cup of chopped walnuts, one cup of sunflower seeds, one cup of golden raisins, and two cups of bittersweet chocolate chips (I prefer Ghirardelli's brand). You can also substitute or experiment by blending in butterscotch, white chocolate, or peanut butter chips. Heat over a stove or in a microwave until the chips are melted. Stir the ingredients until they are all well-coated with melted chips. Spread the mixture onto a well-greased cookie sheet and form it into a flat sheet about two inches thick. Chill the sheet and then cut into squares and wrap in plastic for your hike.

## Snacks, sweets, and drinks

All of the following are pretty easy to fix, though you do have to be patient drying out the chewy ones.

### Peanut brittle

I love peanut brittle — it's practically indestructible, even if it does get a little tacky when hot. You can buy it at any candy store, but it's a lot more fun to make your own, and making it is quite easy. Take 4 tablespoons of butter, 2 cups of sugar, and a pinch or two of salt, and cook over low heat until the mixture is smooth — use a Teflon pan! Keep a bowl of ice-cold water nearby. When the mixture forms into a hard ball after you drop it into the cold water, it's done cooking. Now you can get creative. Tradition calls for two cups of peanuts to be added, but I prefer to use two cups of mixed nuts including chopped walnuts, pecans, and cashews. Pour the mixture onto a greased cookie sheet and place the sheet in the refrigerator. After the mixture is cool, you can break the sheet into chunks and package it in plastic bags.

### Apple/apricot fruit chew

When wandering through the woods, there is nothing quite as good as a flavorful fruit and nut treat followed by a cool water chaser. Making your own fruit treat is easy if you follow the recipe shared with me by a client when I was guiding backpacking trips in southern California many years ago:

Mix together 2 cups of finely chopped and dried apples, 2 cups of finely chopped and dried apricots, and ½ cup instant dried milk (your choice whether you use nonfat). Add 4 tablespoons of frozen fruit juice concentrate (I prefer apple or orange), 2 teaspoons of cinnamon, 4 tablespoons of honey and 4 tablespoons of light corn syrup. Roll the mixture into one long fruit log about one to one and a half inches in diameter. If you wish, and I highly recommend it, roll the entire log over one to two cups of chopped walnuts and then through powdered sugar to thoroughly coat the fruit with sweet and nut topping. Dry the entire mess until firm.

Although drying fruit and other foods works much better if you own a dehydrator designed for that purpose, an ordinary oven serves as a capable makeshift dehydrator, churning out tasty trail foods adequately enough. In this case, prop open the oven door about six inches so that the moisture from the drying fruit roll can escape. Set the oven temperature to 140 degrees, using an internal thermometer to correctly gauge the temperature — on most ovens, you will arrive at 140 degrees by selecting the middle range of the warm setting on the temperature knob. When the log is firm, take it out of the oven, allow it to cool, and then slice it into one-inch-thick sections. Wrap each section in plastic and hit the trail.

### A taste of jerky

Beef or turkey jerky is a wonderful taste treat that I just refuse to leave home without. Homemade jerky is so superior in quality and flavor to most commercial brands and it is so easy to make that I wonder why more hikers don't resort to their kitchens to turn the tasty strips of meat out.

My favorite cut of meat to slice for jerky preparation is flank steak. Figure that three pounds of meat yields approximately one pound of jerky. Before you begin slicing, firm up the cut of meat in the freezer — your cuts will be more even. First remove any excess fat. Second, slice the meat across the grain to a thickness between ⅛ and ¼ inches. Marinate the sliced meat overnight in a refrigerator in a tightly sealed container. I prefer teriyaki, which you can make easily enough by taking 1 cup of soy sauce, ½ cup of dark brown sugar, 2 teaspoons of ginger, 4 to 6 cloves of crushed garlic, and ½ teaspoon of freshly ground black pepper.

Spray your oven racks with a vegetable spray and then spread the strips of meat across the racks. Be sure to place a sheet of aluminum foil over the bottom of the oven to catch the drippings unless you particularly enjoy creating an awful mess. You will need an internal oven thermometer since on most ovens, 140 degrees, the ideal temperature for drying meat, is toward the middle setting of the warm label on the knob. Prop the oven door open a few inches using a pot lid or something nonflammable so that the moisture can escape easily from the drying meat. Your jerky should be ready in approximately eight hours — it should be dry but not brittle to the touch.

### Making fruit leather

When I am trekking in the desert, I love to nibble on a good fruit leather. It tastes great, won't spoil, and doesn't sap the water supply by making you feel far thirstier than you should. To make fruit leather, spray a large cookie sheet with a vegetable spray or coat it lightly with vegetable oil. Puree the fresh fruit of your choice (I am partial to peach, apricot, nectarine, and apple) in a blender until it is smooth — no lumps, wayward seeds or other items to mess up the consistency. If the fruit puree is not sweet enough for you, add white corn syrup or, if you are more naturally oriented, honey to taste. Do not use sugar as it makes the leather grainy and brittle. Add a few drops of lemon juice to enhance the fruit flavor. Pour the puree onto the greased cookie sheet so that the mixture spreads out at an even ¼-inch thickness. Place the cookie sheet into your oven set to 140 degrees. You need an internal oven thermometer since on most ovens, 140 degrees is toward the middle setting of the warm label on the knob. Prop the oven door open a few inches so that the moisture can escape easily from the drying puree. The fruit leather is dried to the correct consistency when it is pliable, but not sticky. Peel it gradually off the cookie sheet and roll it into one large roll as you go. Cut the giant roll into 4- to 5-inch-long sections. Wrap each section in plastic wrap and keep it cool until you are ready to hit the trail. Yummy!

### Flavoring the water

For a "fruit smoothie," trail style, add equal parts of powdered whole milk and powdered fruit drink (I prefer dehydrated orange juice) to your water. I have found that the best way to ensure a smooth smoothie is to add no more than one-half cup of each mix to a one quart bottle and then add water to fill the bottle one-quarter full. Shake vigorously to completely blend the ingredients and dissolve the powders. Fill the bottle the rest of the way with water and shake again to completely mix the ingredients. If you use orange juice, your drink will resemble an Orange Julius — remember those? Sheesh, I'm really dating myself.

If you prefer your mixes prepackaged, AlpineAire makes a fruit smoothie drink that is to die for — on the trail at least. I'm not sure I would opt for this over a blender version using fresh ingredients at home, but then again, it does taste pretty darn good.

# Meals

If you are going car camping and can keep fresh food on ice for a couple of days, try these:

### High-trail stir-fry

Combine 4 cups of chopped peppers, onions, and zucchini with 2 cups sliced or chopped chicken, 2 teaspoons of sugar or honey, 2 tablespoons of soy sauce, 1 tablespoon of ginger, and 1 tablespoon of cornstarch and cook in a well-oiled (I prefer sesame oil) frying pan over medium heat. Serve over steamed rice (quick-cook variety is the best and aim for ½ cup per person).

### Foil dinner delight

In the center of a large square of heavyweight aluminum foil, combine the following: ¼ pound hamburger meat, one chopped or thinly sliced potato, one carrot thinly sliced, one onion cut into wedges or sliced, dash of salt, a sprinkle of pepper, and ketchup (more or less depending on your flavor requirements). Fold the aluminum foil inward and seal it tightly so that none of the juices can leak out during cooking. Add a second layer of foil if in doubt. Place the entire package directly on the hot coals of a fire or on the bottom rack of a barbecue grill and cook for 30 minutes (plus or minus a few minutes depending on how full the foil is and how hot the coals are).

### Wild and wacky salad

Mix one 16-ounce can of red beans, one 16-ounce can garbanzo beans, 1 cup chopped celery, 1 cup diced cucumber, 1 cup diced green pepper, 1 cup diced cucumber, 1 cup mild salsa, ½ cup Italian dressing, 1 tablespoon chopped cilantro, 1 avocado chopped, 2 large tomatoes chopped, and ½ pound bacon cooked crisp and crumbled.

# Desserts

I like fruit-based desserts, but keep the Hershey's handy.

### Baked fruit

This dessert was a camp favorite of mine! Cut the center out of an apple and slice a banana (don't peel!) down the middle. Stuff the middle of the apple with sugar or honey and cinnamon and the middle of the banana with chocolate chips, miniature marshmallows and chopped nuts. Wrap both fruits securely with heavyweight aluminum foil. Place the packet directly on hot coals in a fire or on the lowest grill level in a barbecue over very hot coals and bake the apple for 30 minutes and the banana for 15 minutes (plus or minus a few minutes depending on how hot the coals are).

### Sweet-tooth kabobs

In a large bowl, add the following: three apples peeled, cored, and cut into 1-inch chunks; three bananas peeled and sliced into 1-inch-thick slices; one drained 16-ounce can of pineapple chunks or 2 cups of freshly chopped pineapple chunks. Cut a pound cake into 1-inch chunks and place on a plate. Place banana, apple, pineapple, and pound cake chunks on six skewers. Drizzle each skewer of fruit and cake with sweetened condensed milk and sprinkle with flaked coconut. Heat slowly over coals until toasted. Drizzle Hershey's dark or milk chocolate syrup over each cooked skewer and serve. YUMMY!

## Food tips to ensure camping culinary delight

Little touches and techniques can help make campground cookery very pleasant experiences, for cooks and diners both. Here are a few ways to take the ho-hum out of mealtime in the wilderness.

✓ **Modify the goods.**

Instead of freeze-dried foods, create a superb and nutritious dinner soup by adding any or all of the following ingredients to a Knorr or Lipton instant soup mix: instant rice, noodles, elbow macaroni, potato buds, dried tomatoes, dried mushrooms, or chunks of cheese (adds flavor divine!). Sprinkle any soup with dried Parmesan cheese for the gourmet touch — it will impress your traveling companions.

✓ **Premix the batter in a zip bag.**

Tired of gooping up a pot to mix biscuit, bread, or cake batter when camping? Try mixing the batter in a freezer-weight zip-lock bag instead. Add the mix and the correct amount of water (slowly to avoid lumping) and then knead the bag with your hands until the desired consistency is achieved. Clip one corner of the bag with scissors or a knife and simply squeeze the mix onto an awaiting hot griddle, Dutch oven, or other baking implement. No mess, no fuss. Pack out the bag.

✔ **Concoct hot drinks.**

When the campfire's dancing and snapping, there is nothing better than curling up close to it with a good book, good friends, and a hot drink. Wow your campfire companions with a simple concoction. To each cup of coffee add: one dash of almond extract, one cinnamon stick, and a sprinkle of sugar to bring out the flavor. Camp mocha may be made by adding coffee to a cup-sized package of instant hot cocoa. Top with mini-marshmallows or whipped cream.

✔ **Get the kids into the act.**

Children will have fun baking Bisquick horns if you can stand the mess. Mix six parts Bisquick mix to one part water. Knead the dough until it is firm but not too sticky. Divide the dough into equal parts and then roll each part into long snakes. Find fairly sturdy sticks about three feet long (don't ever cut green wood for this) and whittle a smooth, six-inch surface on one end. Wrap the dough snakes around the smooth ends of each stick tightly and bake over hot coals (not flames) until golden brown. When they are done, the horns should slide easily off each stick, leaving a steaming pastry to fill with jam or honey.

# Catching, Cleaning, and Cooking Fish

Ah, yes, fresh fish. Baked, broiled, poached, mixed into eggs, added to pizza (trout pizza is superb), or served as a high-country sashimi, the mere thought of eating freshly caught and cleaned fish brings a smile to almost any outdoor adventurer.

## Learning to fish

If you've never fished before, casting your hook onto the waters with grace and efficiency takes a bit of practice. But for simple food-gathering effectiveness, nothing beats spin casting with a lure and, if allowed, bait. The requisite equipment is relatively light and inexpensive. Fly-fishing, on the other hand, requires a great deal more knowledge, equipment, and patience if you are pursuing a meal and not simply a Zen-like interlude of outdoor contemplation. Either way, I'd suggest picking up *Fishing For Dummies* and *Fly-Fishing For Dummies,* published by IDG Books Worldwide, as the best and easiest to understand backgrounders I've come across.

## Cleaning the catch

Cleaning fish is relatively easy. Before you begin, remember that cleaning a fish can leave a significant impact on the environment and become a danger to you if bears are nearby or likely to frequent the area.

### Safety and low-impact cleaning suggestions

Follow these rules:

- ✔ Always clean fish far away from your campsite. If you are in an organized campground, clean your fish in the designated area.

- ✔ Always clean your fish far away from the nearest water source. Fish guts and goop do not improve rivers, lakes, or streams. But note the exception, following.

- ✔ If bears are a concern, it's okay to throw the entrails into cold mountain lakes or streams. Covering odors that may attract unwanted bear attention is more important than aesthetics in a case like this.

- ✔ In areas of high use, dispose of the fish entrails in a cathole dug four to six inches deep in loose soil.

- ✔ In remote areas that see little human visitation, scatter the entrails widely and well away from camp, where they can decompose or be consumed by animals or birds.

- ✔ Be sure to clean your hands thoroughly, and if bears are a concern, keep clothing that may carry odors of fish well away from your sleeping area.

### Cleaning guidelines

1. **Carry your catch to an appropriate cleaning area.** Be sure to take a sharp knife and some clean rinse water along with you. Firmly grasp the fish in one hand, belly up. Slit the belly open from the anal vent just behind the back fin to just behind the head.

2. **If your preference is to cut off the head, do that now, cutting on a diagonal line (more or less) from behind the front fins and through the spine.** This is a little more difficult than Step 1 because the fish is very slippery and the spinal column can be quite tough. Use caution that you do not take off your fingers or cut deeply into your hand whilst performing this task — it has happened to more than one person I know, putting an immediate end to camping trips.

3. **With the fish now open, dump the entrails into the hole you have dug, or into a pan for scattering.** Using your thumbnail, scrape away the tissue and any remaining gunk from along the backbone.

4. **Rinse the fish and put it into a zip-lock bag for safekeeping.** Clean your knife and hands and dispose of the rinse water and entrails as I advise earlier in this chapter.

## Preparing the catch

Entire books are devoted to preparing and serving fish. What follow are some of my favorite methods — ideas for you to adapt to your own fish-eating adventures.

### Going caveman

Be sure your campfire coals are hot and the flames aren't leaping. Rub the inside of the fish with lemon juice concentrate, a light dash of salt, a dash of garlic, and a smidgen of dried cilantro. Moisten the skin and lay the fish directly onto the coals. Yes, the fish gets charred, but the skin protects the tender meat inside, and you don't mind the odd black speck or two in your dinner anyway, do you? Carefully remove (using a stick, tongs, or fork) your fish after three to five minutes and scrape off the charred skin. Mmmmm, good groceries!

### Baking

Rub the cavity of the fish generously with butter or margarine and then season it with slices of fresh garlic, a light dash of salt, a sprinkle of pepper, and any other herb your heart desires. If you want to get exotic, add some pine nuts to the cavity too. Wrap the fish tightly in aluminum foil. Place the foil-wrapped fish onto hot coals and cover with another layer of hot coals. Keep an eye on the coals because they will cool, requiring you to place more hot coals on the cooking fish. Baking this way takes between 15 and 25 minutes, depending on the size of the fish and the heat of the coals. The fish is cooked when a fork can be poked through the foil and easily into and out of the fish.

### Grilling

Every gathering in a campground must involve some manner of grilling. Why? Because the grill is there and using it is considered very outdoorsy. Need a better reason? Then perhaps you should stay home.

First, oil your fish to prevent or minimize sticking to the grill. Place the grill five to six inches above the red-hot coals and let it get very hot before adding the fish. Stuff the cavity of the fish with garlic and ginger slices and sprinkle inside and out with soy sauce. Place the fish on the grill. Turn it in about five minutes using tongs or a spatula. Your fish is done when the skin flakes easily after being pried up with a fork — don't test too much or you'll have fish flakes all over the grill and an unsightly mess to eat.

### Poaching

Place the fish in a frying pan and pour in enough water to barely cover the fish. Season the water with salt, herbs, and spices to taste. Put the pan onto the grill or the camp stove, and bring the water to a low boil. The fish will curl, but resist the urge to turn it or otherwise play with it. In approximately 10 minutes, the fish should be done. You can tell it is done when the skin peels off effortlessly and the flesh is no longer transparent.

Remove the fish from the water carefully (the water and fish will be very hot) and, using a fork, peel off the skin and begin separating the flesh from the bones. In many cases, as you pull the backbone, it will take most of the skeleton with it. However, don't forget to warn your friends and family that bones may still be hiding in the flesh, and they should eat with caution. Best served with rice or greens.

Toss the water well away from camp and dispose of the skin and bones as you would entrails.

### Sashimi

Raw fish, you say? Don't knock it until you've tried it. Be sure to have a small container of wasabi (Japanese green horseradish) and another container of soy sauce. But before you indulge in sashimi, you must know that unless the fish is absolutely fresh — and I do mean caught and cleaned no more than one hour before and kept stored on ice — you're asking for trouble.

First, skin the fish by cutting under the fins with a very sharp knife and then pulling the fins firmly back toward the head. Next, slit the knife blade along the backbone from head to tail. Using the tip of the knife, loosen the skin around the gills. Finally, work your fingers (and the knife if the skin proves incredibly difficult) under the skin at the head and peel it back toward the tail.

After the skin is removed, begin cutting the flesh from the skeleton, starting at the backbone and working downward. Place the raw fish into a baggie or a pot with a lid to keep flies away.

Now, what are you waiting for? Take a strip of raw fish, dip it into the wasabi and then into the horseradish, and belly up to the sushi bar.

### Fish pizza

Okay, it's not pizza as you may know it, but around camp, fish pizza is darn close. Take a piece of melba toast, top it with a slice of tomato and a strip of poached or baked fish, sprinkle with Parmesan cheese and soy sauce or other flavoring, and enjoy.

# Chapter 9

# Taking a Hike

● ● ● ● ● ● ● ● ● ● ● ● ● ● ● ● ● ● ● ● ● ● ● ● ● ● ● ● ● ● ● ● ● ● ●

## In This Chapter

▶ Getting ready for your hike

▶ Being aware of where you hike

▶ Tackling tricky terrain

▶ Venturing off trail

● ● ● ● ● ● ● ● ● ● ● ● ● ● ● ● ● ● ● ● ● ● ● ● ● ● ● ● ● ● ● ● ● ● ●

Although vast tracts of wildlands, urban greenbelts, and designated wilderness areas are available throughout North America and the world, the trend of weekend recreating focuses the majority of impacts upon areas of the land that are readily and easily accessible. Broad reaches of backcountry regions see light use, while certain trailheads, trail camps, picnic areas, scenic stops, and other places where the fishing or scenery are especially wonderful, suffer from dramatic overuse. We are in danger of loving selected wild areas to death.

One of the best ways to minimize the trace you leave on the land is to reduce the number of visits you make to areas that are subject to overuse. Check with land managers for the backcountry places that you frequent to find out which sites see the most visits, and then plan your trip accordingly. So much wild country goes untouched and relatively undiscovered that you may be happier for the extra effort and time it takes to camp away from heavily used and impacted locations.

## Preparing for Your Hike

Heading out on a hike from your campsite, or simply going for a dayhike from home, is as simple as putting one foot in front of the other. Making sure your hike is eventful because of sights seen and not emergencies encountered requires some basic preparation and packing, though. No matter how long or short your hike, remember always the axioms, "Plan your hike and hike your plan," and "Be prepared." There's no need to get elaborate with charts, maps, scrolls, notes, research interviews, and books for a simple hike. Planning and preparation mean simply this: Cover the basics to ensure your safety and comfort while away from camp or home.

# Planning your hike

Although I cover trip planning in some detail in Chapter 1, here are a few things to keep in mind whenever you are considering heading off on a hike:

✔ **Always have some idea where you are heading and be sure you are carrying a topographic map of the area you are heading into.** Simply toting along a free park map is a good way to ensure your hike will be adventurous for the wrong reasons. City, regional, and state park maps — and just about all free public land maps — are typically not printed to scale and are relatively useless unless you want to get lost.

✔ **Spend a few minutes chatting with park rangers either at the park visitor center or in the campground.** This short talk is a fantastic way of learning about recommended hikes in the area. Rangers typically (though not always) know the area better than anyone and love to share their knowledge with you. Bring your map with you when you talk with the rangers and they can help you plot your hike effectively to best match your hike goals and effort expenditure.

✔ **Bring a daypack along.** Even though you are heading out on a simple hike, bring a daypack along that is large enough to hold extra clothing, rain gear, food, water, and so on. Always pack the "Ten + One Survival Essentials" that I discuss in Chapter 14.

✔ **Take into account when the sun rises and sets as well as the prevailing and anticipated weather conditions before traipsing off.** No sense in planning to reach a particularly tasty overlook that is only 5 miles away for a sunrise if early morning fog is going to obscure the view. Also, that easy 5-mile hike can quickly turn into an epic march if you discover halfway there that yesterday's snow and this morning's freeze have turned the route into something resembling a toboggan run more than a trail.

## Deciding how long and how far to hike

How far you are going to hike depends on a combination of things, including what the purpose of the hike is, the mood of the hikers at the time, the type of terrain you are hiking on, and what time of day it is.

Let's start with the terrain and how fast you can expect to hike. Most people will hike at a rate of 3 to 4 miles per hour on flat to rolling terrain without too many obstacles to step over and around. Uphill hiking slows down the pace to approximately 1 mile per hour or less. If your travels take you onto very rugged terrain or off-trail, plan on averaging 2 miles per hour or less. Now I know this is a stretch, but if you reach back into your memory banks, you'll remember math class and you'll begin to calculate that 3 miles per hour over a 4-hour time frame means you cover 12 miles.

So, now we move to the time of day. If you are leaving early in the morning and there are 10 to 12 hours of daylight, you have a lot of time to play with. But please, don't even think about trying for a 30-mile hike just because the math works out. I would suggest hikes of no more than 10 miles round-trip, unless your group is ambitious and in very good mental and physical shape. As the day gets later, and you begin to think of hiking, your options narrow. Afternoon hikes when there are no more than 4 hours or so of daylight should not exceed 6 miles.

Before you lock and load on a hike plan, consider the hike's purpose. If it is to watch nature and enjoy a casual stroll, take that into account and plan on a much shorter hike to ensure plenty of time for stopping and enjoying.

Also consider the mood and physical fitness of the hiking group. You may be able to hike up one side and down the other of Everest in a day, but if your partner or friends have trouble with even a few miles, then that is what you are hiking — only a few miles.

### Choosing a trail

Three types of trails exist: loop trails, out-and-back trails, and one-way trails that require a shuttle or other transport to return you to the start. Which type of trail you take depends entirely on your resources and how much variety and effort you want to put into a hiking plan. Loop trails are easy. You start hiking, wander around the loop, and end back where you started, assuming you read the map correctly and stayed alert at trail intersections. Out-and-back trails take you out one way until you have to turn around and return the way you came. These have a certain pleasure to them and are ideal if the time is short and you want to speed your return trip. Keep in mind that very often a trail does look decidedly different when viewed from another direction, though, so it is still important to stay alert. One-way trails are a lot of fun and often run along riverbanks and through canyons where loop trails are not possible. With proper planning (placing a vehicle at one end of the trail and then getting a ride, or driving another vehicle back to the start) you can enjoy a wonderful hike that is full of variety. Just remember to factor driving time as well as hiking time into your trip planning.

### Marking your route on the map

It's okay to act like an automobile club trip planner and highlight your route on the map you are carrying — I prefer a yellow or blue highlighter, but the color choice is yours. Pick a color that will show up easily, and remember, if you get the map wet, the highlighter ink will run. By plotting your route before you head out, it becomes much easier to "hike your plan."

If you are utilizing a Global Positioning System (GPS) receiver while on your hike, you will be able to enter "waypoints" — marked points along your route determined by a landmark, trail intersection, and so on, that are entered into the GPS utilizing latitude/longitude coordinates. (And for more on using the GPS system, see Chapter 11.)

# Hike with trekking poles

When Moses strode out on his great adventure, leading his people to the Promised Land, he carried one very important piece of equipment with him — a walking stick. The walking staff is regarded as one of the earliest tools known to man. While the staff must have been used for protection or to clear an area, its primary benefit continues to be weight bearing and stabilizing. If one stick is good, then two must be better; so enters the trekking pole.

A widely circulated medical study, conducted in 1981 by Dr. G. Neureuther, a medical affiliate of a German mountain guide association, reported that hikers using a pair of trekking poles over an eight-hour trek experienced up to 13 tons of cumulative load relief when walking on flat land, 28 tons of relief while walking uphill, and 34 tons of relief when walking downhill. In other words, less load means less impact and less impact means longer life for the joints and less fatigue for the muscles.

What are the essential features to look for in a good trekking pole?

- Comfortable and secure grip. Cork or rubber is best.
- Adjustable wrist straps with no buckle to minimize chafing on bare hands.
- Replaceable tips. Carbide are the most durable.
- Light in weight.
- Internal shock absorbing system to soften the impact when poles are planted.
- Stowable by collapsing down to 30 inches or less.
- Adjustable system that is easy to expand or compress and stays securely at the length selected.

# Securing permits

Even though the land you are hiking on is public land, you may still need a permit. Most federally designated wilderness areas and an increasing number of national parks and forests require permits even for day use. This is done to limit the number of folks trekking through an area on a given day so as to minimize impacts and make the outdoor experience more enjoyable — queuing up along a trail in a line of humanity is not a quality outdoor experience.

Permits are also a way that land managers try to ensure every visitor to an area is aware of the rules and regulations that govern the visits to and use of that area. Permits for day use are usually very easy to obtain the day of your hike simply by showing up at the area ranger station. In areas subject to high visitation, you may want to reserve a permit ahead of time (if possible) by mail. Each public area has its own set of rules and regulations, so I advise you to call ahead to determine if first-come-first-served or advance reservation is best for your needs.

### Providing your itinerary

Contrary to what most folks think, just because you fill out a permit to go hiking doesn't mean the rangers will come looking for you if you don't return as expected. They retrieve the permit if your loved ones call in a missing person report, but typically not until then. It is always a good idea to notify the rangers of your hiking plans. If they have a registration log that allows you to sign in, they'll point you to it. But remember that what you sign in, you must also sign out, or a very expensive rescue may get triggered.

I do not advise leaving your itinerary posted in obvious view in your vehicle as an invitation to thieves. A better alternative is to place your hiking plans in an envelope placed where officials, if they discover your car still parked after an extended period, will be able to find it on investigation. This won't help you in the short term but may assist rescuers should a rescue be needed after a few days.

The best alternative is to always be sure a loved one knows when you are leaving, where you are going, and when you will return. Giving that person a copy of your map and hiking plans is also a great idea should you need help. Once again, I remind you to always check in the minute you are home safely. Concerned folks who believe that their friend or family member is lost when in fact they are already home and snug in bed initiate too many rescues.

### Getting information about trails

When you walk in to see the ranger, have all your ducks in a row and know what kind of trail that you want to hike on, for how long, how far, and what things you and your group are interested in. The more information you can offer the ranger, the more likely it is that he or she can point you in the perfect direction. You may want to ask about nature walks led by docents — volunteers — and other guided hikes. Many parks offer these services during the height of visitor season — sometimes throughout the year.

# Treading Carefully

The majority of backcountry and urban greenbelt travel is done on an existing network of trails. Problems occur when the trail is of a poor design, when visitors travel several abreast and widen an existing track, when an obstacle blocks the original trail and multitudes of visitors create an alternative trail, or when visitors decide that cutting a switchback is a better and more convenient alternative to staying on the trail.

You can easily minimize impacts upon trails and the surrounding areas by adhering to a few guidelines.

## Pacing yourself

Always hike at a speed that is most comfortable for the slowest member of your hiking group. This ensures that everyone enjoys the hike and that no one becomes exhausted. Take rest breaks about every 20 minutes and use this time to sip on a little water and munch on some energy food.

When hiking uphill for extended periods, use a step mountaineers call the "rest step." This is a slow, methodical approach to moving uphill; and properly executed, this step should keep you truckin' all day long. The motion is a rhythmic one. First, you step forward with one foot. As your weight moves onto that foot, you allow your leg to straighten so that all your body weight is supported by your leg bones, not your muscles. Hesitate for a second and then swing your other leg forward and straighten it as you bring your weight to bear. Pause and then rock forward on the other foot again.

## Traveling in single file

Perhaps the most common impact on the environment that can be avoided is traveling two abreast, whether on foot, on horses, or on bikes. Always travel in single file. By doing so, you are helping to prevent damage to the sides of the trail and the potential widening of the trail by erosion. Traveling in single file also eliminates the opportunity for the worst impact of all — two or more paths side by side, cutting an ugly latticework across a meadow.

There is an exception to the single file rule, though: When hiking across surfaces that are more durable than alpine soil, spread out. By not following the same route and limiting impact to footprints of one person, the grasses or vegetation are more likely to recover. Hiking single file in these instances risks creating a permanent scar across the land.

## Yielding the right-of-way

When encountering others on the trail, be they other hikers, horseback riders, or bikers, practice trail etiquette. Hikers always yield to equestrians; bikers yield to hikers and equestrians; uphill travelers always yield to those moving downhill within the same user group (hiker/hiker, biker/biker, equestrian/equestrian). When moving out of the way, step off the trail completely so as to allow the other group to pass completely. Never continue to walk or move when off the trail as this results in either widening the trail route or creating an entirely new trail location.

## Rest stops

Frequently, significant trail damage is done when you or others are not traveling on the trail at all. How? During rest stops adjacent to a trail. Choose your rest stops with care. The area selected should be off the trail, out of the way of other users, and on a stable and durable surface such as rock outcroppings or sandy areas. As in a campsite situation, take precautions to minimize damage to the surrounding vegetation and soil. After a rest break is over, be careful to replace all gear and litter back into your pack, panniers, or saddlebags — the most common time to forget gear or inadvertently litter is during a rest break.

# Reading trail markings

As you travel across wildlands you will encounter a wide variety of marking trails or routes of travel. Please, resist the urge to add signs of your own to the trail. There are enough signs as it is — too many, in my opinion — and simply adding more not only clutters the landscape, but can lead to confusion, too. What follow are a few of the signs and markers you are likely to see:

- **Paint:** I personally hate this kind of marking, but you'll see it often on rocks, sometimes on trees. Simply follow the same color paint along the route and you'll know you are still following the track you started out on. Paint markings appear on either side of a rock or tree trunk so they are visible from both directions of the trail. Markings are usually a straight brush stroke or a circle.

- **Blaze:** You can still see these in the old growth forests of Canada and the U.S. — more frequently back east. A blaze is a physical cut into a tree that leaves a mark (if it doesn't kill the tree) that you can follow. Like paint, blazes are cut into both sides of the trunk, most often with an axe, so you can see the trail marking from both directions on the trail.

- **Cairns or ducks:** Cairns or ducks are stacks of rocks along a rocky, tree-less route that help to guide you where otherwise you may wander off-route. Cairns are frequently used through boulder fields or in alpine environments where no other means for providing a sign exists.

# Tackling tricky terrain

Mud, loose rocks, snow, fallen logs, water, and trailless terrain each present a different challenge to the hiker trying to negotiate the land on a hike. What follow are a few, though by no means definitive, suggestions for what to do when encountering various challenges either on the trail or off.

### Trail obstacles

An obstacle on a trail can take many forms, from a fallen tree to other trail users (which is why it is important to move off the trail during a rest break). Should you come across a fallen tree or other obstacle, first try to move it. If you are able to move it off the trail without hurting yourself or damaging the trail, then do it. Otherwise, attempt to go over the obstacle without creating an alternative trail. If moving the obstacle or going over it is impossible, then carefully select a route around the trail blockage that will minimize lasting impacts. Inform the land manager (or ranger) of the trail blockage so the obstacle can be removed and the alternative trail covered up.

### Steep or fragile terrain

You should skirt extremely steep or unstable terrain unless it's unavoidable. If at all possible, restrict your ascents and descents on steep slopes to those areas that have snow or rocky areas for you to walk on. Otherwise, realize that the act of digging in your toes or heels will leave highly visible gouges that can lead to significant erosion problems. If you must travel across very steep and unstable or soft soils, spread out. Move carefully and deliberately. Do your best not to dislodge small or large landslides, rocks, or other scree. Be cautious that other members of your group are not in the path of falling debris.

### Mud

Although it may seem somewhat distasteful on foot and a tad messy by bike, hiking or pedaling through the muddy sections of a trail is typically the more suitable alternative to creating an entirely new trail that skirts the problem areas. I recommend waterproof boots and gaiters that prevent water and mud from leaking in over your boot tops.

### Snow

Hiking early in the season often means encountering snowbanks that partially or totally cover the trail. Walk across the snowbank if it poses no danger to yourself or the rest of your party. Attempt to create a path across the snow that closely duplicates the route followed by the original trail lying somewhere underfoot, under snow. By doing this, when the snow is almost melted away, hikers following your route will find themselves walking back on the trail and not walking either beside it or in an entirely new location. If the snowbank is too steep to negotiate safely, the best option is to walk next to the base of the snowbank and risk widening the trail rather than walking elsewhere and beginning the development of a new trail.

## Hiking with children

Although there are plenty of hiking boots on the market for children, I would recommend that you stick to shoes that are designed for trail running or low-top hiking shoes. Your children will appreciate the freedom of movement while hiking and scrambling and you'll appreciate the slightly lower cost of footwear — not to mention the fact that running shoes or low-top hikers are more likely to be worn everyday, and not just a few days out of the year.

Always bring along extra sets of clothes for the children. Mud, water, dirt, and other stains you didn't even know existed will flock toward the kids in layers. As far as colors of clothing are concerned, I would recommend bright ones, making it much easier for you to spot the little ones wandering through the trees.

Carry the bare minimum in your daypacks. Make everything count. Extra weight is not worth the extra pain. Children want to and should participate, even the younger ones. My daughter Nikki was carrying a small pack when she was just 3. Granted, all she carried was a small teddy bear and a box of juice, but it was important to her to feel involved — and quite frankly, for Nikki the teddy bear and juice were essential.

Everyone should carry a signal whistle and signal mirror and know how and when to use them. Teach your children never to blow on the whistle or use the mirror for signaling unless they are in trouble. Also, teach them that signals in threes (three sharp and distinct blows on the whistle, three flashes of light from the mirror) indicate someone is in trouble and will alert folks that help is needed.

Always have an emergency plan in place. You never know when a real need or emergency will arise, so it is best to always be prepared. Know where the nearest emergency room is. Involve your children in every plan that you make. They are never too young to hear how to take care of themselves. Learn basic first aid and CPR at the very least.

Child carriers by Tough Traveler, LL Bean, Kelty, and Madden, to name a few, are super ways to get outside on a hike with children who are either too young to walk or too young to walk very far. Don't overlook the fact that while you are using energy and perhaps feeling hot, your child is simply sitting there and may need warmer clothing. Be sure to protect your child from biting insects and the burning rays of the sun while they're along for the ride.

### Eroded and washed-out areas

Sometimes, because of a poorly designed trail or damage caused by unthinking trail users, erosion begins to occur. There is not much you can do in these instances other than walk as carefully as possible across the impacted areas, trying to step only on durable and more stable surfaces such as rocks, sand, or snow. Notify the area land manager (or ranger) as soon as possible so that appropriate trail repair measures may be taken. If the problem continues, it may worsen to the point of becoming irreparable.

ECO ETIQUETTE

## Don't take shortcuts

Shortcutting a switchback in a trail is never a justifiable alternative to staying on the trail. These secondary routes, created by selfish and thoughtless trail users, serve only to encourage erosion and scar the land. If you have the time, when coming upon a shortcut, take the initiative to block it with rocks, small logs, and other brushy debris that may be available. Inform the land manager of the situation and what you have done to reduce the problem.

## Traveling off-trail

Although cross-country travel is not for everyone, it is a marvelous way to leave the potential crowds behind and view a slice of wilderness that few have an opportunity or willingness to visit. Cross-country travel is not a viable alternative for those who cannot travel without leaving a trace — such as mountain bikers in all instances or equestrians in most cases. "Take only memories and leave only footprints" is a general, though appropriate, adage. Preferably one takes only memories and leaves nothing, but that would require floating through the land without touching it — not a very practical outlook on the realities of wilderness travel. Cross-country travel also is not for those who don't possess solid — and I do mean expert — map and compass skills. And simply knowing how to use a Global Positioning System (GPS) does not qualify.

I want to repeat the idea of leaving no trace because that's the pledge you take when traveling off-trail. When you head off the beaten path:

- ✔ Do not blaze (mark or cut) trees.
- ✔ Do not build cairns or ducks (rocky piles) across open, treeless land.
- ✔ Do not leave markers or messages of any sort for others following.
- ✔ Do not flag branches with flagging tape or any other material.

If you or others following cannot move off the trail without artificial aids like those listed, you and they have no place traveling cross-country. What's your alternative? Hone your backcountry skills to the point you can travel freely across the land without the encumbrance of markers and signs. Chapter 11 covers the basics.

# Chapter 10

# Fun, Games, and Photo-Ops

. . . . . . . . . . . . . . . . . . . . . . . . . . . . . . . . . . . . . . . .

. . . . . . . . . . . . . . . . . . . . . . . . . . . . . . . . . . . . . . . .

**Y**ou can do an infinite number of things to entertain everyone in your camping party, whether they're adults or children, or adults acting like children.

As with any activity you choose, be sure that it always adheres to the following guidelines: It must be safe; it must not disturb the wildlife; it must not damage the environment in any way; it must not disturb other campers; and it should be fun.

That said, turn your campers loose! Youngsters (all ages) are limited only by their imaginations when it comes to having fun on a camping trip. Choices include such all-time favorites as tree climbing, crawfish hunting, firefly chasing, cloud watching, meadow crawling, and hide-and-seek, among many tantalizing alternatives.

## Anyone Bored? Slim Chance!

When your campers finally run out of their own great ideas for fun, you can be ready with a long list. The following are some of my favorite games and nature activities to enjoy with children or an adventurous group of adults.

### Night-world vigil

Going on a night walk with your children in the wilderness is a wonderful experience you shouldn't miss. It can, however, be somewhat unsettling for first-timers and is best enjoyed if a little forethought and preparation go into the adventure. So, if you can rehearse a night-world vigil at home, so much the better. Here's how:

Pick a night that is going to be clear with no moon. Turn out all the lights in the house so there is a minimum of artificial light illuminating the backyard. With a flashlight, walk out into the backyard and sit down under a tree or somewhere that is comfortable. Bring a blanket along if you wish. With the flashlight on, show your child that although it seems lighter with the flashlight, your vision is really limited to the beam of the light. Now, turn off the light and sit quietly. Explain and talk about each sound as you hear it: a dog barking, a bat flitting through the air, a siren, or a mouse rustling in the compost pile. Begin to help your child distinguish between those sounds that are heard in the day and those heard at night. Ask him or her why some animals only come out at night and what makes them different from daytime animals. How does the backyard seem different in the dark? Why? When the time seems right, walk back to the house without the flashlights. Point out to your child how much better your vision is without the light.

## Hug a tree

This is an excellent exercise that teaches children to tap into their perceptual skills. Blindfold your child and lead her to a nearby tree. Ask her to get to know the tree by hugging it, touching it, smelling it, tasting it, and listening to it. Ask her to describe the tree to you: its size, its age, and its shape. After your child feels that she really knows the tree, lead her away, spin her around, and remove the blindfold. After you remove the blindfold, ask your child to find her tree. Children discover that doing this requires all their senses and that it is possible to "see" and "know" an object without eyes. Be a participant in this activity, too: Let your child blindfold you and lead you through the exercise.

## Stream walk

A stream walk is one of my favorite exercises. Be sure that everyone wears old tennis shoes and that the day is warm. Beware of slippery rocks, sharp sticks and other objects, poisonous snakes, and hypothermia. Do not stay in the cold water too long. Bring along magnifying glasses, aquarium nets, and several face masks, clear plastic dishes about six inches across, or your homemade underwater viewing can. (See "Tide-pooling," later in this chapter, to find out how to assemble your own viewing can.)

Choose a section of stream that is not too difficult to navigate through, not too long (and with easy exit points), and not too deep. The idea is to wade down the middle of the stream slowly and methodically. Look for minnows, frogs, tadpoles, and crawfish. Use the net to scoop up animals and look at them in the dishes. Use your masks or place the dishes in the water for a glass-window view of the stream below the surface. Romp, play, and get dirty. Wallow in mud holes and explore every nook and cranny. If you come upon a still pool, have your children stand quietly, observing the world below them through masks or the glass dishes floating on the surface. If they are able to stand quietly enough for longer than a minute, they will get a peek at another dimension or world swimming around their legs.

## Swamp mucking

This is a variation on the stream walk that I discuss earlier in this chapter with one major exception: You get really muddy. Talk about immersing yourself in nature! When I led groups into the swamp at camp, squeals of happiness and curiosity overcame the nervous apprehensions of things slimy and gross. (Interestingly, when parents heard about the activity through letters from their children, they wanted to know if they, too, could go swamp mucking.) The idea is to actually crawl through the swamp following open waterways and animal paths.

Use obvious caution before diving into a swamp that may be home to alligators, water moccasins, leeches, or snapping turtles.

## Fox and hare

This is a fun game that teaches anyone to become aware of his surroundings to such an extent that he is able to follow the trail of something because of the signs it leaves. Begin by designating the hare, usually an adult, and the foxes, usually the children and another adult for supervision. Initially, the hare should get a two- to five-minute head start — enough that the foxes lose sight of the hare. The hare leaves signs for the foxes to follow, such as bits of colored paper on the ground or in branches, that are not too obvious yet distinct enough to be followed with minimal effort. As the foxes gain more and more experience, the hare should get a longer head start and should begin leaving bits of paper that more closely match the color of the terrain. As a variation, the hare can drag a branch behind him or her, leaving a more subtle trail for the foxes to follow. The goal of the game is for the foxes to successfully follow the trail of the hare and catch the hare. Use your imagination to adapt the hare's role and the trail he leaves any way you wish.

## Blind trust

Blind trust teaches participants to listen carefully to directions and to learn to use their other senses of awareness. It also teaches folks important communication and leadership skills.

Play this game in a fairly wooded area with some small hills and narrow gullies or other obstacles. Blindfold all in the group except the designated leader. For the first time around, the designated leader should be an adult. The idea is for the leader to guide his group through the woods, going over, around, and under obstacles using only voice commands to give directions. At no time is the leader allowed to move obstacles or touch the players.

A parent or other adult should keep a watchful eye on the group at all times to maintain a margin of safety. I once had a child try to lead his group over a gully using a narrow log as a bridge. The ten-foot fall that could have resulted was not my idea of a good learning opportunity.

## Snapshot

This game is great fun, and you can play it anywhere. It teaches children to use their observation skills efficiently and accurately. One person plays the role of the camera or lens, and the other person works the shutter or picture-taking button. The person guiding the camera searches for beautiful, interesting, or creative images that the camera can photograph. He sets up the camera, who must keep her eyes closed until told to open them, so that a picture can be taken. The camera guide snaps the photo by tapping the camera on the shoulder or hand. The camera opens her eyes without moving or twisting about and stares at the image in front of her. After about five seconds, the camera guide taps the camera's shoulder or hand, and the camera closes its eyes. Allow your child to be the "photographer," using you as the camera, and you will be afforded a unique and quite possibly very moving look at how your child views what is fascinating and beautiful.

## Barefoot in the woods

Going barefoot is a most natural and yet rarely enjoyed experience. Going barefoot encourages you to slow down, feel the ground underfoot, and relive an almost primeval instinct. Be sure that the ground you are going to walk over is relatively free from sharp rocks, thorns, and yes, even glass. Lead your youngsters through the woods single file. Teach them to walk as if they are hunting: Take a very small and very careful step forward to the outside ball of your descending foot. Very slowly, and without weighting it, roll the foot to the inside of the ball. If nothing that may break with a loud snap or pop is felt underfoot, carefully lower the heel and then fully weight the foot. If your child becomes adept at this, he or she will be able to sneak up closely to birds and animals without spooking them. The key is slow and steady movements.

## Stalking

One person, the prey, sits with his eyes closed at one end of a clearing about 25-feet wide. Everyone else tries to stalk the person without being heard. If the prey hears a sound, he points to it and opens his eyes. If the stalker is able to freeze and not move while the prey is watching, then the game continues. If, however, the prey opens his eyes after pointing and the stalker moves at all — even a flinch — the stalker becomes the prey.

## World above/world below

This activity is a quiet observational game that only works if your children are feeling calm and not overly agitated. This game can be played anywhere and is limited only by imagination. To study the world above, everyone lies still on their backs looking up at the world above. (It is most effective to play this game under a dense canopy of leaves or swirling clouds, or in dense, tall grass.) Looking down is, appropriately, the opposite of looking up. Everyone lies on their stomachs and watches the world as it passes by their faces. Looking down works outstandingly well at a stream or lake edge, above a tide pool, or in a dense patch of grasses or fallen leaves. If the ground is cold or hard, bring ensolite (sleeping) pads for everyone to lie on.

## Tide-pooling

Tide-pooling, especially with a young child or an older adult who is young at heart, is an absolute hoot. Poking and peering into pools searching for crabs, sea urchins, seashells, sea cucumbers, octopi, starfish, and the like can keep the explorer occupied and entertained for hours. I've whiled away many an afternoon wandering from pool to pool, or along northwestern beaches at a neap (minimum) tide, searching out what was previously untouchable.

To make the trip more enjoyable, bring a viewing "eye." I use an old diving mask, that, when pressed up against my face and then placed in the water, allows me to visually and clearly enter the world below. You can make your own, quite easily enough, by cutting the end off an old #10 coffee can, covering it tightly with clear plastic wrap and securing the wrap in place with a rubber band. When you get to a deep tide pool that you want to look into, just place the can in the water, plastic end down, and look through the can like a viewing window. You'll be amazed by how clearly you can see.

Sometimes, you may want to turn over a rock or log to see what lives under it. Do so carefully and gently, taking care not to crush what lives underneath. Replace the rock, with equal care, when you are finished looking.

Don't collect anything from the beach that is living — in most cases, doing so is illegal. Besides, marine animals are much better cared for in a wild environment. Finally, as you wander, remember that most beachfronts are considered public property right along the waterline, but after you head up the beach, above the high tide limit, you enter a zone that may or may not be private. It is your responsibility to know whether you are treading on public or private beachfront. If in doubt, ask at the public access point before venturing out. One more thing: Never, ever turn your back on the ocean — you risk getting drenched by a sneaky wave.

## Stargazing

The lights of a city mask the stars, leaving no chance to see the world beyond earth unless you step away from the city and gaze skyward from a mountaintop or an open field. For most city-trapped folk, seeing a million pinpricks of light twinkling against the inky-black backdrop of a night sky is a new experience. Stargazing takes practice and patience, but with a star wheel (available at most nature, outdoor specialty, or hobby stores) and a star guide, you'll open up a new world for yourself and your family or friends.

The following are some favorite and easily found stars and constellations:

- **North Star.** You can locate this star, also known as Polaris, if you can find the Big Dipper. The beauty of the North Star is that it stays in one place in the sky, and always to the north of you. To pick it out of the mass of other twinkling stars, find the Big Dipper and then look to the two stars that make up the lip of the dipper's ladle. The North Star lies above the two stars, known as *pointer stars*, in a relatively straight line, approximately four to six times the distance between the two stars.

- **Cassiopeia.** This star was named for the wife of King Cepheus, an Ethiopian king. According to mythology, she was turned into a constellation. Look for a five-star cluster shaped like a "W" or an "M" on the north/northeast horizon just before midnight in a summer sky.

- **Ursa Major.** You can find this constellation (also known as the Great Bear) near the Big Dipper, which actually makes up a part of the bear. The dipper makes up the bear's back, with the handle standing in for the bear's nose. Three pairs of stars make up the bear's paws.

- **Bootes.** Also known as the Herdsman, this constellation resembles a large kite and is located below the Big Dipper. At the constellation's base lies Arcturus, the fourth-brightest star in the sky (look for the star's distinct orange color).

- **Leo.** You can find the lion just below the bear's paws between the Great Bear and the western horizon. The bluish-white star Regulus sits near the lion's chest and behind its front leg.

# Sledding

All it takes is one wild, snow-spraying ride on a sled to bring out the youth that's hibernating in many of us. Winter play is all about snow and getting around on it. But you don't have to shell out big bucks to experience the thrill of sledding. Look around for the following free or inexpensive sled substitutes:

### Garbage bags

Get a box of 20 or more 36-gallon-size, heavyweight, garden-variety garbage bags — $1.99 or less at most discount stores. Double up the bags, slide your legs inside (if you can fit) or sit on top (although this method is not nearly as secure), and rip off a run or two before the bags shred into oblivion.

### Discarded inner tubes

Find these at a local truck stop or truck repair center. If they have unusable ones, you can often get them for free and the price of a few patches to seal the holes. If not, be prepared to shell out a few bucks — a small price to pay for a steed that will carry you hurtling downhill in the winter and surfing downstream in the summer.

### Cafeteria tray

If you went to high school or college in any state that had snow on the outdoor menu, you're probably familiar with a favorite pastime: racing downhill perched on a serving tray pinched from the school cafeteria. The ride is wild, fast, uncontrolled, and monumentally unforgettable. Find a tray for about $1.50 at a restaurant supply store.

### Air mattresses

For a cushy ride at high speeds, opt for a cheap plastic air mattress available for $10 at any camping or sporting goods store. If the mattress survives the day, you can sleep on it that night.

### Snow shovel

Yes, there's even a school in New Mexico that teaches you the finer points of shovel racing. Suffice it to say that all you really need is a large snow shovel, a steep hill, and smidgen of insanity. Sit on the shovel, holding the handle in front of you, lift your feet, and hang on! Buy a snow shovel for $15 at any hardware store, or simply borrow your neighbor's — tell him you'll shovel his driveway when you return.

# Night sounds

Encouraging folks to tune into the world around them is important. When I was a mountain guide in the '80s, I was amazed by how many of my clients, young and old, were completely unfamiliar with the sounds the night air in the mountains or desert brought. For many, these sounds were a source of discomfort and anxious moments only because they did not know what they were. I found that by walking them away from the campsite to a preselected area for us all to sit and listen to night sounds was a valuable experience and went very far to teach them to respect, but not fear, the dark. As you hear sounds, take the time to explain them — or ask what they are. Cover all sounds like wind, a gurgling stream, an owl, squeaking mice, a coyote howl, and the rattle of rocks falling from a cliff cooling in the night air.

# Storytelling

There's nothing quite like sitting around the campfire telling stories and munching on s'mores (melted chocolate, toasted marshmallows, and graham crackers). I like reading aloud from a selection of Robert Service poems or readings from naturalists such as Siguard Olsen and Henry David Thoreau. Another fun thing to do is create your own group adventure so that everyone contributes to the story. One person begins a tale and then hands off the story to the person to his right or left. That person continues the story, embellishing it as he sees fit. Use your imagination! Although ghost stories are considered a camping tradition, I offer one word of caution: Tell ghost stories only to older children. *Campfire Stories*, written by William Forgey, is a good source, as is my favorite ghost story guide, *Campfire Legends, Twisted Tales for Storytellers* by John Long. The latter offers crib notes for telling the tales rather than simply reading them — much better for the best storytelling effect.

# Sunrise hike

Getting up before the sun rises probably isn't high on your agenda unless you are a mountaineer seeking to reach a summit before the sun softens the snow. However, many campers miss out on a very special and spiritual time out-doors by experiencing sunrise only from the protected confines of a tent and sleeping bag.

Though the groans were loud and clear as I woke folks an hour before dawn on every trip I guided for five years, the grins, oohs, and ahs following a sunrise breakfast experience were unanimous. I'd select a safe route up to a suitable lookout point that was no more than a 30-minute hike from camp. Headlamps and flashlights are a must. After we safely nestled into the lookout area, I'd quiet the group, and we'd watch the thin sliver of light appear on the eastern horizon. Colors often dance in the sky as the sun pushes fingers of light through the velvet curtain of dawn before exploding onto the scene as a warm, golden orb.

After the initial show is over, it's time to fire up a camp stove, whip up hot cocoa and coffee, and hand out bagels, cream cheese, dried fruit, or whatever your breakfast dreams desire — within reason of course. (See Chapter 8 for more on cooking and eating in the wild, and check out Chapter 16 for some of my favorite campground recipes.) After you have experienced one sunrise, you'll want to see hundreds more.

## Singing campfire songs

Singing around the campfire is a time-honored tradition. If you are completely inept at remembering songs (as I am), latch onto *Campfire Songs* by Irene Maddox. The book features 192 pages of rounds, songs, and ballads — many with guitar chords, should you be more musically inclined than I am.

## Just hanging round

There is an art to doing nothing, which is, frankly, one of the things you should specialize in when outdoors. For that very reason, I tote along a couple of hammocks whenever I car-camp. No, there aren't always places to hang them in camp, but when there are, a hammock's presence announces to the world: "Mellow dude in camp — do not disturb."

Swinging gently in the late afternoon sun while the breezes tease the leaves in the trees above is perhaps one of the most relaxing moments I can imagine. However, don't just flop into a hammock, because relaxation will be the farthest thing from your mind.

Folks who lie end-to-end in a hammock find little rest and relaxation — their hindquarters drag the dust while their head and feet point skyward. The secret, my friends, is in positioning. If you lie diagonally in a hammock, forces that you learned about in high school physics come into play and — presto — your body gains support, and your mind finds peace. I tuck a stuff sack filled with a soft parka under my head and keep a water bottle and favorite book handy for good measure. If mosquitoes or biting flies are a problem, keep a head net handy, too.

# Watching Wildlife

Everywhere you look, nature is there. To see nature, all you have to do is open your eyes and ears. When you go traipsing off into the wilds, however, remember to respect private property (always get permission before venturing out) and keep in mind some simple tips:

- **Do not pick plants or disturb nature in any way when on public property** — look, don't touch, is the creed here. Touching and picking disturbs the beauty for others who may want to experience in the future what you are enjoying at the present.

- **Respect nature by treating habitats with care** — no turning over rocks, breaking apart downed logs, or poking sticks into holes. Animals live in these places, after all!

- **Picking wildflowers or plants on private land, when you have permission, is okay as long as you do not decimate the habitat in the process.** Pick selectively and conservatively, and only if there are many plants to choose from.

- **Never pick an endangered plant or wildflower, no matter where it may grow or how many you see in the meadow or forest** — it may be the last meadow or forest in which these plants are growing! (How do you tell what's endangered and what's not? Ask a ranger or other informed person. When in doubt, don't touch.)

## Gear for viewing and identifying wildlife

What naturalist gear you need varies depending on your level of expertise. Junior naturalists (beginners) should choose only from those items that I specifically list in the "Junior naturalist" heading. Casual naturalists (I think of them as avid novices) should choose from everything that I list under the "Casual naturalist" heading as well as all items that I list under the "Junior naturalist" heading. Hard-core naturalists (experienced, even a little) may choose their gear from the entire list.

Choose from the following lists when assembling your gear for viewing and identification purposes:

### Junior naturalist (beginner)

- Mini field guides, such as *Peterson First Guides*
- Aquarium net (for viewing aquatic life)
- Bug viewer
- Crayons in various shades

✔ Envelopes (for collecting leaves and seeds)

✔ Notebook and pencil

✔ Plastic hand lens

✔ Plastic minibinoculars

✔ Six-inch ruler

### Casual naturalist (avid novice)

✔ Binoculars (7 x 35 is an adequate and versatile choice)

✔ *Peterson Field Guides*

✔ Plastic containers for specimens

✔ *Audubon Pocket Guides*

✔ Magnifier (5x to 10x magnification is best)

✔ Microcassette recorder

### Hard-core naturalist (experienced, even a little)

✔ Camera (a waterproof point-and-shoot is best for all-around use)

✔ Butterfly net for collecting insect life

✔ Compass

✔ Plaster of Paris mix to make impressions of animal tracks

✔ Pocket knife

✔ Reference books

✔ Small plastic vials for collecting specimens

✔ Small trowel

✔ Small waterproof paper notebook

✔ Tape measure

✔ Thermometer

✔ Tweezers

✔ Yardstick

# Capturing Moments in Freeze-Frame

A picture is worth a thousand words. It's true, I guess, providing the picture is a keeper. Many are not. You know the kind I mean — we've all taken them: snapshots that are too light, too dark, too far from the subject, full of distracting stuff.

## *Making shots worth showing*

The following tips can help you insure that your shots are worth showing to friends (see *Photography For Dummies*, published by IDG Books Worldwide, for more tips on capturing the perfect image):

- ✔ **Centered subjects in a photo look stiff and posed and also downright amateur.** Place the subject of the photo off to one side and let the light or surrounding landscape add to the story you are trying to tell.

- ✔ **Remember to use a sense of scale in your photos.** A giant sequoia or a distant mountain that looks huge to you appears as nothing more than a tiny image on a screen unless you place an object of known size in the picture to establish a relationship of scale. For macro photography, I often slip a penny into the picture next to tiny flowers to show just how small they really are.

- ✔ **A flare across your favorite shot can be prevented if you use a lens hood or learn to cup your hand just above or to the side of the lens to block out stray light.**

## *Deciding which camera to use*

Many cameras are on the market, so which one you should use depends on your budget and how much gear you're willing to schlep along. Most of the time, I'm perfectly happy using my compact point-and-shoot 35 millimeter Pentax. If the mood strikes me, however — and it frequently does — I'll carry along my Nikon with two lenses: a 28mm to 75mm telephoto and a 75mm to 300mm zoom. I prefer 100 ASA speed film, but if the light is going to be low, as it often is in the woods, I turn to 200 ASA or, rarely, 400 ASA (this gets much grainier). I always shoot slide film — prints are just too limiting.

If very little of the preceding paragraph makes sense to you, go to a camera store and talk to a clerk there. Tell her where you're going and what kinds of things you're thinking of taking pictures of, and she can direct you to the right film.

Although disposables can't match the optical quality of their more expensive point-and-shoot cousins, they come as close as needed for most vacation and photo album shots as long as you remember a few key points:

- ✔ Specify 5 x 7 (or smaller) prints for sharp, colorful, and relatively grain-free photos. If you choose larger prints, the quality will start to deteriorate.

- ✔ When shooting underwater or at the water's surface, make sure that you're shooting in the sun. Shadows darken photos dramatically.

- ✔ Never try to shoot deeper than five to eight feet underwater — your shots will turn out lifeless and dark.

> ✔ For shots above the water, always place your back to the sun and make sure that your subject is well lit. To correct for shadows, use the flash as fill-in lighting.
>
> ✔ You can't focus the lens, so don't shoot anything closer than three and a half feet unless you want to look at blurry shots.

The essence of most amateur wildlife photography is defined by animal butts — way off in the distance. Learn to anticipate a shot, move in front of the action, and then set up the photograph so your image fills as much of the frame as possible. You will be best served using a 300-mm lens.

## Keeping the camera handy

No camera does you much good if you can't get to it. It's not uncommon for well-intentioned photographers to spend an entire day hiking without burning one shot because the camera sat safely secure inside the pack on their back. The key to taking photographs during the day is to make your camera accessible. SunDog, LowePro, Tamrac, and PhotoFlex are some of the better known manufacturers of padded camera cases which can be carried as a chest pouch or attached to a waist belt. I prefer a chest pouch, although it does limit your "at the feet" visibility, which is a drawback if you are negotiating difficult terrain. Some of my friends prefer an ordinary fanny pack, which they spin around so the pack carries in front. I can't fault the ease of access, but it's a nuisance on steep climbs since the fanny pack is always in the way of your thighs and knees.

# Buying and Using Binoculars

Binoculars are an important addition to any outdoor adventurer's equipment list. They bring the distant world close enough to view, allowing you to visually leapfrog up a mountain, capture the intricate detail of a hawk's feathers high overhead, or scan the surface of a lake — all without moving a step. Choosing the right binocular, however, can be confusing, especially because hundreds of models are available, with prices ranging from $10 cereal-box sport glasses to $700 autofocus binoculars utilizing the latest in microchip technology.

## Assessing your needs

Before you shop, do your homework and make a list of your needs. Are you going to use your binoculars primarily for viewing wildlife, sports, stars, or a combination of these subjects? Will you use them in normal lighting, in the shadows of late evening, or in the deep forest? Will they be routinely exposed to elements or relatively protected? Is durability a factor?

# Caring for your binoculars

Follow these tips to keep your binoculars in top condition:

✔ Never touch binocular lenses with your fingers. Instead, remove grit and grime with a few puffs of a blower brush (found in most photo stores) and then brush away any remaining particles. Remove haze and fingerprints by gently wiping with a lens tissue dampened with a drop of lens cleaner.

✔ Don't leave your binoculars in the hot sun, the trunk of your car, or anywhere else where heat may warp the casing.

✔ Keep your binoculars stored in a padded nylon or leather case. Add a packet of silica gel to help absorb any moisture.

✔ Clean the exterior of your binoculars only with a lint-free cotton cloth or a silicon-impregnated cloth that some manufacturers supply with your purchase.

How much you are willing to spend is the final decision. If you are only going to use the binoculars once or twice a year, you can probably get away with a lower-priced model. But don't settle on the cheapest pair that you can find. You may regret your choice later. Generally, the higher the price, the better the optical quality and the more durable the housing — to a point. Beyond $250 to $300, you probably won't notice the difference.

## Talking the talk

When you compare various makes and models of binoculars, here are the key terms to keep in mind:

✔ **Power or magnification** determines how much an object is enlarged. A 7x binocular magnifies seven times (makes an object appear seven times closer). You may find some binoculars with a 10x magnification, but unless you plan to use a tripod, stay away from these models. Any gain in magnification is lost by the corresponding magnification of movement.

✔ **Objective size** refers to the diameter of the front (objective) lenses. A 7 x 35 binocular's objective lens measures 35 millimeters across. Larger objective lenses allow more light through and are better in low-light situations.

✔ **Exit pupil** is determined by dividing the larger number by the smaller number. For example, a 7 x 35 binocular has an exit pupil of 5 millimeters (35 divided by 7). The larger the exit pupil number, the more light being transmitted to your eyes. A 3-millimeter to 5-millimeter exit pupil is generally adequate for normal viewing. An exit pupil of 7 millimeters is best for low-light use.

✔ **Field of view** is the width or amount of area that you are able to see through binoculars at 1,000 yards. The field of view for a 7x binocular is typically seven degrees or 369 feet. This information is always printed on the instruction sheet, if not on the binocular body. Any binocular with a nine-degree or more field of view is considered a wide-field model. A wider field of view is helpful for wildlife viewing.

✔ **Prisms** are the little gizmos that bend the light entering the binoculars, allowing you to see an upright image with increased magnification and brightness. Porro prism binoculars are bulkier and heavier but offer an accurate sense of depth of field. Roof prisms are more expensive but offer a lighter and more compact alternative with virtually the same features as a porro prism model. (Depth of field is not as good, however.)

✔ **Focusing** is either fixed, center, or individual. Fixed is convenient but loses in overall image quality and versatility. Center focusing adjusts both eyepieces at once and is usually the preferred option. Individual focusing is a pain!

✔ **Waterproof housing** is the best choice when you anticipate using your binoculars in dusty or moist environments, although the housing won't handle prolonged underwater submersions well.

✔ **Lens coatings** help with contrast, light reflection, and color saturation. Multicoated lenses are best but are no substitute for an adequate exit pupil rating.

# Usage chart

Binoculars fill virtually any indoor and outdoor need imaginable, from opera to football to wilderness exploration. However, no binocular will meet every need. The following is a recommended application for a select sampling of magnification powers:

✔ **6 x 30:** Stadium sports, indoor sports, theater, bird-watching at a home feeder

✔ **7 x 25:** Hiking, bike touring, nature observation, stadium sports

✔ **7 x 35:** General purpose, bird-watching, boating, stadium sports, wildlife observation

✔ **7 x 50:** General purpose, stargazing, boating, hunting, bird-watching

✔ **8 x 40:** Wildlife observation, stargazing, long-distance bird-watching

# Part IV
# Staying Safe, Staying Found

The 5th Wave          By Rich Tennant

"That perfect stack of perfectly shaped rocks? It's a trail marking. It says, 'this is a warning', and 'I am obsessive'."

## In this part. . .

Going camping isn't much fun if you don't stay found. In Chapter 11, you learn enough navigation skills to guide you into the wilds and back again — safely. In Chapter 12, I turn you into an amateur meteorologist and teach you how to predict weather patterns — a very useful skill if you're planning a hike or a climb while at base camp. And no section on safety would be complete without a discussion of first aid. Chapter 13 focuses on dealing with minor scrapes, bumps, blisters, and bites and teaches you preventative skills to help you stay accident-free.

# Chapter 11

# Staying Found Simply

● ● ● ● ● ● ● ● ● ● ● ● ● ● ● ● ● ● ● ● ● ● ● ● ● ● ● ● ● ● ● ● ● ● ● ● ● ●

## *In This Chapter*

▶ Finding your way without street signs

▶ Using your map and compass like a pro

▶ Getting from A to B like a homing pigeon (well, almost)

▶ Going high-tech with Global Positioning System

▶ Sharpening your survival skills

● ● ● ● ● ● ● ● ● ● ● ● ● ● ● ● ● ● ● ● ● ● ● ● ● ● ● ● ● ● ● ● ● ● ● ● ● ●

*W*hy do people get lost? For many reasons, and the majority are completely avoidable. The most common mistake is not packing a map and compass because you're "just going out for a quick hike on a clearly marked trail." All you have to do is be daydreaming or chatting with your partners to walk off one trail and onto another, completely unaware. Another mistake is lack of preparation. You can imagine the routine — the trip is on so you grab a map, toss the compass in the pack, and go, with no forethought or map homework. I always study my maps before I go out, which is why I probably have an easier time staying on course. Yet another reason for getting lost is trusting your partner, who may be just as hopelessly lost as you are. Everyone who wants to safely enjoy the great outdoors should master basic navigational skills and be able to use them.

Having been a member of several search-and-rescue teams and also a professional mountain guide, I am continually amazed by the number of people I encounter who dutifully carry a map and shiny new compass, yet have absolutely no idea where they are, where they are heading, or where they came from. Sure, packing along a topographic map and a compass fulfill the "be prepared" mandate, but what good are they if you don't know how to use them? Not much! You may as well bring a world atlas or road map — they'll be as much help as a topographic map in the backcountry if you don't have map and compass skills.

The art to staying found involves using one's head, remaining observant, and applying map and compass skills properly.

# Use Your Eyes, Ears, and Nose

No one I know can claim to have a homing pigeon's infallible sense of direction. However, with a little practice and an observant eye, combined with the skilled use of a map and a compass, you can claim the title of "skilled navigator." I earned the nickname "Navgod" while competing as captain of Team Media in the 1995 Eco-Challenge, a 360-mile, nonstop adventure race across the wildlands of Utah. As confident as I am about navigating outdoors, I am often the brunt of family jokes regarding my consistent ability to become completely turned around in a mall or crowded city. Why? Simply, skilled navigation requires using your senses — all of them. In the wilderness, I am always on edge, listening, watching, hearing, and smelling. In the city, I tend to tune out, and as a result, I miss clues that will point me in the direction of my car — one of thousands parked somewhere in the garage where I left it hours ago.

## Navigation requires 360-degree awareness

Keep your eyes alert and moving in 360-degree scans as you move down or up a trail. You must always be searching for clues that can help you to remember the course you are on, and then catalogue those clues in your mind for reference when you need them. Pay very close attention to the following:

- Stream crossings
- Trail intersections
- Rocky outcroppings that stand out
- Trees that are different from all others
- Unique features in the landscape — even if man-made

Look over your shoulder often so you can gain an image of how the landscape appears from more than one perspective. Why look over your shoulder? Because things look very different when you look at them from other angles and directions. When I was teaching advanced map and compass skills to students, they would invariably navigate the course I'd set before them with confidence, getting from Point A to Point B quickly. But when I asked them to retrace their route, using only the map as a point of reference, confusion set in. Nothing looked familiar to them anymore because they forgot to tuck away the essential clues.

As you walk, always look forward, to the sides, and over your shoulder. Remember key landmarks and points of reference from multiple directions and tuck away the clues in your mental catalogue. Worried you may forget? Jot notes on the map margin or a small notepad.

# Place yourself in the picture as you walk

You need to remain aware of your surroundings from the minute you step away from your car, cabin, tent, or whatever your starting point is. Think of your travels as a puzzle that you assemble as you move. Each landmark or point of reference becomes another piece that you fit into the puzzle. Keep asking yourself, "If I had to return to where I started, which direction would that be and how would I get there?" Every hill you move around, every landmark, every stream crossing, every direction change, every elevation change becomes a critical part of the navigation puzzle you are assembling. Each piece will fit logically if you put it in place as you go.

Don't forget to take into account the sky as well. Although the sun moves across the sky (and the moon does, too!), learning to associate times of day with the sun's position in relation to landmarks you are passing can be immensely helpful in determining where you are should you need to retrace your steps.

# Navigation requires more than your eyes

How do your ears and nose play into the navigation game? While you may not be able to see a stream, you can certainly hear it. Where is it? To your left, right, far below, nearby? Where is the stream in relation to your location right now? Make a note and keep moving. Listen to how sounds change as you move. Breathe deeply. That smell — wild onions? Perhaps it's cedar or the earthy smell of a damp meadow. Make a mental note about what you smell relative to your location. As the trail moves in and out of the woods and in and out of valleys, does one area in particular feel much colder or warmer to you? Make mental notes of all these signs.

Using your eyes, ears, and nose to stay on course is the way pioneers and Native Americans successfully crossed terrain much wilder than it is now, all without the aid of a compass or map. With practice, you can do that too.

# You're not lost — just simply disoriented!

In our modern world where wildlands are surrounded by civilization and rescuers have technology at their fingertips to aid in searches, it is rare that anyone remains lost for long. Most often, being lost simply means you'll be a bit late for dinner or perhaps have to spend a cold night on an unplanned sleepover. Staying found is not hard if you follow the following tips and suggestions:

 ✔ **Always tell a family member or close friend where you are going, when you will be leaving, and when you plan on returning — and then stick to your plan.**

✔ **Be prepared for the worst.** Just because you are heading out for a day hike under sunny skies doesn't mean you won't be forced to spend a night out under adverse weather conditions. Always carry the survival essentials that I mention in Chapter 14.

✔ **Become skilled at using a map and compass.** Another book that I authored, *Compass & Map Navigator*, published by The Globe Pequot Press, is an excellent place to begin, but reading is not enough! You must get out and practice, practice, practice. Joining an orienteering club near you is a great way to gain experience and to have a lot of fun.

✔ **Should you get lost, don't panic.** Recognize the difficulty and then rationally work your way through it. Most often, if you sit down and calmly reflect for a few minutes, mentally retracing your steps, the way out becomes clear.

✔ **If you come to the conclusion you are definitely lost, STAY PUT!** Although it is tempting to wander, there are numerous tales of lost persons being found dead weeks or months after a search was begun, simply because they wandered out of the area where the search party expected them to be.

✔ **Drink plenty of water.** Your body can do without food for a few days, but it cannot function without water. Signal your position by building a smoky fire. If you run out of food, don't begin grazing or gnawing on branches and leaves unless you are sure you can identify them as edible.

✔ **Shelter yourself from the elements as best you can.** I talk about this in detail at the end of this chapter, beginning at the heading "Seeking shelter."

# Understanding Your Map

A topographic map is a one-dimensional representation of a three-dimensional environment. How cartographers do this is by using contour lines (see Figures 11-1 and 11-2) to show where hills, mountains, valleys, and canyons are located. A trained eye can look at a flat map with all the contour lines and see valleys, mountains, ridges, and more.

Topographic maps are printed in color, with green depicting forested or vegetated areas and white indicating open terrain. Contour or elevation lines are printed in brown. Blue indicates water, either as a lake, river, or stream. Black is used for man-made features such as trails, roads, and buildings.

Man-made features on topographic maps should always be suspect, even on privately printed maps that claim to be up-to-date. Why? A building that existed when the map was printed may have vanished due to fire, weather, flood, or other reasons. Or, the building that was there when the map was printed may have turned into a tiny suburb, full of many buildings.

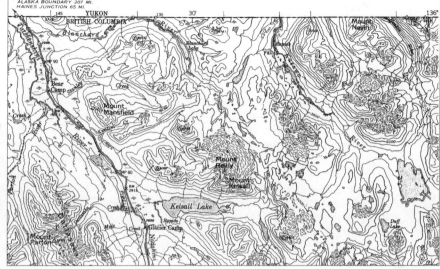

**Figure 11-1:**
Portion of
topographic
map with
contour
lines at
500-foot
intervals.

Many other symbols are used to depict such things as mines, ghost towns, marshes, swamps, waterfalls, caves, and the like. The key to the symbols does not appear on the map but on a separate sheet that may be obtained free from the United States Geological Survey (USGS).

Map reading takes more than simply understanding the symbols, though.

## *Do you have the right map?*

Somewhere on the map will be information regarding what area the map covers. With a USGS map, the area information appears in the lower left corner along the white border surrounding the map itself. The area the map covers is also indicated in the upper right corner along the white border on a USGS map. The United States is divided into quadrants based on lines of latitude and longitude, and each quadrant most often carries the name of a significant geographical feature or municipality falling within the quadrant's boundaries.

USGS maps print adjoining map information along their borders so that you can effectively link maps of the same series and scale. Typically, the names of corresponding and adjoining maps are printed at each corner, one at each side, and one at both the top and bottom of the map. You can also find a silhouette picture of the region the map series covers, divided into equal quadrants — the map you are using will be the one that is shaded. This way you can see where the map fits into the entire region's mapping picture and how many adjoining maps you may require to navigate across it.

# *What is the map's scale?*

USGS prints its maps in what are known as series (7.5-minute, 15-minute, and so on) Although you can still find 15-minute series maps, the USGS publishes mostly 7.5-minute series maps these days. To explain minutes, the earth is divided into 360 degrees of latitude (east/west) and 180 degrees of longitude (north/south). Each degree is divided into 60 units of measurement called *minutes,* and each minute is divided into 60 units of measurement called *seconds.* In navigational terms, minutes and seconds have absolutely nothing to do with time and everything to do with a unit of distance measurement. A 7.5-minute series map then represents an area of the earth's surface that is 7.5 minutes (one eighth of a degree) of longitude wide by 7.5 minutes (one eighth of a degree) of latitude high. Typically, in a 7.5-minute map, the scale will be 1:24,000, which means that one unit of measurement on the map equals 24,000 units of the same measurement full-sized. In a 1:24,000 scale map, one inch equals about one eighth of a mile or nearly 2,000 feet. At the bottom of most maps is a bar scale that allows you to make to-scale measurements that correspond to foot, mile, or kilometer distances.

# *Determining latitude and longitude*

Degrees of latitude and longitude are indicated in the corners of most maps. Reading up from the bottom left or right corner of a map, black ticks and/or fine black lines indicate changes in minutes and seconds of latitude. Latitude in the Northern Hemisphere (north of the equator) increases as you move north and toward the top of the map. Black ticks and/or fine black lines indicate changes in minutes and seconds of longitude when reading from the bottom right or top right corner of a map. Longitude in North America increases as you go west.

# *Universal Transverse Mercator (UTM)*

How can the round earth be transformed into a flat map? Glad you asked! One method is to apply the Universal Transverse Mercator system. UTM is the system grid that divides the entire world into 60 zones that are 6 degrees wide. The zones begin at east/west longitude 180 degrees and continue at 6-degree intervals. Each zone is then removed from the globe and flattened, losing its relationship to a sphere and introducing a certain amount of distortion. Since UTM projections distort the regions above 84 degrees north latitude and below 80 degrees south latitude far too much, they are not used on maps referencing the UTM grid. The UTM grid is based upon the meter, and grid lines are always 1 kilometer (0.62 miles) apart, making it much easier to estimate distance on a map. UTM coordinates are printed on a map in an east/west and north/south position. Numbers along the right side of a map are called *northings* (indicating the exact position in a north/south relationship). Numbers along the top of the map are called *eastings* (indicating the exact position in an east/west relationship). Making sense of the numbers is quick and easy:

✔ Increasing easting numbers indicate you are heading east; decreasing indicate you are heading west. Increasing northing numbers indicate you are heading north and decreasing indicate you are heading south.

✔ A reading of full UTM positions written along the right side of your map may go as follows: first mark (435000m.N.) and then the second mark (436000m.N.). What does this mean? The larger numbers (35 and 36) indicate thousands of meters, and because a thousand meters equals one kilometer, the two ticks are 1,000 meters or one kilometer apart. The last three numbers are printed smaller and indicate hundreds of meters. If the readings of the marks were (435000m.N.) and then (435500m.N.), this would indicate the ticks were 500 meters or one-half kilometer apart.

Does this UTM stuff seem a tad technical? Well, it is, but if you want to use one of those nifty little electronic gadgets called a GPS — a global positioning system — that I describe later in this chapter, you need to know UTM. Many guidebooks and directions provide UTM bearings rather than latitude/longitude.

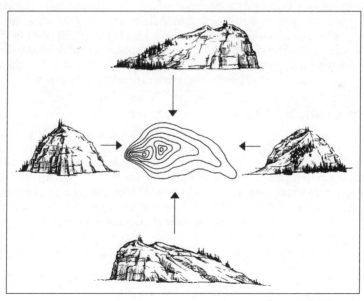

**Figure 11-2:**
Topographic
map adds
height and
depth to a
flat picture.

*Courtesy Jon Cox, Brunton Co.*

### Seeing in 3-D when looking at a map

Learning to translate the one-dimensional image printed on the sheet of paper you call a map into a three-dimensional representation of the world takes practice. Figure 11-2, for example, shows a topographic map of a twin-peaked mountain plus four two-dimensional views. Have patience and take heart — seeing 3-D on a flat map is not as difficult as it may appear at first. Think about it this way:

- **Widely spaced contour lines** indicate a gradual slope.

- **The more packed the contour lines** are together, the steeper and more severe the terrain. Closely spaced contours may mean a cliff.

- **Contours that roughly form circles,** each getting smaller in size with each gain in elevation, indicate hills or mountain peaks. A summit is often marked with an X, with a number printed next to it indicating the exact elevation of that peak.

- **Contour lines that bend into a "V"** (the V's may look more like U's if the terrain is sloping very gently) represent either a canyon or valley or a sloping ridge. If the V is pointing uphill, toward a point of higher elevation, then the V's are forming a canyon. If the V is pointing downhill, toward a point of lower elevation, then the V's form a ridge. It stands to reason that a stream in a V would indicate that the V is a canyon and pointing toward higher points of elevation.

- **V-shaped valleys** on a map are typically steep and more difficult to navigate. On extremely pronounced V shapes, expect the sidewalls of the canyon to be steep and almost impossible to scramble up or down. If you are on the canyon floor, you'll probably be there to stay until you exit either upstream or downstream. U-shaped valleys, on the other hand, are far more gentle and easier to navigate through.

### How significant is the map's contour interval?

Aside from telling you how steep the terrain is, the interval should alert you to something else. Consider a map with a contour interval of 50 feet. This means the cartographer drew a contour line on the map for every 50 feet of elevation change up or down. But what this also means is that the map may not include some pretty impressive stuff — like that 30-foot-high chunk of rock you see ahead, or a 35-foot cliff or 25-foot-deep wash. The reason they don't show up is simply that they are all smaller in scale than 50-foot up/down intervals.

### Use your map's scale to estimate trip distance

Although the bar scale printed at the bottom of your map is a straight line, I have never once seen a trail that remained straight for more than several hundred yards. And trails have a nasty habit of gaining and losing elevation, so while a trail line on a map may look like one mile, you could clock several miles as you hike it. Still, measuring your route somewhat accurately does allow you to plan your trip with some idea of how long it will take.

Photo by Brian Drumm.

**Figure 11-3:**
Measuring
trail dis-
tance with a
piece of
wire.

My preferred method of measuring distance relies on either red or white narrow gauge electrical wire. Electrical wire, the kind used in model building, is very flexible, holds its shape, doesn't stretch, and can be marked with an indelible ink marker. Cut a 12-inch section of the wire and then mark ¼- and 1-mile increments on it with a fine-tipped indelible black ink marker. I have found that using dots for the ¼-mile marks and a complete band around the wire for the 1-mile marks works best. Be sure to meticulously match your marks to those on the map's bar scale.

Place one end of the wire at your starting point and then gradually bend and contour the wire to match the twists and bends of your trail or route of travel. (See Figure 11-3.) Once the bending and contouring is finished, you can count up the miles and determine just how far your planned route is, how far it may be to your estimated rest points, and how far it is to points of scenic interest, water, and so on.

### Folding a map

A properly folded map — yes, there is such a thing (see Figure 11-4) — makes it a simple matter to open and close your map even in windy weather. Further, the accordion configuration collapses to pocket size with ease. After you establish the creases, any map folds up and down almost without effort.

## Waterproofing a map

Making a see-through, waterproof cover for your maps is an easy way to prevent your much-needed map from turning into a shredded pile of unreadable mush when the weather turns damp — and you know it will at some point. All you need is a large, freezer-weight zip-lock bag and a few sections of sturdy, waterproof tape such as duct or packing tape.

Simply cut the tape into a strip long enough to completely adhere to one edge of the bag from top to bottom. Press one-half of the tape, length-wise, onto the side edge of the bag, leaving the other half of the tape hanging over the edge. Now flip the bag over and fold the tape down on the other side of the bag. Repeat each step twice more, once for the bottom and once for the remaining side. You now have a wonderful waterproof map container that is reinforced on three edges.

Several other ways to waterproof a map are:

✔ Paint on a product called "Stormproof" or other map-waterproofing treatments by Aquaseal or Nikwax, available at most map and outdoor specialty stores. The clear chemical coating renders the map waterproof, flexible, and able to be written on.

✔ A coating of "Thompson Water Seal" or other brick and masonry sealant will make a map water-repellent, but not waterproof.

1. Lay the map flat, printed side up. Fold it in half vertically, with the face inside the first fold to establish the first crease. Make this and every subsequent crease clean and sharp.

2. Working with only the right half of the map, fold the right side in half toward the center, resulting in quarter-folds.

3. Fold the outside quarter-fold back to the edge, producing an eighth-fold. Use this fold as a guide and fold the other quarter the same way — trust me, it's easier than it sounds.

4. Half the map should now have four accordion-style folds.

5. Repeat Steps 2 and 3 on the map's other half so that you end up with a full accordion of eight folds in a long ruler-like shape.

6. Finally, fold the map in the shape of a Z so it's in thirds. Voila! Now you can look at any section without having to completely unfold the map, and it snaps into place almost by itself.

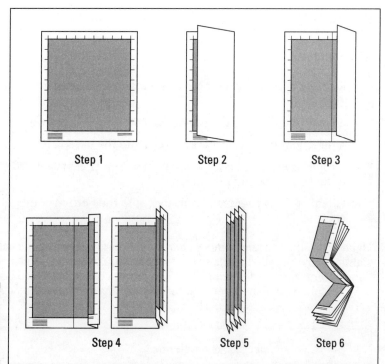

Step 1        Step 2        Step 3

Step 4        Step 5        Step 6

**Figure 11-4:**
Six steps to
a properly
folded map.

## A map has its limitations

Because a map can provide only so much information, a complete picture of how easy or difficult the terrain is to negotiate may not be evident until you are actually attempting to navigate your way. I have encountered vast swampy areas that I had to spend hours walking around and deep sand that turned each step into a thigh-burning adventure. I have also encountered raging rivers where the map shows only a seasonal stream, and boulder fields that stretched for miles over terrain that showed flat on the map, as well as other challenges. Never forget that a map is but a tool, and not the gospel on what you may or may not encounter.

# Buying a Compass

At a minimum, a compass should feature the following:

- ✔ Rotating bezel or azimuth ring with a 360-degree dial in 2-degree graduations
- ✔ A clear baseplate with inch and millimeter scales
- ✔ A direction-of-travel arrow engraved into the baseplate
- ✔ A rotating magnetic needle mounted in a clear capsule filled with liquid to reduce shake and movement
- ✔ Orienting lines engraved or printed onto the bottom of the rotating capsule

Figure 11-5 shows basic compass features. Additional features, such as a sighting mirror (called a prismatic compass), built-in adjustable declination, clinometers, and a magnifying glass add to the cost of the compass but are very useful if you plan to become serious about your navigational skills.

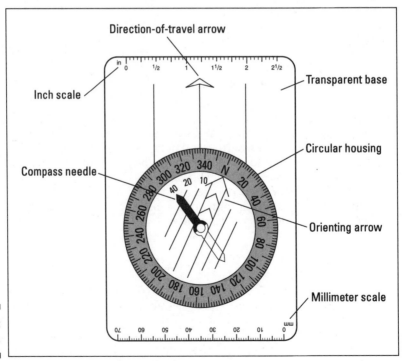

**Figure 11-5:** Compass.

## Caring for your compass

Compasses are designed to work even when you subject them to rough handling like banging against rocks, dropping them onto hard surfaces, and using them in the dirt. Still, if you want your compass to work when you need it, a little TLC is in order.

✔ **Protect your compass as much as you can.** I tuck my compass inside my shirt to protect it when it is hanging around my neck and not in use. If you have a sighting compass with a cover, keep it closed when not in use.

✔ **Never leave your compass sitting in an extremely hot environment.** Places such as on a rock under intense desert sun or on the dashboard or in the glove compartment of your car are horrible places to leave your compass. Extreme temperatures can cause the damping fluid in your compass to rupture the housing and leak out, rendering your compass useless.

✔ **After applying insect repellents, be sure to clean your hands thoroughly before touching your compass.** The chemicals in repellents (most typically DEET) can eat the ink off your compass's housing. Worse, DEET has been known to affect the plastic housing of a compass, causing it to cloud up and even crack.

✔ **From time to time, you may need to disperse a static charge that builds up on your compass.** Over time, the needle on your compass may begin to act sluggishly, even appear to stick to the bottom of the liquid-filled housing. Most often, this is due to a build up of static electricity within the housing and you can easily correct it by simply rubbing a small amount of water directly over the housing to disperse the static charge.

✔ **It is not uncommon for a small bubble to appear in the liquid-filled housing when you are using your compass in high elevations or in temperatures below freezing.** The bubble forms because the fluid within the housing contracts or expands at a faster rate than the housing, resulting in a "vacuum" bubble. This bubble will not affect the performance of your compass as the liquid's sole purpose is to dampen or slow down the movement of the magnetic needle. Typically, any bubble will disappear when the compass is returned to room temperature or to a lower elevation. If the bubble remains, it is possible to correct the situation by placing the compass in a warm (not hot) spot, such as a sunny windowsill. Should the bubble grow in size, you might have a small, almost imperceptible leak in the liquid-filled compass housing, and that means you need a new compass.

## A word on declination

I recommend that you purchase a compass that has a declination adjustment feature built in — it costs $20 or so, but is well worth it.

Declination is simply the difference between true north, which is what all maps are based on, and magnetic north, which is what all magnetic needles point toward. In a perfect world, they would be the same, but, as ours is not a perfect world, magnetic north and true north are often very different. For example, using a compass as your guide, if you ignore declination on a simple two-mile hike from your car to a nice lakeside campsite, you could end up in a valley several thousand yards away!

Declination is either west or east depending on which side of true or geographical north the compass needle points. On USGS topographic maps, arrows printed on the bottom margin of the map indicate declination. The arrow with a star above it indicates true north. The shorter arrow with an "MN" above it indicates magnetic north. So unless you are using a compass with the declination adjustment feature built in, you have to resort to math every time you take a bearing. If the MN arrow is on the left side of the true north arrow, declination is west and you need to add the indicated degree amount to correct your bearing. If the MN arrow is on the right side of the true north arrow, declination is east and you need to subtract the indicated degree amount to correct your bearing.

Now, I know you just love to add and subtract all day long, but frankly, with a compass that features a built-in declination adjustment, all you do is simply turn a screw or adjust the housing once and the compass will read true. Doesn't that sound simpler? Of course, you do have to remember that each time declination changes, often from map to map, you need to manually adjust the compass to the new setting.

## Understanding compass parts

Besides a needle and a big "N," how complicated can a compass be? Oh, not very complicated, but there are some parts to talk about, including features that come into play every time you take a bearing and set a course.

- **Azimuth ring (housing):** The circular housing with textured edges on the compass, often liquid-filled, that rotates within the compass base for taking or setting bearings. Degree markings, from 0 to 360, are typically etched into its surface, making up the azimuth ring or graduated dial.

- **Gun-type sights:** Most often found on prismatic (sighting) compasses, they are used like the sights on a gun for sighting and taking bearings with maximum accuracy.

- **Index line:** The mark on the front of the sight or compass baseplate where you will read the indicated bearing.

- **Line of travel or direction of travel:** A line or arrow engraved on the baseplate of your compass that points you in the direction you need to go to get to your desired destination.

✔ **Liquid damping:** Liquid damping allows the needle to come to rest rapidly and helps to hold the needle steady, allowing for faster and more accurate readings. Compasses that do not have liquid damping leave the user waiting for what seems a lifetime for the needle to stop spinning — and squinting to determine which point the bouncy needle is actually pointing to. The better compasses use a kerosene-based fluid or some other additive to ensure the liquid does not freeze or boil from minus 40 degrees F to plus 120 degrees F.

✔ **Mirror:** Incorporated into a hard-case lid that folds down over the top of the compass housing, the mirror is used to make prismatic in-line sightings, the most accurate method of using a handheld compass. A prismatic compass allows you to hold the compass at eye level, sighting both the distant object through the gun sight and the compass face at the same time.

✔ **Orienting arrow:** This is the outlined arrow engraved into the base of your compass housing and often lined with red paint. The arrow is made to exactly outline the outside of the magnetic needle. By centering or "boxing" the magnetic needle within the orienting arrow's outline, both pointing in the same direction (unless back-sighting), you are able to determine your bearing or direction of travel.

✔ **Protractor:** Some models have this feature that allows you to more easily plot a bearing on a map.

✔ **Sighting line:** This is the line you sight along on a handheld compass to take a bearing.

# Navigation Basics: Using Your Tools

By using the natural means of navigation I describe in this chapter, combined with your basic tools — the map and compass — you have the means to travel anywhere you want without fear of getting lost. That does not mean you will never be disoriented, but disoriented and lost is the difference between having confidence in your navigational abilities and feeling hopelessly over your head because you haven't practiced enough. Practice does make perfect. I will offer you a few basic tips that will get you into the navigational mood, but by no means should you consider this the complete word on navigation. To become really proficient, you need to read, study, and practice, practice, practice. I recommend joining an orienteering club — they are in almost every major city throughout North America. By going out on a regular basis with the club, you will find your skills becoming sharper and sharper, and before long, you'll never get lost either. Me? Lost? Never! Okay, I'll admit to my wife I've been mighty disoriented for a day or so, but I have *never* been lost.

# Finding yourself on the map

To find where you are on a map, you must first orient the map so that it represents a two-dimensional image that comes as close to exactly paralleling the three-dimensional world you are standing in as possible. You can do that with or without a compass.

### Orienting a map without a compass

The quickest way to orient a map is by using easily identifiable landmarks. If you can identify a nearby peak, for example, or a rock outcropping, lake, or point where two trails intersect, or a point that is unique enough to have a map symbol or designation, then placing yourself on the map is easy.

After you know your exact position on the map, just spin the map until other points of reference on the map line up with the same points of reference that you see on the surrounding landscape. Good navigators should keep their maps in constant orientation to the surrounding landscape as they travel.

### Orienting a map with a compass

No matter how good you are, eyeballing your map to the lay of the land is only roughly accurate. For complete accuracy you need to use your compass to correctly orient your map to the surroundings. Because the map is printed with the edges lined up with true north, and because the compass needle always points toward magnetic north, you have to account for declination to correctly align your map. Here's how:

1. **Correctly set your compass declination adjustment.**

2. **Place the edge of the compass baseplate along the printed edge of the map.**

3. **Carefully rotate the map until the red end of the magnetic needle is centered (boxed) in the orienting arrow.**

Your map is now oriented to magnetic north and the surrounding landscape.

### Establishing a bearing in the field

Imagine that you are hiking toward a distant landmark that you can see from where you are now but will soon disappear when you enter the woods or descend into a valley. How can you be sure you will stay on course? Figure 11-6 shows how you hold the compass as you follow these steps:

1. **Hold your compass level at waist height and point the direction-of-travel arrow at the landmark. If it's a prismatic compass, you need to hold it at eye level, sight through the gun sight, and view the housing in the mirror.**

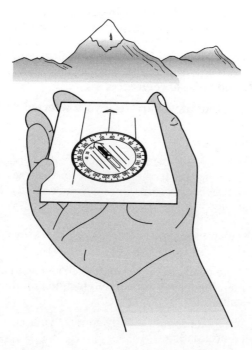

**Figure 11-6:**
Taking a
bearing in
the field.

2. Rotate the compass housing until the red end of the magnetic compass needle is centered (boxed) within the orienting arrow.

3. Read your bearing in degrees at the center *index point* — where the compass housing meets the direction-of-travel arrow on the compass baseplate.

4. To follow the bearing you get from Step 3, pick the first significant point of reference in line with the direction-of-travel arrow — a rock or a large tree, for example — one that you will not lose sight of until you reach it. Also, look over your shoulder and select a major landmark (say, a rocky outcrop) directly behind you — again, one you will not lose sight of.

5. Do not touch that compass dial! Walk directly toward the point of reference and don't worry that you can no longer see the original landmark you are hiking to because your compass reading has already been set at the index.

6. When you reach the reference point, hold the compass level once again, turn your body until the north end of the compass needle centers itself exactly inside the orienting arrow, and find another point of reference in line with the direction-of-travel arrow.

7. **Before you head out, take a back bearing by turning around with the compass still held level until the white end of the compass needle is now centered inside the orienting arrow. Do you see the rocky outcrop in line with the direction-of-travel arrow? If so, you're on course for the original landmark as planned. Turn around and head directly to your next selected point of reference.**

8. **Repeat the procedure until you arrive at your selected destination.**

### Taking a map bearing

You have your map out and you know where you want to go, but you can't see it — kind of like not being able to see the forest for the trees. No worries, gang! A couple of quick procedures with your map and compass and you're on course and on your way.

1. **First, orient your map using your compass, as I describe earlier in this chapter.**

2. **Place the edge of the compass baseplate like a ruler with the direction-of-travel arrow pointing from your current location on the map toward your intended destination.**

   The edge of the baseplate should exactly connect your current location and your intended destination.

3. **Being careful not to move either the map or the compass, rotate the compass housing until the north end (red end) of the compass needle centers itself exactly inside the orienting arrow.**

   The index point indicates your degree bearing.

4. **Without moving the compass housing, stand up holding the compass level at your waist and rotate your body until the north end of the compass needle centers itself exactly inside the orienting arrow.**

   The direction-of-travel arrow indicates your course.

To coach you along the way, follow the navigation directions in "Orienting a map with a compass," earlier in this chapter.

### I see it on the map, but . . .

You can see where you are on the map, that much is certain. You've even picked out an interesting-looking summit on the map, not too far from where you are now, and you want to explore it. But in scanning the terrain, you're having a hard time picking the summit out of the several others clustered nearby. What do you do?

1. **Follow the steps in "How do I take a map bearing?" earlier in this chapter.**

2. **After you have established a bearing and rotated your body, holding the compass at waist level until the magnetic needle is boxed or centered within the orienting arrow, you should be able to determine which summit is the one you want to explore.**

   The correct summit is the one that the direction-of-travel arrow is pointing toward. For a prismatic compass, you will hold the compass at eye level, sight through the gun sight, and view the housing in the mirror. The summit will be the one your gun sight is lined up on.

### I can see the landmark, but where is it on the map?

You can see that distant summit, and you know where you are on the map, but you have no idea which summit on the map is the one you are looking at in the field (Figure 11-7). Let "Navgod" help you (that's me).

1. **Orient your map.**

2. **Hold your compass level at waist height and point the direction-of-travel arrow at the mountain's summit.**

   For a prismatic compass, you hold the compass at eye level, sight through the gun sight, and view the housing in the mirror.

3. **Rotate the compass housing until the red end of the magnetic compass needle is centered (boxed) within the orienting arrow.**

   Your bearing may be read in degrees at the center index point — where the compass housing meets the direction-of-travel arrow on the compass baseplate.

4. **Taking care not to move the map, place one edge of the compass baseplate directly on your current location on the map.**

5. **Now, without moving the compass housing or moving the map in any way, pivot the compass around your known location point until the red end of the magnetic compass needle is centered (boxed) within the orienting arrow.**

**Figure 11-7:**
Finding on the map what you can see on the horizon.

6. **Draw a line, either in pencil or an imaginary one, along the edge of the baseplate toward the summits indicated on the map.**

   The summit you are looking at in the field is the one intersected by the line drawn from your location.

### Working your way around obstacles

What happens if you come to a natural obstacle you hadn't counted on, an obstacle that stands directly in your path and established compass bearing? No problem! (See Figure 11-8.)

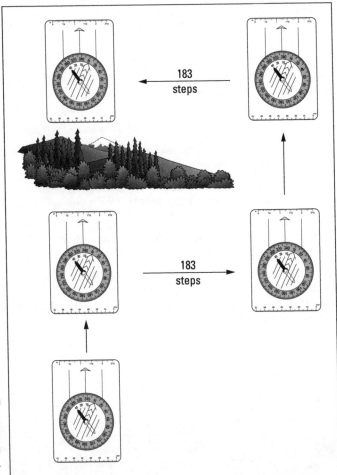

183 steps

183 steps

**Figure 11-8:**
Working around an obstacle.

1. Take as close to a 90-degree bearing (hard right or left turn) as possible and begin walking beside the obstacle, counting your steps.

2. After you reach a point where you can resume hiking in the direction of your original compass bearing, stop counting and remember how many steps you took.

3. Turn 90 degrees back so that you are walking on the same heading you were on when you encountered the obstacle, and walk until you are clear of the obstacle again.

4. Turn 90 degrees in the opposite direction you originally took in Step 1 and retrace your steps, counting until you walk the exact number of paces you noted in Step 2.

You are now back on your original course, this time on the other side of the obstacle you encountered.

## Trail markings, cairns, and blazes

How do you know if you are on the right trail or not? Trails are marked in many different ways throughout North America. Blazes — a blaze is a diamond, circle, or dotted "i" carved into a tree about 6 to 8 feet off the ground — are common. Painted blazes or metal plates nailed to a tree are also common. These identifiable trail markers are placed on both sides of the tree and at regular intervals so that you can spot the next blaze within a few feet of leaving the last one. Sometimes, finding the next blaze involves a little search-and-find mission. Don't panic and, above all, don't head out blindly along a route just because it "looks like a trail." Thousands of trails exist in the woods simply because animals use them and not because humans created them.

When the trail heads above the treeline or through open and treeless areas (deserts, vast plains, and so on) trails often are marked with "ducks" or *cairns* — piles of rocks. Sometimes, in challenging terrain where route-finding is a matter of life and death, cairns have been replaced by 5-foot-high wands with reflective tape or paint. Mount Washington in New Hampshire and Mount Katahdin in Maine are two such areas.

*Do not* add to trail markers that already exist — for example by flagging (very unsightly) or building new cairns. Just because you think the trail needs a marker doesn't mean you are right. For one thing, you could be off route, and adding a marking may only confuse those who follow. If you're tempted to add a trail marking, my advice is to improve your navigation skills first, and then, if you still feel the urge to build markings, join a volunteer trail crew that maintains the area.

# Using the Global Positioning System

Though it doesn't replace a map, a compass, and an observant nature, the Global Positioning System (GPS) is an amazing product of the space age and a useful tool to add to your standard navigation kit. With a GPS radio receiver, you can determine your exact location on the map simply by pressing a button. You can enter a location from your map as a "waypoint" in the GPS memory, and the GPS will help to guide you there. You can also store information in the GPS as you travel, and it will help to guide you back.

GPSs are not without serious limitations in the backcountry, though. High mountains, deep canyons, dense forests, and jungle canopy all obscure the satellite signals a GPS relies on, making the unit useless and leaving you lost unless your map and compass skills are up to the task.

Originally developed by the military, the GPS is a network of 24 satellites orbiting the earth and transmitting precise time and position information. A GPS receiver works by listening to the signals from three or more satellites and calculating the distances from the satellites to the user. Using some fancy math footwork, the handheld device (see Figure 11-9) displays numbers on a small screen that tell you where you are.

**Figure 11-9:**
A GPS
receiver.

Photo courtesy of GARMIN® International.

You must acquire three satellite signals for the GPS to accurately display longitude and latitude. You must acquire four satellite signals to add elevation to the mix. Keep in mind that the U.S. Department of Defense controls the signals broadcast to civilian receivers and intentionally distorts them (so that some hostile force won't use GPS to drop a bomb on your campfire). So while GPS is amazingly good at telling you where you are, it's not accurate down to the diameter of your campfire. The horizontal accuracy of a GPS reading will vary from 40 feet (15 meters) to 327 feet (100 meters). Altitude or vertical accuracy is even wider from the mark, varying between 327 feet (100 meters) and 510 feet (156 meters).

## A GPS is only as good as its owner is skilled

GPS receivers are electronic devices, and as such can break down or fail. What happens if you drop the GPS or the batteries die and you are in the middle of nowhere? Nothing will happen if you are skilled at navigating with a map and compass, save perhaps the need for a bit more concentration and effort. But I think that too many folks are heading outdoors these days enabled by the ease of navigating with a GPS. This thinking is a fool's paradise and the reason many more rescues are occurring.

## Essential features of GPS

Most GPS receivers will display information in either longitude/latitude, *Universal Transverse Mercator* (UTM, the grids that many Bureau of Land Management and other survey maps use), or military grid. Some, such as the Trimble, display actual map quadrant names and give inch measurements to aid in position location on the listed map. As a minimum, your GPS receiver should support both UTM and longitude/latitude grids, because with those two, you can use the GPS anywhere in the world.

"Route" and "GoTo" functions are essential. The Route function allows you to program a route of travel using numerous waypoints and automatically switches from waypoint to waypoint as you hike along your route — you don't have to touch a button. The GoTo function also will guide you, but it is a single application only, meaning that you have to enter the next waypoint into the system each time.

Steering is perhaps the most useful tool that your GPS offers if you are willing to hike with your GPS on all the time, because a GPS cannot calculate direction if you are standing still. While a compass simply points you in the direction you need to go, a GPS in GoTo or Route mode will not only direct you toward your next waypoint, but also tell you how far you have traveled, how far you have to go, if you have wandered off course and how to get back, and when you reach your destination.

Personally, I use my GPS to establish a bearing, which it easily does when in either the Route or GoTo function. By simply pressing a button, it displays my bearing and next waypoint. It's a simple matter for me to turn off my GPS (or place it in battery-save mode if I'm planning to use it again soon), whip out my compass, set the bearing, center (box) the orienting arrow, and hike off in the direction that my direction-of-travel arrow points.

## Putting your GPS to use

Before you use your GPS, you must set it to local time. Next, determine whether you want it to read in feet, meters, or miles for distance measurement and select the coordinate system you want to use, such as latitude/longitude, UTM, or another one if it's available. Finally, you need to initialize your GPS either by turning it on and letting it establish its own coordinate fix (this can take up to 15 minutes from a cold start) or by entering in the UTM or latitude/longitude coordinates for where you are standing, if you know them. After your GPS establishes your current coordinate fix, save it by giving this fix a name and number (For example: Trlhd 1). Now, plot your course by entering the coordinates along your route and giving each waypoint a name and a number (I prefer to number sequentially).

As you move along, your GPS gives you a current position fix every time you turn it on. From this position fix, you can use the GPS to determine a straight-line bearing toward and distance to your next waypoint or final destination. Here is where your compass and map skills come into play. (While the information your GPS is giving you is very valuable, it is almost useless until you apply it using your basic navigation tools.) After the GPS has given you a bearing, you need to use your compass to orient yourself to follow that bearing. True, you can use a GPS for this direction finding as long as you leave it on and are in GoTo mode, but it takes much longer. Also, while the GPS gives you a bearing to follow and also provides distance information in a straight line, it can tell you nothing about the lay of the land. It could be pointing you right at a cliff for all you know. A quick glance at your map with the bearing information in hand tells you all you need to know about how easy or difficult the terrain ahead is. Then, using your compass and map together, you can plot a safe and easy route to get you to where you need to be.

# Honing Your Survival Skills

Fear and panic are by far the greatest dangers to any human being in the outdoors. While it is true that natural acts and other unforeseeable circumstances claim injuries and lives each year, most deaths and injuries can be prevented by staying calm and thinking through the situation. Staying calm is not so easy to do, however, if you have only a limited knowledge or information source upon which to draw to help you in times of crisis. This is why it is so important to learn basic wilderness skills that will help you in the event of an emergency. Learn how to stay oriented, how to build a fire (see Chapter 7), how to look for shelter, where to find water, and other basic skills necessary to stay alive.

# The art of staying found

When Daniel Boone was asked if he was ever lost, his reply was, "Disoriented for a couple of days, maybe. Lost, never." The major difference between Mr. Boone and the majority of weekend wilderness explorers is one of skill. Mr. Boone could always hunt, trap, find water, build a shelter, make a boat, and gradually find his way out of most predicaments. The average family, however, has neither the acquired wilderness skills to survive off the land nor the time to spend wandering aimlessly.

It is important for you to realize that anyone can get lost. All it takes is a dense mist, a few unplanned turns in the woods, nightfall, or a storm to disorient most people outdoors. The so-called instinctive "sense of direction" is only as good as the information provided to create that sense. I have seen people who swore up and down that they had infallible senses of direction get utterly lost after I led them on a short, albeit circuitous, hike away from camp.

## Staying aware of your surroundings

A good sense of direction comes from keeping your senses wide open to all sources of information — sights, sounds, smells, and even feel. Teach yourself to be aware of significant landmarks such as a tall tree, a prominent rock, or a large meadow. Learn to look in 360-degree sweeps — look at the route you are traveling from front, side, and back. Quite often, a tree that looked so unique and significant in one direction looks completely different when viewed from another.

Sounds such as a river, cars on a road, and a foghorn on a lighthouse are also important bits of information. Don't overlook the smell and feel of an area. A valley may feel damp and smell a certain way. Water can quite often be smelled from a distance. Individually, each of the senses contains a fragment of information to help you stay found. Combine all the fragments into careful and complete observation, and you begin to create a "good sense of direction."

Many of us have heard it hundreds of times, but I am going to say it again: "Plan your hike and hike your plan." Good planning goes tremendously far in insuring a safe trip.

Teach your children about the area you are going into as well. Most children will find topographic maps confusing and impossible to understand. Try, instead, to draw a special map for your children. Show them where major landmarks, roads, and water sources are; how the trail looks; where you plan to camp; and where some of the nearby towns are.

## What to do if you become lost

I'm lost! That initial moment of panic surges through the human mind and body like a runaway train. If not controlled, the body soon follows the urge to act like a runaway train and very often takes off plowing through bushes, trees — anything — in a desperate effort to be found. This type of panic is all too common and can lead to complete exhaustion, dehydration, injury, and even death.

### Sit and think

It is imperative that you sit down and think quietly if you believe that you are lost. It is when people panic and begin to frantically attempt to find their way back to home or camp that they usually get into deeper trouble. If you learn to sit down and think carefully, a solution usually becomes evident. Learn to look around painstakingly, retracing your steps in your mind. Very often, after some calm thinking, you can discover the trail or route home.

### Explore methodically

Sometimes, however, the route home is not clearly evident, and you may feel a need to get up and explore the surrounding area in search of a trail. This is okay if you can accurately mark the area you are now standing in so that you can return to it after the initial search. From that original sit-down point, you can begin working your way outward in a circular pattern until you discover a familiar piece of ground or terrain. While working your way out in this circular fashion, always keep your original starting position in sight.

## Children and strangers: A word of caution

I feel somewhat strange mentioning molestation in the context of what to do if a child is lost, but it is an important consideration. In this day and age, children are molested and come to harm, often when they are perceived to be the most helpless. It is vitally important that you teach your children not to thankfully run into the arms of a waiting stranger who seems to be offering help. Give your children some idea of whom to trust and who should be treated with caution so they can make that decision for themselves should the need arise. I taught my daughter to trust a police officer or ranger and adults in groups. Individual men offering help are immediately suspect. It sickens me to have to teach her not to trust, but with the rate of abductions and molestations on the rise, I have no choice.

From each familiar point that you discover, establish another landmark that now identifies this area, and repeat the process. Essentially, you move from familiar point to familiar point and mark your progress along the way. After you discover a trail or road that is recognizable, you can then head out in a straight line toward home or help.

It is equally critical for your children to understand the importance of staying in one place if they have no idea where they are. Wandering children make for extremely difficult rescues.

# Seeking shelter

If you are really lost and have no idea in which direction home or camp lies, then finding shelter should be your priority. Although small caves, deadfalls, hollow logs, and eroded overhangs appear to be good shelters in warm and sunny weather, these natural shelters often are not ideal. At best, natural enclosures usually can provide only temporary refuge, and at worst, they can become death traps.

### Sheltering naturally

With any shelter you look for or build, your primary considerations should be wind protection, rain or snow protection, and heat retention.

#### Wind protection

Wind protection is extremely important since a strong wind coupled with rain can cause your body to lose heat rapidly — you can die of hypothermia, even at 50-degree air temperature. Wind also rapidly increases the rate of dehydration. Wind protection is the easiest to find, since almost anything — a fallen log, a dense bush, or a large rock — can protect you from the sides and break the wind.

#### Rain or snow protection

Rain or snow protection is more difficult to find since the shelter must provide protection from above as well as from the sides. Dense bushes, thick brush piles from logging road construction, downed trees, natural caves, and large rock piles are all candidates for a natural shelter that will protect you from wind and rain.

#### Heat retention

Most natural shelters can't provide the third important criterin for shelter selection — heat retention. If you study the way animals construct their burrows or nests, you will find that they hollow out an area in a tree or the ground and then line it or stuff it with leaves, grasses, twigs, and even fur. Thinking like a wild animal, then, you should gather dead leaves, twigs, and grasses to line and stuff the natural shelter you select to help you stay warm.

Natural shelters can be dangerous, and you must learn to identify the dangers. Deadfalls (fallen dead trees), rock piles, and caves are all potential homes to a variety of animals and insects. You must take care not to suddenly disturb a nest of bees, a poisonous snake, or a bear. Perhaps even more dangerous is the possibility that the natural shelter could collapse at any moment, trapping you inside or under something heavy. Be very cautious around deadfalls. Where one tree has fallen, more may be ready to tumble, given a strong enough wind.

Another possible hazard of a natural shelter is that it camouflages whatever is in it very well. When I was actively involved in search-and-rescue missions, I can vividly recall one particular rescue where we were looking for an older man who had been missing for several days. It had snowed heavily, covering up all previous signs and making it difficult for the dogs to find any scent. All we had to go on was instinct and educated guesses based upon the lay of the land and our deductions as to how this individual would have traveled.

We swept the area for several days, back and forth, covering every inch with what we thought was a fine-toothed comb. We found no sign of the man and were forced to give up. Later that month, after all the snow had melted away, a gentleman hiking in that area stumbled across the man's pack near a downed tree. Looking further, he found the man huddled inside the trunk with branches pulled in front of the opening to protect him from the snow. He had frozen to death, and we had walked back and forth in front of that tree on several occasions without realizing he was in there.

After that particular search, I now recommend that anyone using a natural shelter leave some sign outside the shelter that someone is there. The sign should be somewhat obvious and visible enough so that snow or debris falling on the ground will not obscure it.

### Building your shelter

Building a shelter is perhaps the best way to stay warm, dry, and secure, and a constructed shelter does stand out from the surrounding environment. While many survival books teach you to build lean-tos, A-frames, igloos, and even cabins, the quickest and most efficient shelter to create is one I was taught to build at camp when learning about Indian lore. It uses only available material lying on the forest floor and requires no tools to build. A child can construct this shelter in about one and a half hours.

1.  **Pick an area that has good drainage, is not going to get washed away, and will not get buried under a falling tree or avalanche of rocks.**

    It is also a good idea to make absolutely certain that the area you have selected is not over an animal hole, an ant's nest, or a thicket of poison oak, ivy, or sumac.

2. **At the shelter site, find a large rock, stump, log, or other support.**

   I was taught to use a log or downed tree as one wall, but downed trees with trunks large enough are not always present. Ideally, the log or rock support should be about three feet high.

3. **Find a large stick several inches across and approximately five feet long — or longer if the person using it is taller.**

4. **Lean one end of the stick on the rock, log, or stump so the other end rests on the ground, forming a ridgepole for your shelter.**

5. **Collect a large number of smaller sticks to lean along each side of the ridgepole, creating a frame for your shelter.**

   Remember to leave the opening or door to the front and one side, facing away from the wind.

6. **Crawl inside the shelter, making sure that there is enough room to lie down comfortably so that you do not kick or disturb the sides when moving about.**

7. **Pile twigs, dried leaves, and small branches on top of the framework you have built.**

   Make this a generous layer of leaves and twigs — approximately two to three feet thick is appropriate.

8. **On top of that layer, add a snug layer of small branches and twigs that is heavy enough to help hold the inner layer in place, even in a strong wind, but not so heavy that it crushes or compresses the leaves and twigs making up the inner lining.**

9. **Stuff the inside of the shelter full of dried leaves, pine needles, ferns, and so on, so the interior is loosely filled from top to bottom.**

10. **With the shelter now complete, squirm and snuggle feet-first inside.**

    This type of shelter will keep a person (adult or child) warm and dry for days, even in the worst conditions.

# Finding water

Finding water is second only to finding shelter in the scale of importance for survival situations. Dehydration is a killer. Remember that with a good shelter and a supply of water, a person can survive for a very long time, even with no food. That said, be wary of any water. Most water on the earth today is polluted to some degree. Chemically or biologically, these pollutants can turn a very basic survival situation into a critical emergency. For this reason, water must be treated or purified to be considered safe.

### Treating the water

There are several ways to treat water. The boiling method is the best guarantee of purification. If you have a pot or cup with you, build a fire and bring the water to a rolling boil to purify it. Boiling water destroys all biological pollutants.

Filtering in a survival situation doesn't remove most dangerous pollutants. In a survival situation most folks are not usually carrying a commercial filter with them. To filter very muddy or debris-filled water, pour the water through a bandanna or other piece of cotton clothing so that particles are filtered out.

Chemical purification works very well in removing biological but not chemical impurities. Products made of iodine such as Potable Aqua or Polar Pure are easy to use and very effective chemical treatments for water. If you camp with children, teach your child how to use these properly and safely. If your child carries a compact survival kit with him or her, include a bottle of Potable Aqua in it.

### Discovering water

You can find water or create it. The easiest way to get water is to discover a stream or moving water source. Moving water is the least likely to be polluted. Tree stumps, potholes, and stagnant ponds are other water sources, but these are typically the most likely to be dangerously polluted. Sometimes, digging down into a damp streambed uncovers a water source that will regularly fill the hole. You can even obtain water from dew-soaked leaves and grasses. Instead of crawling around licking the leaves, soak up moisture using a cotton cloth and then squeeze out the water into your mouth. As a last resort, you can opt to create water using the solar still method discussed in the next section.

### Making a solar still

Water distillation using a solar still is a method of creating water where there is none evident. This method requires a large piece of plastic, a cup, and a length of plastic tubing (see Figure 11-10). Knowing how to create a water distillation system is very useful, and the water is pure.

Follow these steps to set up a solar still:

1. **Find an area that is damp or located in a dry streambed or at the bottom of a gully and dig a hole about two feet deep and three feet across.**

    The earth you are digging in should be damp near the bottom. However, if the dirt is dry, drop in green leaves, urinate in it, or add a small amount of water to provide moisture for condensation.

2. **Place a cup in the center of the hole and rest one end of the plastic tubing in the bottom of the cup.**

3. Cover the hole with the clear plastic sheet, leaving the other end of the plastic tube protruding out to one side.

4. Seal the edges with dirt so that no moisture can escape and no air can get in.

5. Weight down the center of the plastic sheet with a rock so that the point of the inverted cone is directly above the cup.

The sun, even on a hazy or partly cloudy day, will warm the earth and cause moisture from the soil to evaporate and condense on the underside of the plastic. The condensation rolls down the plastic and drips off the weighted end into the cup. You will be able to drink out of the cup using the plastic tube sticking out of one side of the plastic sheet. This method works well, and the condensation or distilled water is pure, even if the moisture source is not (for example, if the moisture source is urine or badly polluted water).

**Figure 11-10:**
The water from a solar still is pure. (Drinking tube is not shown.)

# Chapter 12

# Weathering the Outdoors

*A*lthough you can't do much about the weather, by learning to read and understand changes in weather patterns and what those changes mean, you can experience the vast difference between blind reaction and reliable preparedness. Often, that difference alone may determine the margin of comfort and safety that separates disaster from adventure.

Keep a weather eye on the sky. The more you are aware and the more you learn about what causes weather, the more perceptive will be your observations and the more accurate your guesses as to the weather's outcome. But never forget — weather forecasts are only educated guesses, never statements of fact. Always be prepared for the worst.

In this chapter, I provide some basic tips for predicting changes in weather patterns and suggest some safety precautions for riding out the inevitable storms. If you'd like to learn more than I can cover in this short chapter, check out another book I wrote, *Basic Essentials Weather Forecasting* (published by the Globe Pequot Press), for a deeper look at meteorological concepts.

# Predicting Weather Changes by Reading Clouds

Cloud watching is more than simply picking out shapes that look like pirates or giraffes. By observing clouds and identifying them, you can gain a fairly good insight into what the next 12 to 24 hours of weather may bring.

# What is a cloud?

Clouds form whenever vapor from the earth condenses and is lifted skyward. In simple terms, a cloud is visible because the moisture has cooled below the dew point and condensed into particles that reflect light. The hotter and more humid the air that is rising, the more dense the clouds that form — think of thunderheads in the Midwest on hot, humid afternoons.

# Getting to know the basic cloud formations

These are the main types of cloud formations you need to concern yourself with when letting your eyes surf across the sky:

### Cirrus

Made up predominantly of ice crystals, cirrus clouds are arguably some of the most beautiful of the cloud formations, leaving milky white swirls and curls etched across the sky (see Figure 12-1). Cirrus clouds, with the exception of cirrostratus (thicker, sheet-like clouds which can mean snow or rain coming), indicate fair weather will hold for a while.

### Cumulus, cumulonimbus

Often referred to as *heap clouds*, cumulus formations are typified by heaped or fluffy formations (refer to Figure 12-1). Grayish, puffy clouds, they form in masses early in the day and are often precursors to an afternoon thunderstorm. As cumulus clouds stack vertically and begin to form a flat base with a towering center and an anvil-shaped upper, they form the classic thunderhead which can mean heavy precipitation, thunder, lightning, and hail.

### Stratus

Stratus means *layered*, essentially formless with no real defining base or top. Fog is a type of stratus cloud that lies close to the ground and is caused when the earth's surface cools. This cooling effectively lowers the air temperature, resulting in condensation.

- **Cirrostratus:** High-level (usually around 20,000 feet) veil-like cloud formations composed of ice crystals and often spreading out over a very large surface area. Halos are very often observed in cirrostratus clouds, indicating a lowering of the cloud ceiling and possible precipitation within 48 hours.

- **Altostratus:** Medium-level clouds (usually hovering around 8,000 feet) that are flat or striated, dark gray in color. A darkening of the cloud cover indicates possible precipitation within 48 hours.

✔ **Nimbostratus:** Low-level, dark and thick clouds, often without any real defining shape. Its ragged edges, known as scud, produce steady precipitation.

✔ **Lenticular clouds:** Well known in the Sierra Nevada, lenticular clouds, known formally as *altocumulus lenticularis*, are lens-shaped clouds that form at or around mountain peaks due to a cresting or wave in the airstream passing over the peak. As air is forced up the mountain ridge, it cools, condenses, and forms as a cloud near the peak. As the air passes over the peak and heads back down the ridge, it warms and moisture evaporates. Since condensation is occurring only at the peak, the cloud forms only at the peak, and even though winds are whipping through it, the cloud remains stationary.

**Figure 12-1:**
Clouds.

You can make some general predictions about the weather without even knowing a cirrus cloud from a stratus cloud.

If clouds are massing and generally increasing in size and density, the weather is possibly changing for the worse. Clouds moving more quickly across the sky indicate a change in wind velocity and also a change in pressure, indicating an approaching storm.

Since the various cloud formations take on different appearances and altitudes, it is possible, although sometimes difficult, to observe the movements of two or more different cloud formations across the sky. Cloud formations that are moving in separate directions and at different altitudes often announce an impending storm.

Finally, observe cloud movements and wind direction together. If both the cloud movement and wind direction are the same, any weather will come from the direction the wind is blowing.

# Geographic Weather Variations

Although the weather may be warm and sunny on the ridge above, it is entirely possible for temperatures to be downright cold in the valley below. How is this possible? The answer is microclimate influences. Differences in temperature and humidity in various microclimates are created by different degrees of solar warming, radiation, and evaporative cooling. Knowing what these are and how they work can make the difference between a chilly night huddled in your sleeping bag under a cold air-sink, or basking comfortably several hundred feet away under moonbeams. Of course, if the weather is foul, microclimatology is a moot point — foul weather is a constant with no microclimate sanctuaries.

## Adiabatic fluctuations in temperature

Here's a word to drop into your next weather conversation: *adiabatic*. Sounds like diabetic but it's not related. Adiabatic is the term explaining why air cools as it rises and warms when it falls. To get just a little more technical, air cools approximately 5.5°F for each 1,000 feet of elevation gain. It warms at about the same rate during elevation loss. As air meets a mountain and is forced over it, the air pressure falls, and the temperature also falls as the air expands. Once the air pours over the peak and begins to descend, air pressure and temperature both rise again.

Condensation throws a monkey wrench into the entire process, however. Just as adiabatic cooling lowers the temperature of air, any condensation that may occur warms it. The net effect on humid air being pushed up over a mountain peak is an average cooling of the temperature of 3.2°F per 1,000 feet. Once at the peak, the air begins to warm as it descends, and no further condensation occurs. Adiabatic warming of this air happens at the normal 5.5°F for each 1,000 feet of elevation loss.

# Mountains and valleys

Hike anywhere in any mountain range and you will note one constant feature: Wind blows up the mountain during the day (Figure 12-2) and down the mountain at night (Figure 12-3). Why? Two forces are at work, both caused by radiation as the earth's surface loses more heat than it absorbs during a clear night. As the ground gives off heat, the heat rises and the earth cools. The air close to the ground becomes colder more quickly and, because it is denser than warm air, begins to flow, rather like water, downhill — toward valley bottoms and desert floors. As the cool air rushes down the mountain (this is the breeze you feel), it displaces the warm air, forcing it upward and keeping a cycle of air going. As the warm air gets forced out, the cool air pools and collects in the lower reaches, creating places often referred to as cold sinks.

In broad valleys covered with dense meadow grasses, frost pockets may form, even though the temperature just 500 to 1,000 feet higher is a comfortable 50 degrees. The broader the valley and the more vertical the surrounding mountainous ridges, the more marked the temperature contrasts will be. The narrower the valley, the less dramatic the temperature differences between top and bottom will be, since the walls tend to radiate heat from one to another, trapping potential heat loss from the valley bottom.

As the early morning sun begins to warm the valley, the winds will reverse themselves and begin rushing up the mountain as the warm air begins to rise. Remember, however, that the air can only be warmed if the sun hits it, which explains why the side of the valley that is getting the sun first will experience upslope winds, while the side of the valley still in the shade experiences cool downslope winds.

Cloudy conditions or a presence of strong winds in the area will alter the topographical variations in the wind and temperature pattern. Cloudy conditions act as an insulator, reducing radiant heat loss and holding a thermal layer of air closer to the earth's surface. Windy conditions may overpower the gentle nature of upslope or downslope winds and also alter the potential temperature variances.

Winds that flow up and down a valley or canyon floor operate in a similar manner to winds that flow up and down a valley's walls. As temperatures fluctuate between higher elevations (mountains, ridges, or foothills) at one end of the canyon or valley and the lower elevations (desert, plains), winds also fluctuate in intensity and direction. Canoeists and rafters know this well, as many an afternoon wind blowing upstream from the heated elevations below has thwarted efforts to paddle into it successfully. It is important to note, however, that canyons and valleys channel wind, too, and it is entirely possible — probable in fact — that winds will roar up or down the canyon or valley no matter what time of day it is.

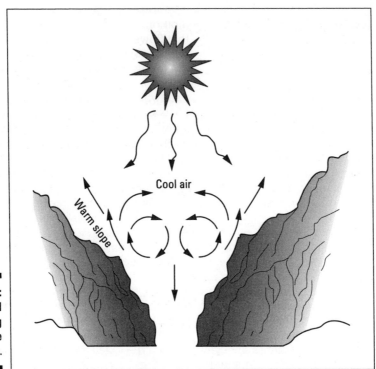

**Figure 12-2:**
Day wind
blowing
up the
mountain.

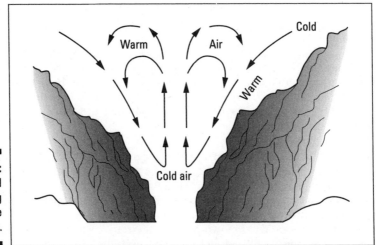

**Figure 12-3:**
Night wind
blowing
down the
mountain.

# *Snowfields, glaciers, and wintry environments*

In many mountain environments, the presence of year-round snowfields and glaciers creates localized wind conditions in the valleys directly below. These winds are caused by the cool air that flows off the glacier or snowfield, displacing the surrounding warmer air that hugs the valley floor. The winds are fairly gentle and warm and dissipate quite quickly.

Winds originating from glaciers or snowfields will occur as long as there is a sufficient temperature differential between the surface temperature of the snow and the surface temperature of the ground below the lip of the glacier or snowfield. The cold wind that emanates from ice caves underneath a glacier also has a significant effect on the growing season of plants. In the Cascade range near the Canadian border, there are several ice caves I have camped adjacent to where the growing season of the plants and flowers begins consistently several weeks after those of plants only several hundred feet away. This is because the colder air near the ice makes the plants think the growing season has not yet begun. This knowledge works well if you are trying to get a photograph of various flowering alpine plants, as I was, and miss the first bloom due to miserable photography weather, as I did.

## Estimating wind speed

Devised by Sir Francis Beaufort in 1805, the wind speed chart, now known as the Beaufort Scale of Wind Force, is an excellent and extremely accurate method of estimating wind velocity.

Wind speed in miles per hour

0-1 Smoke rises straight up, calm

1-3 Smoke drifts

4-7 Wind felt on face, leaves rustle

8-12 Leaves and twigs constantly rustle, wind extends small flag

13-18 Dust and small paper raised, small branches moved

19-24 Crested wavelets form on inland waters, small trees sway

25-31 Large branches move in trees

32-38 Large trees sway, must lean to walk

39-46 Twigs broken from trees, difficult to walk

47-54 Limbs break from trees, extremely difficult to walk

55-63 Tree limbs and branches break

64+ Widespread damage with trees uprooted

# Windchill index

The windchill equivalency index demonstrates the actual cooling effect on bare skin when exposed to air under the following temperature and wind conditions. Although understanding windchill has very little to do with being able to predict weather patterns, it is important to realize the impact wind and temperature have on the body so that the outdoorsman or -woman can make safe decisions about dress and travel. In the table, for example, if the temperature is 20° above zero and the wind is blowing 15 miles per hour, the windchill equivalent is 6° below zero.

| Temp: | +40 | +30 | +20 | +10 | 0 | −10 | −20 | −30 |
|---|---|---|---|---|---|---|---|---|
| Wind Mph : | | | | | | | | |
| 5 | 37 | 27 | 16 | 6 | −5 | −15 | −26 | −36 |
| 10 | 28 | 16 | 2 | −9 | −22 | −31 | −45 | −58 |
| 15 | 22 | 11 | −6 | −18 | −33 | −45 | −60 | −70 |
| 20 | 18 | 3 | −9 | −24 | −40 | −52 | −68 | −81 |
| 25 | 16 | 0 | −15 | −29 | −45 | −58 | −75 | −89 |
| 30 | 13 | −2 | −18 | −33 | −49 | −63 | −78 | −94 |
| 35 | 11 | −4 | −20 | −35 | −52 | −67 | −83 | −98 |
| 40 | 10 | −4 | −22 | −36 | −54 | −69 | −87 | −101 |

## Oceans and lakes

Anyone who has spent anytime at all hiking, boating, or camping near the shore of a large body of water, such as the ocean or any one of the Great Lakes, is probably familiar with the daytime onshore winds and the nighttime offshore breezes. As with snowfields and glaciers, temperature differences between the land and sea must be sufficient for winds to occur. Unlike snowfields and glaciers, clouds will reduce the temperature contrasts. Winds typically are most common when the days are sunny and warm and the nights are clear.

Generally, onshore breezes begin around mid-morning and continue until early to mid-afternoon. The wind is typically steady and can result in a dramatic drop of onshore temperature, sometimes as much as 10°–15°F. Evenings and early mornings are usually calm. The offshore breeze often begins shortly after dusk and continues until early morning.

## Deserts

Thermally created low-pressure systems often develop in desert areas. As superheated air rises skyward, it creates a void, a low-pressure area that must be filled. The resulting effect is strong horizontal winds that rush in as the pressure attempts to equalize, creating dust devils and sandstorms.

# Turning to Mother Nature for the Forecast

Mother Nature provides a lot of weather clues, some in the form of rhymes but all fairly simple and easy to remember. Here are some of my favorites — you may already know them:

## Morning or evening sky

"Red sky at night, sailor's delight. Red sky in morning, sailors take warning." This weather proverb means that if the clouds take on a reddish hue in the morning, you can expect rain by the end of the day. If the evening sky is red, the weather will probably remain clear the following day.

## Geese and seagulls

Geese and seagulls have a reputation for not flying before a storm. Biologists theorize that this is because they have a harder time getting airborne in low-pressure (thinner-air) conditions. Or maybe they're just a lot smarter than we give them credit for.

## Mosquitoes and black flies

Anyone who has camped beside a body of fresh water prior to a storm's arrival knows that mosquitoes and black flies will inevitably swarm and feast heavily up to 12 hours before the storm hits. You can bet the storm is almost upon you when the feasting frenzy subsides and the little buggers fly away to hide — about an hour before the weather turns.

# Frogs

Frogs of all shape and color have an uncanny tendency to increase their serenading several hours before a storm arrives. The reason they do this is not so much that they're reliable weather forecasters but that the increased humidity in the air from an incoming storm allows them to stay comfortably out of the water for longer periods — their skin must be kept moist at all times.

# Halo around the sun and moon

In the summer, the sight of a hazy halo or corona around the sun or moon is a good indication that a change in the present weather pattern is in the forecast — most often rain.

# Frost and dew

The presence of heavy frost or dew early in the morning or late in the evening is a fairly reliable indicator that up to 12 hours of continued good weather might be expected.

# Wind

"Wind from the south brings rain in its mouth." Low-pressure systems create cyclonic winds that rotate in a counterclockwise direction. Since low-pressure systems are frequently associated with rainstorms, the rhyme proves quite accurate. Counterclockwise wind rotations create wind that blows from the south — wind that brings in the rain.

High-pressure systems are often associated with clear or clearing weather, with clockwise rotating winds. Keep aware of wind directions and you will keep your finger on the weather's pulse: Is it beating fair or foul?

# Campfire smoke

By observing the smoke from your campfire, you can tell what pressure system is in the area, low or high. If the smoke from the fire hangs low to the ground and dissipates into the branches, that means a low-pressure system is present, and rain is possible. If the smoke rises in a straight, vertical column, high pressure rules, and you can anticipate fair weather (see Figure 12-4).

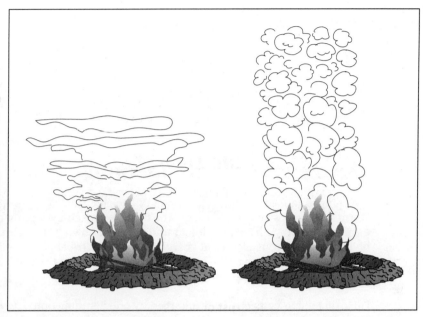

**Figure 12-4:**
Low-hanging campfire smoke indicates rain, but smoke rising in a vertical column indicates fair weather.

## Crickets

Believe it or not, you can estimate the air temperature in Fahrenheit degrees by counting the number of chirps a cricket emits over a 14-second period and adding 40 to the number. So, if a cricket chirps 25 times over 14 seconds, you add 25 to 40 and arrive at 65° F. Scientific studies have proven that crickets are correct within a degree or two over 75 percent of the time. Keep in mind, though, that air temperatures closer to the ground where the cricket resides will differ from the temperatures a few feet higher by as much as several degrees.

## Deer, big horn sheep, and elk

Animals such as these, which are common in mountainous areas, will commonly move down a mountain and into sheltered valleys as a storm approaches and will begin to move back up mountain as a storm gets pushed out. The trouble with this weather indicator is that by the time you see the animals moving, the storm is already bearing down.

# Surviving Weather Emergencies in the Great Outdoors

Lightning, flash floods, tornadoes, and avalanches — all are powerful, natural events that result directly or indirectly from weather phenomena. And all can be safely avoided in most cases by following a few precautions.

## Thunderstorms and lightning

Lightning is caused by the attraction of unlike electrical charges within a storm cloud or the earth's surface. The friction caused by rapidly moving air particles, churning from the violent updrafts and downdrafts of air, leads to a building up of strong electrical charges. As the electrical pressure builds, charges between parts of the cloud or from the cloud to the earth are released, taking the form of lightning.

Up to 30 million volts can be discharged by one lightning bolt, and it is this power or explosive heating of the air that causes the compressions of thunder.

Thunderstorms are a dangerous companion to have when traveling exposed on a mountain peak. If a thunderstorm approaches when you and your hiking party are on an exposed peak or ridge, take the following precautions:

- **Get off the ridge or peak if at all possible.** Even moving to a few feet below the highest point around you is better than not moving at all.

- **Get away from your pack.** The metal in the pack will conduct electricity.

- **Position yourself on a dry surface — preferably an insulated one such as a sleeping pad.** If the sleeping pad has become soaked in the rain, however, it will be useless and even dangerous since water conducts electricity.

- **Do not lie down or sit.** Instead, crouch with your feet close together. The idea is to minimize the available surface area through which possible ground currents from nearby lightning strikes may move.

- **Do not huddle next to a lone tree.** That is rather like hugging a lightning rod and expecting to be safe. Choose a cluster of trees instead and place yourself in the middle, preferably in an open area.

- **Spread out the people in your group so they're at least 25 to 30 feet apart.** If lightning does strike, the idea is to minimize the potential damage and injury. With the group spread out, chances are only one person will be injured if at all, and this leaves the rest of the party to provide lifesaving assistance once the storm moves on.

- ✔ **Avoid any depressions or caves.** Such areas usually have moisture in them, making them more susceptible to conducting electricity.

- ✔ **If you are caught on a lake in a thunderstorm, assume a crouching position toward the middle of the boat.** Try to minimize your contact with wet objects.

- ✔ **If you are at your campsite when a thunderstorm rolls through, the same general precautions apply.** Position yourself on a dry, insulated surface, such as a sleeping pad. Keep away from metals, like your backpack structure or tent poles. Presumably you've had the good sense not to pitch tent beside a lone tree in the wilderness.

# Tornadoes

Tornadoes are perhaps the most violent and intense of all known storms, with winds in excess of 300 miles per hour recorded in the vortex. Man-made structures seem to literally explode as the extremely low pressure within the vortex of a tornado causes the normal pressure trapped within structures to expand rapidly, ripping buildings to shreds from the inside out.

Violent updrafts recorded between 100 to 200 miles per hour within the center of the funnel cloud have been known to suck anything within the tornado's path hundreds of feet in the air before hurling the objects some distance away. Over bodies of water, funnel clouds lift water into the air creating what is known as a *waterspout*.

Most injuries and deaths that are tornado-related are caused by debris flying through the air and objects falling over. If a tornado approaches, take the following precautions:

- ✔ **If you're outside:** Curl up in a tight ball in a drainage ditch, a culvert, or any other depression that will protect you, and cover your head.

- ✔ **If you're driving:** Get out of your car and seek shelter under a highway overpass if possible. Do not attempt to wait out the passing tornado inside your car.

- ✔ **If you're indoors:** Leave the windows closed and seek shelter in a basement, if you have one, or in a room located in the center of the home with no windows or the fewest number of windows possible. Curl up against a wall and cover your head.

- ✔ **If you're in a mobile home, RV, barn, or small building that you know is not firmly anchored to the ground:** Get out. The tornado will toss it about like a house of straw, and you are in more danger inside than you are outside.

## How far away is that thunderstorm?

It is possible to roughly judge the distance of an approaching storm by observing the lightning's flash followed by the resounding boom of thunder. For this method, count slowly, "one-one thousand, two-one thousand, three-one thousand" and so forth. This will approximate one second elapsed for each thousand counted.

After the lightning has flashed, begin to count. When you hear the thunder, stop counting. Every five seconds of elapsed time indicates one mile of distance. In other words, if the count reaches "seven-one thousand," it is safe to assume that the approaching thunderstorm is approximately one and a half miles away.

# Chapter 13

# Health and Safety Are No Accident

*In This Chapter*

▶ Staying cautious, staying safe

▶ Saving the day with first aid

Chances are, you'll never have to use your first-aid kit or knowledge for anything more than patching up a few minor scrapes, bumps, blisters, and bruises. Of course, this assumes you also are wise enough to pack your kit with the necessary items to meet the needs of more serious emergencies, and to have the requisite first-aid skills to match. First aid is not magic or a performance of miracles. It is simply the act of using your head and common sense. In this chapter, I provide you with the basic resources and accompanying tips to prepare you to meet and, hopefully, prevent any simple emergency.

## Avoiding Nature's Nemeses

The very best first aid of all is the act of prevention. Everyone, especially children, should be cautious around fire, sharp objects, and camp hazards such as tent lines. But not all dangers are so obvious. In this section, I list some of the more subtle hazards that any outdoor traveler should be aware of.

## Finding your footing among rocks, rubble, brush piles, and fallen logs

All of the above are potential injury traps. Loose rocks, rubble, brush piles, and logs can all give way, causing slips and falls that lead to bruises, open wounds, sprained ankles, and broken bones. Rocks can slide, creating a much more dangerous situation. Logs or rocks supporting larger logs and rocks also can shift and give way, trapping unfortunate victims. Children and adults — including me — love to climb on fallen logs, but being cautious is important. Loose bark, moss, and debris can all lead to a nasty fall.

## Watch out for that tree!

Climbing trees is great fun, but you must exercise care. Learn to look for weak or dead branches that may break under your weight. Moss growing on tree branches can cause an untimely slip. Never break branches or try to pull branches out of trees for firewood — unless in an emergency. Pulling branches out of a tree is not an environmentally sound practice. It can pull down the tree itself or cause an avalanche of broken branches.

I know everyone has heard the phrase "Put that down or you'll put some-one's eye out!" Protecting your face when traveling through dense under-brush, walking at a safe distance behind the person ahead, and making sure that branches don't snap back in the face of someone following behind you can help prevent eye injuries.

## Exercising caution around water, mud, wet sand, and riverbanks

Water attracts campers like ants to a picnic. You should instruct children, especially, not to go near water except in slow-moving and very shallow areas. Children should never enter the water without adult supervision. Even in these seemingly safe areas, potential hazards exist for both adults and chil-dren. Mud and wet sand on a riverbank or lake edge are sometimes quite deep. Sprinting to the water without first checking the stability of the mud or sand can result in a child becoming stuck, making rescue very difficult.

Riverbanks are notorious for giving way without notice. Never overlook the potential dangers of sitting or standing on the edge of high riverbanks that may be undercut by the water flow. Anytime the water is moving swiftly, the riverbanks should be suspect. If a riverbank gives way and pitches you or your children into rapids or cold, deep water, hypothermia or even drowning may result. (See "Cold-related illnesses and injuries," later in this chapter, for hypothermia treatment guidelines.)

## Avoiding the big chill: Staying alert around snow and ice

Staying alert is important in snowy or icy conditions. Snow-covered trees, rocky ledges, and ice overhangs can all give way without notice, burying whatever or whomever is underneath. Snow at the top of ravines or on ridges can slide or avalanche. Snow also melts into clothing, causing chilling and putting you at risk for hypothermia (see "Cold-related illnesses and injuries,"

later in this chapter, for treatment advice). Ice is deceptive. Stay away from ice-covered lakes, rivers, riverbanks, and ponds. There really is no safe way to determine the absolute strength of the ice, and a fall into the icy water can be deadly.

## Pointing out poisonous plants

Most campers, especially those with children, worry about running into poison oak, poison ivy, or poison sumac. Not all of these plants grow in every area of the United States, so check with your local park service before heading out. (Typically, poison ivy and sumac grow in the Midwest and East, and poison oak grows only in the West.) Everyone should know how to identify the plants' leaflet clusters and colors so they can avoid nasty skin reactions. See Figure 13-1.

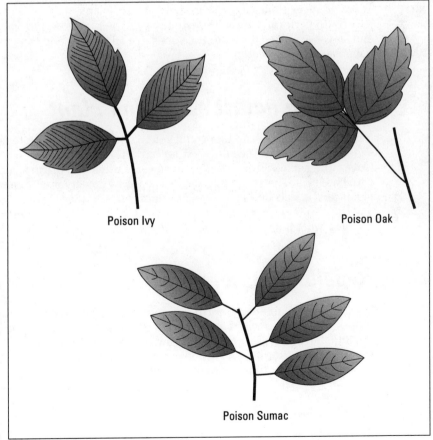

Poison Ivy

Poison Oak

Poison Sumac

**Figure 13-1:** Learn to identify — and strive to avoid — poison oak, poison ivy, and poison sumac.

Poison oak and ivy both go by the rule "leaflets three, let them be." The main difference between the two is that poison oak is a tree or a shrub and poison ivy is a vine. Also, poison oak leaves are lobed, while poison ivy leaves are somewhat jagged. Poison sumac is a shrub that grows mostly in swampy areas and has smooth leaves growing opposite one another in a single line along each stem. All three plants secrete a noxious oil that severely irritates the skin and can be transmitted by direct contact, contact with contaminated clothing or pets, or breathing the smoke. (See "Poison ivy, oak, and sumac," later in this chapter, for rash treatment suggestions.)

If you suspect you are going to be in an area where either poison oak, ivy, or sumac are present, I recommend wearing long pants and long-sleeved shirts as a barrier of protection. Be sure you do not touch your eyes or mouth with your hands until you wash your hands thoroughly. Always wash your clothing in hot water and soap immediately upon returning home. Simply tossing the clothes into the hamper can contaminate other clothes with the urushiol — the oily secretion from the plant that causes the skin irritation.

Teach younger children to ask for help identifying plants — otherwise, they may try to perform dangerous taste tests on their own. Berries, mushrooms, and leaves are all tempting to the young eye and palate and can invite potential poisoning accidents.

## Avoiding nature's stinging plant

Nettles will sneak up and bite you if you're not careful — not bite in the literal sense, but you'll feel the sting. Nettles have thousands of hairs on their leaves that act like little hypodermic needles when you brush against them with bare skin. The stinging feeling is caused by a nasty brew of natural chemicals. It feels like a bee sting, no more serious. (See "Scrapes, scratches, and open wounds," later in this chapter, for advice.) To avoid nettles, do the obvious: wear long pants and long sleeves.

## Repelling insects

Insects have inhabited the earth for more than 350 million years and, frankly, it does sometimes seem that mankind's only reason for being here is to give the little buggers a meal. Since the dawn of civilization we've been trying to repel the biting hordes every time we head outdoors. Just watch us flail our hands and arms as they buzz around with disdain!

## Animal fears and children

Although educating yourself and those in your family or traveling group about the risks of poisonous animals, insects, and other potential animal hazards is important, don't add terror and fear to the mix. To say that bears are dangerous and then leave it at that is not in the best interests of you, your child, or the bear. Teach caution and respect, not fear. Children should learn all that the outdoors has to offer — or at least as much as you are able to share. You may find yourself having to "de-Hollywood" their images of animals. Read books together at home and go to museums and zoos — anything to present the most complete picture possible.

The more that you and your child know about animals, the more you will all be able to appreciate the outdoors, the animals that live there, and the behaviors necessary to safely coexist in that environment. If you and your children are aware and alert, then you will rarely encounter a situation where you are bothered by a "dangerous" animal.

Mosquitoes, fleas, ticks, and black flies all have bites that can cause painful irritations at best and debilitating or fatal diseases at worst. Repellents, when used properly, can prevent bites and thus help you and your family avoid the serious health risks associated with disease transmission by infected insects. (If you do get bit, see "Insect bites and stings," later in this chapter, for treatment suggestions.)

Besides dressing in light-colored clothing that protects as much of your skin as possible, applying an insect repellent can reduce your chances of getting bit. Deciding which repellent is best and safest for your needs depends on your recreation plans and traveling situation. In the following sections, I provide answers to some common questions about repellents so that you can choose the best product for your situation.

### What is DEET?

You're not likely to find the words DEET on any repellent label. That's because DEET stands for "N,N diethyl-m-toluamide." If the label contains this scientific name, the repellent contains DEET. Despite fears of DEET-associated health risks and the increased attention given natural alternatives, DEET-based repellents are still acknowledged as by far the best alternative when serious insect protection is required.

### What health risks are associated with using DEET?

In recent years, the press has attributed a number of medical problems and even deaths to DEET — events that those manufacturers who produce DEET-based repellents vehemently deny as being specifically DEET-related, pointing to reams of scientific documentation as evidence. It does seem logical to assume that if DEET can peel paint, melt nylon, destroy plastic, wreck wood finishes, and damage fishing line, then it must be hell on the skin — or perhaps worse.

Although nothing definitive has been published, a growing number of people in the scientific community believe that repeated applications of products containing low-percentage levels of DEET can be potentially dangerous. They theorize that repeated applications actually put consumers at a greater risk for absorbing high levels of DEET into the body than if they had just used one application of a 30- to 50-percent DEET product with an efficacy (effective repelling time) of four to six hours. Also being studied is the possibility that low levels of DEET, which may not otherwise be of toxicological concern, may become hazardous if they are formulated with diluents (considered inactive ingredients), which may enhance the absorption rate.

### Are natural alternatives a safer choice?

To imply that essential oils are completely safe because they are a "natural" product is not altogether accurate. Although essential oils are derived from plants that grow naturally, they are chemicals, too. Some are potentially hazardous if ingested, and most are downright painful if they find their way into your eyes (common with children's wandering fingers) or onto mucus membranes. For example, pennyroyal is perhaps the most toxic of the essential oils used to repel insects, and it can be deadly if taken internally. Other essential oils used include citronella (perhaps the most common, it's extracted from an aromatic grass indigenous to Southern Asia), eucalyptus, cedarwood, and peppermint.

### How effective are natural repellents against ticks?

According to the EPA, natural repellent manufacturers aren't supposed to advertise that their products repel ticks because data regarding their effectiveness against ticks is inconclusive.

### How effective are natural repellents against mosquitoes and biting flies?

Although data differs from study to study, the average efficacy (effective repelling time) of a citronella product appears to range from one and a half to two hours. Tests conducted at England's Cambridge University in 1993 comparing Natrapel to DEET-based Skintastic (a low-percentage DEET product) found citronella to be just as effective in repelling mosquitoes.

Citronella products work for up to two hours and then require reapplication (the same holds true for other natural formulations). Products using a low-percentage level of DEET also require reapplication every two hours to remain effective. So if you or your child are going outside for only a short period in an environment where insect bites are more an irritant than a hazard, you would do just as well to "go natural."

### What other chemical alternatives are there?

Another line of defense against insects is the chemical *permethrin*. What makes permethrin so good is that the chemical is applied directly to the outer fibers of gear or apparel, dramatically minimizing the risks to humans. Permethrin chemically binds to the fibers, minimizing inward migration and reducing the risk of skin contact. Permethrin-based products are designed to repel and kill crawling insects, making them preferred tick repellents.

### Can DEET-based or natural products also be applied to fabrics?

Although you can use DEET on apparel items, the chemical's application should be limited to natural fibers. DEET will quickly melt synthetic fibers, and it's most embarrassing to watch your pants melt right off your body. As far as long-term application, naturals do not lend themselves well to either skin or fabrics. An herbal alternative is being tested as a fabric treatment, so there may in fact be a place for natural repellents being used for this application in the near future.

### What do the experts recommend to prevent tick bites when adventuring in tick country?

Wear long pants tucked into your socks as well as long-sleeved shirts tucked securely into your pants and cinched with a belt. Wear light-colored clothing to make spotting ticks easier, and choose tightly woven fabrics so that ticks have trouble hanging on.

You must perform tick checks regularly, especially in those dark, moist areas and crevices around the waistline, knees, breasts, armpits, ears, and crotch. (Can't tell a tick from a housefly? Check out Figure 13-2.) Use a buddy system — this is not a good time to be modest. Applying DEET insect repellents to the skin and permethrin repellents to clothing, tents, sleeping bags, and any surface other than your skin are considered to be the most effective lines of defense against ticks.

**Figure 13-2:**
A close-up of a tick. In real life, a tick is about the size of a pinhead.

### Are there child-safe insect repellents?

It is generally acknowledged that children should not use insect repellents with a high percentage of DEET — in fact, the lower the better — with 10 percent being the recommended dosage. Most companies offer lower-percentage DEET-based products. Pump sprays or lotions are often the easiest means of application. Many consider DEET-based products using synergists — a bonding chemical that prevents skin absorption — or other methods in addition to reduced-percentage concentrations to be the safest alternatives. Although not as effective as DEET in repelling insects, natural- or synthetic-based insect repellents offer alternatives to parents seeking potentially less chemically toxic bite protection.

### Do repellents work against bees, wasps, and other stinging insects?

No. However, you can avoid attracting undue attention by following a few simple guidelines. Dress in light-colored clothing. Studies have shown that black, red, and blue are more attractive since bees and their other stinging cousins see in ultraviolet. Do not wear perfume or cologne — the sweet smell seems to attract insects of all kinds. When planning a picnic, keep in mind that serving fruit, red meat, sodas, or food packed in heavy syrup is like ringing the dinner bell for hornets, yellow jackets, bees, and wasps. Should a stinging insect make frequent flybys through your personal space, resist the urge to wave wildly and swat blindly. Instead, use — and encourage your children to use — a gentle pushing or brushing motion to deter the intrusion. Wasps, bees, hornets, and yellow jackets don't react kindly to quick movements. Check out "Insect bites and stings," later in this chapter, for sting treatments.

## Purifying water

Water trickled crystal clear from the mountain pool. I was parched, and I'd left my water filter at home to save weight. Worse, I hadn't packed any iodine tablets, either. I contemplated the apparent purity of the water and elected to slake my thirst. The water flowed coolly and tastefully down my throat, and I smiled.

I wasn't smiling two days later when cramps and other nasty bodily functions doubled me over.

I learned the hard way. Just because your backcountry water appears pure doesn't make it safe. Teensy vermin like *giardia* and *cryptosporidium* can cause nausea, diarrhea, vomiting, or worse, and you'll never see 'em coming. A water filter is a must-have for outdoor travel.

## *Choosing a water filter*

These days, there's really no excuse for going without a filter: Handheld filters are getting more compact, lighter, and easier to use (see Chapter 2). You can find filters ranging in price from $25 up to $300. Unless your needs are very basic indeed, I've found that filters in the $50-and-up range offer more versatility and far more durability and function than their cheaper counterparts.

A filter's purpose is to strain out microscopic contaminants, rendering water clear and somewhat pure, depending on the size of the filter's pores — what manufacturers call *pore-size efficiency*. A filter with a rating of one micron or smaller will remove protozoa like *giardia* and *cryptosporidium*, as well as parasitic eggs and larvae, but it takes a pore-size efficiency of less than 0.4 microns to remove bacteria. (A micron is one thousandth of a millimeter — you can't see it with the naked eye.)

A good backcountry water filter weighs less than 20 ounces and is easy to grasp, simple to use, and a snap to clean and maintain. At the very least, buy one that removes protozoa and bacteria. (A number of cheap, pocket-sized filters remove only *giardia* and *cryptosporidium*. In my book, buying one of these is risking your health to save money.) Consider the filter's flow rate, too: A liter per minute won't leave you dying for a drink.

If you travel in Third World countries, or if any water you encounter may be contaminated by sewage, viruses are a concern. Only one filter that I know of, the First Need filter by General Ecology, claims to meet EPA virus-removal standards by filtration alone, thanks to a fancy matrix system — a convoluted maze of passages that trap little nasties inside.

The other filters require chemical assistance, either by incorporating iodine into the filter or using iodine tablets like Potable Aqua. Iodine tastes awful and can be a health risk to some people, so many filters employing it also have a carbon element that removes the iodine when its job is done. Carbon also gets rid of pesticides, herbicides, heavy metals, and chlorine, but there are a couple of carbon-use caveats: A few recent studies have shown that in certain situations, it's best to leave a little iodine in the water. If you think that your water source is contaminated with sewage, remove the carbon filter. I've found that orange juice crystals (ascorbic acid) can help offset the iodine's nasty taste since ascorbic acid oxidizes or neutralizes the iodine. If you follow my lead, remember to wait 30 minutes after filtering the water before stirring in the crystals. Thirty minutes should be enough contact time for the iodine to kill even the most sturdy of microorganisms.

Folks suffering from thyroid disease, immunodeficiencies, and iodine allergy should not use iodine. Pregnant women should not use iodine for longer than one week.

All filters will eventually clog — it's a sign that they've been doing their job. If you force water through a filter that's becoming difficult to pump, you risk injecting a load of microbial nasties into your water bottle. Some models can be brushed or scrubbed to extend their useful lives. And if the filter has a prefilter to screen out the big stuff, use it: It will give your filter a boost in mileage, which can then top out at about 100 gallons per disposable element. Because a filter's carbon element can reach its limit for absorbing a particular chemical and then let bad stuff through, always replace the filter and the carbon element according to the manufacturer's recommended schedule.

Because each filter has its own idiosyncrasies and care needs, be sure to read a manufacturer's use instructions carefully.

### Exploring filterless options

If you don't feel like carrying the weight or bulk of a filter, you can opt for chemical treatments such as iodine, or you can boil the water. Boiling is virtually foolproof; however, it does take a fair amount of time and a considerable amount of fuel. Additionally, I have yet to meet an adult or child who enjoys drinking hot water on a hot day. Iodine has worked well for me, and I have been very happy with Polar Pure (an iodine crystal-based system) and Potable Aqua (a tablet).

Because Potable Aqua is a tablet system, it is quite easy for children to understand and use if necessary, although it does have a very limited shelf life once the bottle is open. Polar Pure has a much longer shelf life and is more versatile, but may be more complicated to use.

# Coming to the Rescue with First Aid

The information provided in this chapter about first-aid materials and procedures is not a substitute for professional medical assistance and advice. Whenever possible, seek medical help in an emergency. Consult your doctor or local library and become trained and certified in first aid before assembling a first-aid kit and heading outdoors. *Remember:* A first-aid kit doesn't help anyone if it is in the hands of an untrained person — in fact, more harm can be caused than good! Inappropriate administration of drugs or failure to recognize immediate care requirements causes needless injuries — and even deaths — every year. Everyone in your family should become trained in first aid and CPR. The Red Cross, the American Heart Association, and private organizations and hospitals offer excellent training programs. Frequently, organizations like the Sierra Club and other outdoor-oriented outfits offer wilderness first-aid courses. Become trained — become safe!

## Children and first aid

Before heading out on any outing with your children, make sure that they are familiar with some simple first-aid skills. Should something happen to one or more of the adults that they are with, the children need to feel confident in their skills and abilities, no matter how basic they may be. Children should never have to feel helpless. In the house, the backyard, or a nearby park, run through various emergency scenarios and practice first-aid skills that will be useful to your children. The more your children know, the more independently and confidently they will look at emergency or stressful situations. More importantly, they will learn how to prevent injury in the first place.

Having said all that, let me put your mind at ease. In my years of teaching wilderness first aid and guiding trips, I have witnessed some of the finest first aid performed by relatively untrained individuals. These people did not reach into a drug bag and begin administering medicine, nor did they do anything tricky or fancy. Instead, they remained calm and at ease, provided comfort, and tended to the needs of the injured parties as best as they could. That is the essence of first aid — do good if you can, but do no harm.

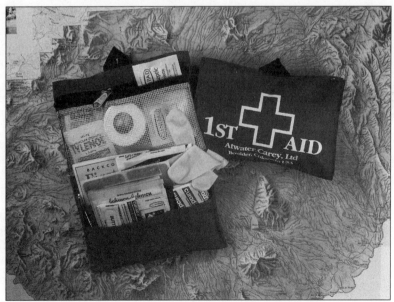

**Figure 13-3:**
First-aid kit.

*Backpacker first-aid kit by Atwater Carey*

## Packing a first-aid kit

Loading your first-aid kit with appropriate supplies takes careful planning. You should consider the duration of your trip, the length of time it will take you to reach qualified medical care if required, the amount of weight the kit will add to your load, and the amount of space you have available in your pack, duffel, boat, bike, and so on. I compile a comprehensive list of items to consider placing in a first-aid kit, but by no means am I suggesting you carry all of the items all of the time. Let common sense, as always, be your guide. And you may wish to purchase a ready-assembled kit — Figure 13-3 shows one brand.

### Medications

Stock your first-aid kit with the following medications:

#### Pain relief drugs

Do not administer any of the following drugs to a child without the express guidance and direction of a medical doctor!

- **Aspirin:** A mild analgesic, anti-inflammatory, and fever reducer. (Bayer is a popular brand.) Aspirin interferes with blood clotting and can cause nausea. Don't give it to children.

- **Ibuprofen:** An anti-inflammatory and moderate pain reliever. Motrin may cause stomach irritation and nausea. Brand names include Motrin and Advil.

- **Acetaminophen**: A pain reliever and fever reducer. Acetaminophen overdose may cause liver damage. *Note:* This drug is the primary pain reliever in many first-aid kits. Tylenol is a popular brand.

- **Tylenol with codeine (narcotic, prescription only):** A pain reliever and fever reducer. Codeine sometimes causes nausea, constipation, and allergic reaction.

- **Lidocaine gel 2 percent (prescription only):** A topical pain reliever and local anesthetic.

#### Allergic reaction drugs

- **Diphenhydramine:** An antihistamine, sedative, and anti-itch treatment. (Benadryl is a popular brand.) Use with caution — this drug may cause drowsiness, constipation, weakness, headache, difficulty in urination, and diarrhea.

- **Anaphylaxis kit (prescription only):** An injection of epinephrine and Chlo-Amine tablets to relieve severe allergic reaction. These drugs may cause headache, anxiety, and heart palpitations. Brand names include Epi-Pen and Ana-Kit.

✔ **Caladryl lotion:** A calamine and Benadryl (diphenhydramine) lotion that relieves minor skin irritations.

✔ **Hydrocortisone ointment 25 percent (prescription only):** A steroid ointment for more severe skin reactions.

### Gastrointestinal drugs

✔ **Diphenoxylate HCl Atropine Sulfate:** An anti-diarrheal. Use this drug only if the diarrhea compromises your safety or ability to travel, because bowel retention can introduce serious infection and start a fever. Common brand name is Lomotil.

✔ **Mylanta or Tums:** Stomach acid neutralizer and indigestion reliever. This drug can produce mild diarrhea.

### Antibiotics

Unless you know what infections you're treating, antibiotics are worthless. Broad-spectrum antibiotics are best, but you should always be aware of what specific type of infections you'll most likely encounter. Consult your physician for guidance.

✔ **Septra DS (prescription only):** Antibiotic for treating urinary tract infections and diarrhea illness. This drug may cause an allergic reaction.

✔ **Keflex (prescription only):** Antibiotic for treating skin, respiratory tract, urinary tract, and inner ear infections. This drug may cause allergic reactions.

✔ **Neosporin ointment:** Antibiotic to help prevent infection in minor cuts and abrasions.

### Other drugs to consider

✔ **Cough suppressant:** Robitussin with codeine.

✔ **Decongestant:** Afrin Nasal Spray (not recommended for prolonged periods or for use at high altitudes); Sudafed; Actifed.

✔ **Antibiotic eye drops:** Neosporin Ophthalmic Drops.

✔ **Vitamin A and D ointment:** To soothe rashes and dry skin.

### Skin preparations

✔ **Betadine:** Cleanses skin around a wound; also cleans blisters before lancing. If cleaning a wound, use one part Betadine to three parts sterile water.

Never use Betadine in a deep wound since it contains iodine, which will kill tissue.

✔ **Tincture of benzoin:** Prepares skin for application of an adhesive.

✔ **Aloe vera:** A 100-percent gel containing aloe used to soothe pain from burns or superficial frostbite.

✔ **Hydrocortisone cream:** A cream ointment used to soothe inflammation from insect bites, poison ivy, poison oak, poison sumac, and other skin rashes. Common brand names are Cortaid, Lanacort, and Cortizone.

✔ **Antibacterial soap:** Cleanses minor scrapes and scratches and sanitizes hands in preparation for first-aid administration.

### Bandages, dressings, and other items

✔ **Sterile gauze pads:** Keep a variety on hand, including 2-x-2-inch and 4-x-4-inch sizes.

✔ **Rolled gauze:** I recommend Kling and Kerlex brands in 2-inch to 4-inch widths.

✔ **Non-adhering dressing:** I prefer Telfa Pads. (Xeroform, which is coated with antibacterial ointment and petroleum, works well, but you have to change the dressing frequently so that it doesn't dry out and adhere to the skin.)

✔ **One-inch-wide adhesive tape.**

✔ **Butterfly bandages** or Steri-strips assortment in ¼ inch to 4-inch lengths. These are used to close wounds that would otherwise require stitches.

✔ **Three-inch-wide elastic wrap:** Ace is one common brand name.

✔ **Large compress:** Sanitary napkins work well and are the most cost-effective means of supplying your first aid kit with compresses. Guys, if you're feeling squeamish, *get over it!*

✔ **Assortment of cloth and plastic adhesive bandages:** Band-Aid is the most popular brand. I recommend carrying some bandages with cartoon characters or other juvenile designs — children seem to love them, and some adults do, too.

✔ **Moleskin:** Prevents and treats friction and blisters. It is adhesive on one side and fuzzy on the other.

✔ **Molefoam:** Prevents and treats friction and blisters. It is thicker than moleskin and can be used to fashion "donuts" and other shapes to alleviate pressure spots.

✔ **Spenco Second Skin:** This is a gel-like substance that comes in sheets that can be cut to size and provides soothing protection against blisters, although I have known it to stick to the wound and create a painful and difficult removal.

✔ **Triangular bandage:** Holds dressings in place, attaches splints, and creates slings.

*Equipment and accessories*

✔ **Tweezers.**

✔ **Vinyl gloves:** Latex gloves can degrade quickly in a first-aid kit. Vinyl gloves protect the first-aid provider from possibly becoming infected with HIV and prevent another disease from coming into contact with the blood or body fluids of an accident victim.

✔ **CPR Microshield or Pocket Mask:** Two brand names for CPR mouth-to-mask barrier devices that offer protection between a victim and a first-aid provider during rescue breathing situations.

✔ **Needle.**

✔ **Single-sided razor blade.**

✔ **Bandage scissors.**

✔ **Irrigation syringe.**

✔ **Low-reading thermometer** (for identifying fever and hypothermia).

✔ **SAM splint or wire mesh:** (a brand name for a thin strip of metal about 4 inches wide and several feet long that is wrapped in a thin layer of foam, for immobilizing sprains and fractures). By bending and shaping, you can immobilize a sprain or fracture very effectively with either of these tools.

✔ **Space blanket** (made of thin foil and used for treating heat loss and shock).

✔ **Waterproof matches.**

✔ **Emergency report form** for documenting when an injury occurred, how it occurred, where it occurred, who treated the injured party, and how the injury was treated. This is immensely helpful information for an emergency room when a patient is first admitted.

✔ **Pencil and paper.**

✔ **Emergency contact numbers.**

✔ **Cell phone.**

✔ **Money for a pay phone.**

✔ **Sawyer snakebite kit** is the only kit I will recommend, and it is also useful for removing venom from insect stings and bites. (Do not use the tiny rubber suction kits, ever!)

✔ **Dental kit** containing oil of cloves (for numbing a nerve), cotton pads (for absorbing moisture), and wax (for creating a temporary filling/cap for a broken tooth).

Anyone in the position of providing first aid is at risk of exposure to infectious diseases. Most serious of these risks is HIV (human immunodeficiency virus) and hepatitis B, which are spread by contact with infected blood and/or body fluids. Always use protective vinyl gloves, eye protection (glasses or sunglasses will suffice), and mouth protection (such as a mouth-to-barrier breathing device used when rescue breathing). Tie a bandanna over your mouth and nose to serve as a makeshift mask for further protection. One last suggestion — don't delay controlling life-threatening bleeding or beginning rescue breathing simply because protection is not available.

# Health tips from a pediatrician

Dr. Barbara Kennedy, a pediatrician, National Outdoor Leadership School (NOLS) graduate, member of the Wilderness Medical Society, mother of four, and author of Adventure Medical Kits' *A Medical Guide to Traveling With Children*, offers the following reminders about child-specific needs in the outdoors:

✔ **You must adapt standard first-aid kits to meet infants' and children's special needs.** Actual items you carry will vary depending on the ages of the children, preexisting medical conditions, length of travel, specific environment traveled in, and the parents' first-aid knowledge.

✔ **Infants can develop infections and become hypothermic, hyperthermic, and dehydrated more rapidly than adults or older children.** Carry a digital thermometer and the appropriate lubricant for monitoring rectal temperatures. Temperatures 100° and over require immediate medical attention in a child younger than four months of age. A bulb syringe is also useful — not only can it be used to suction mucus from the throat and nasal passages of infants, but it also may be used to flush foreign bodies from ears and to administer enemas.

✔ **Blisters bother all ages.** Feet should receive attention the minute you notice friction or irritation. Always leave small blisters intact unless you suspect infection. A fluid, gel laminate (Spenco Second Skin is one brand), and an adhesive pad are very effective in preventing and treating blisters. Drain large blisters carefully using a sterile needle so as to prevent the blister's breaking and becoming an open wound.

✔ **Most children under five can't swallow pills.** Chewable medications are preferred. If chewable drugs are not available, liquids will work, but they add excess weight and can leak. Most children can chew tablets after their first molars are present — usually around 15 months. For children who can't chew, chewable medications may be crushed between two spoons and mixed with food.

✔ **Select first-aid-kit medications and supplies that have multiple uses.** Reduction of weight and bulk is a primary concern in any first-aid kit. For example, Desitin, best known for helping to prevent diaper rash, is also an excellent sunblock because it contains 40-percent zinc oxide.

## *Administering first aid*

In all first-aid situations, the following basics govern action for most procedures:

1. **Identify the method of injury and ensure that no one else in the group, including the potential rescuer, will also be injured.**

2. **Call for help, if possible and/or appropriate.**

3. **Remove the mechanism or situation of injury from the injured person if it is life-threatening (a rockfall, avalanche, or electrical wire, for example) to them. Do not attempt to move the mechanism or enter the situation that caused the injury if it is likely to cause you harm — such as diving into ice-cold water in a bold attempt to rescue a victim. Better to attempt a rescue with a throw rope or by reaching with a branch in that situation.**

   This may involve moving the injured person, but only do so if the immediate situation is life-threatening, and under no other circumstance. Anytime you move an injured person, you risk aggravating her injury and causing permanent damage or even death.

4. **Check the ABC's and respond accordingly:**

   ✔ **Airway:** Is the person's airway blocked or compromised in any way? If so, clear the airway and move to Step B.

   ✔ **Breathing:** Evaluate the person's breathing. Observe the rise and fall of his chest. Is he breathing? If not, start rescue breathing.

   Refer to a first-aid guide or take a CPR training course for specifics.

   ✔ **Circulation:** You can check the person's circulation as you check his breathing in the previous step. Does the person have a pulse? If not, start CPR immediately.

   *Remember:* Establishing an airway and performing CPR can be performed effectively while transporting the patient out of immediate danger. Don't waste precious seconds.

5. **Control any bleeding by holding a dressing over the wound and applying direct pressure.**

   A clean article of clothing, a bandanna, a sanitary napkin, or whatever clean cloth or absorbent material is available will work as a dressing. Add additional dressings to the wound while maintaining pressure until the bleeding is controlled. If the stack of dressings becomes too bulky or ineffective, remove dressings from the top and replace them with fresh ones, but don't remove the one that is in direct contact with the wound — you risk starting the bleeding all over again.

6. **Stabilize any other injuries such as fractures and dislocations to prevent further discomfort and harm.**

Never try to set a fracture or restore a dislocation unless you've been properly trained. Although this is sometimes done in a wilderness situation, it is done only to save life and only by thoroughly trained personnel. Maintaining a calm and comfortable environment for the injured person while stabilizing injuries is essential.

7. **Treat the person for shock.**

Shock is a life-threatening situation, even if the injury is not. An allergic reaction, a severe or not-so-severe injury, a poisoning, or an illness — even as a result of seeing someone else injured — can bring on shock. Some of the classic signs and symptoms of shock are weakness, pale skin color, cool and clammy skin, irregular breathing patterns, nausea, dizziness, and shivering — even in warm weather.

It is important to maintain the person's body temperature. Wrap the person in an emergency blanket or sleeping bag if she's cold. In hot weather, keep the person cool by creating shade. Always attempt to keep the individual insulated from the ground. As a rule, keep the person lying down, comfortable, and resting with her feet raised. In the event of a head injury, don't raise her feet. Listen to the injured person and meet her needs — do not try to restrain her in an attempt to "do what the *Camping For Dummies* book says." If she feels more comfortable sitting up, then let her. However, do continue to encourage her to rest and keep warm.

The following sections describe treatments for some specific ailments and injuries.

## Altitude sickness

Altitude sickness is the body's reaction to a lack of available oxygen in the atmosphere. The higher the elevation, the less the concentration of oxygen, and the more likely the body is to succumb to altitude sickness. Typically, altitude sickness occurs at 8,000 feet or above, although there are a few documented occurrences at lower elevations. Symptoms include nausea, headache, shortness of breath, and extreme fatigue. Rest, food, and water are the only cures — it takes time for the body to acclimate to altitude change. Descending a few thousand feet until the person begins to feel better may be the best solution. The odds of getting altitude sickness are greatly reduced by drinking water, eating well, and gaining altitude gradually.

High-altitude pulmonary edema and high-altitude cerebral edema are much more severe reactions to altitude and require immediate descent and evacuation to a hospital. If the individual develops pneumonia-like symptoms or starts staggering, becomes incoherent, or suffers unbearable head pressure, evacuate him immediately!

## Blisters

Blisters are caused by friction or constant uncomfortable binding pressure — usually from poorly-fitting boots or inadequately protected feet. To minimize your chances of developing foot blisters (assuming your boots fit properly), keep in mind the following tips:

- ✔ Wear two pair of socks — one thin liner and a thicker cushioning outer sock of wool.
- ✔ Take the time to remove debris that falls into your boots.
- ✔ Never hike for extended periods with wet feet.

Should discomfort or a hot spot begin to appear, stop immediately and attend to your feet. If there is evident redness but no blister, applying moleskin directly to the hot spot should take care of the discomfort. If a blister has started to form, cut a donut out of molefoam and surround the blister. You can secure this in place with a strip of moleskin if necessary.

If the blister is broken, treat it as an open wound. Clean the area with soap and water and then dress it accordingly. Applying Second Skin, a gelatin-like sheet, directly over the broken blister and securing it in place with moleskin works well.

If your feet are dirty and somewhat sweaty, moleskin or adhesive tape won't adhere well to the skin. Cleanse the area with an alcohol wipe and then apply tincture of benzoin around, but not on, the wound to prepare the skin for an application of adhesive.

## Burns

Minor burns such as those received from a hot stove, pot handle, or match usually aren't serious enough to warrant medical attention. However, treatment should be taken seriously. Immerse the affected area under cool water to alleviate the pain and stop the burning sensation. Clean the area with soap and water and consider the application of a topical anesthetic to minimize pain.

For more severe burns involving blistering and deep tissue damage, the victim needs medical attention.

## Bruises

Bruising is caused by a blow to the muscle or soft tissue, resulting in bleeding into those tissues, which in turn causes swelling and discoloration. If swelling and pain increase dramatically over a 24-hour period, then a visit to the nearest emergency room is a wise precaution. Otherwise, resting the extremity in an elevated position and applying a cold, but not wet, compress is appropriate.

### Scrapes, scratches, and open wounds

The best first aid for scrapes, scratches, and open wounds is to cleanse the area with antibacterial soap and water. Apply an antibacterial ointment and top it with a clean, non-adhering dressing such as a Telfa pad, and secure the dressing with adhesive tape.

For minor scrapes and scratches, applying a mild antiseptic or lotion can relieve the itching. Aloe vera ointments or gels help relieve the burning sensation.

For serious bleeding, apply direct pressure to the wound with a clean sterile compress. Elevate the extremity if necessary to slow the bleeding. Continue to apply direct pressure and add more compresses to the original dressing until the bleeding slows or stops. After the bleeding stops, secure the wound with a compression bandage and head to the hospital for stitches.

If stitches become necessary, they must be placed within six hours in order to be effective and minimize scarring. Don't allow the wound to get too old or too dirty. Steri-strips or butterfly bandages can be used as an interim stitch to hold incisions or lacerations together until stitches can be used. The wound must be clean and antiseptic before using Steri-strips if at all possible.

### Eye injuries

If any chemical such as stove fuel or chlorine gets in your eye, flush the area with large amounts of water. Be sure to flush from the inside corner of the eye (nearest the bridge of the nose) to the outside to avoid flooding your face or your other eye with contaminant. Keep irrigating until you are sure the chemical has been removed (approximately 10 to 15 minutes). Use a continuous gentle stream of water and not a blast such as the pressurized output from a garden hose — cut a very small hole in the corner of a plastic, resealable bag. Fill the bag with water and seal. By squeezing the bag, you will get a stream of water. Don't squeeze too hard — you don't want to drown the person. After irrigating your eye, remove any coagulated chemical with a moistened cloth. Irrigate your eye again. Don't put medications in the eye. Cover the injured eye with a sterile gauze pad and immediately go to the hospital.

If a person suffers a puncture wound to his eye, do not remove the object if it is still in the eye. Creating a donut out of a bandanna and placing it around the injured eye provides a raised protective surface against which you can bandage the eye without risk of pushing on the object. You will need to bandage both eyes so the injured person is not tempted to move his eyes around and cause greater pain and damage. Evacuate the person to a hospital immediately.

### Impaled objects

A fishhook is probably the most common impaled object for a camper. If you get a fishhook stuck in a finger or elsewhere, push the hook's barbed end all the way through your skin, clip off the barbed end, and then pull the shaft back through your skin. This is very painful, so it sometimes helps to numb the area with lidocaine or ice. If at all possible, this procedure should be performed in an emergency room.

## Splinters

Tiny splinters can be hard to see, but painful, nevertheless. First, clean the area with soap and water. If the splinter is shallow, use a needle to gently pry back the tissue over the splinter. By removing the first layer or two of skin, it is often much easier to pry out the splinter or pull it out with tweezers. If the wound is a dirty one after the splinter removal, clean it thoroughly with soap and water and apply a topical antibiotic cream to the area.

## Heat-related illnesses

Heat-related illnesses should, frankly, never happen. If you drink sufficiently (at least 3 to 4 quarts of water per day), rest adequately (in the shade and frequently if hot), and dress appropriately (in light colored, loose clothing), then you should not suffer from heat problems. The following sections help you to recognize and treat the various stages of heat illness should they occur.

### Heat cramps

Muscle cramps are most often caused by a dilution of the salt in your body fluids. Usually this is due to heavily worked muscle activity and an intake of excessive water without accompanying salt. Drinking fluid fortified with electrolytes helps prevent this painful problem. If a cramp does occur, you can massage and stretch the muscle. You may still experience muscle soreness for several days after a cramp.

### Heat exhaustion

*Heat exhaustion,* usually experienced in hot weather, sets in when the body loses important fluids and salt. You can prevent this condition by eating correctly, drinking two to four quarts of fluids per day, reducing physical activity during very hot weather, and perhaps adding an electrolyte supplement such as ERG or BodyFuel to your water. Symptoms of heat exhaustion include dizziness, pale skin, restlessness, nausea, rapid heartbeat, and headache. Treat a victim of heat exhaustion by removing the heat source or removing the victim from that source — take off his clothing or move him into the shade, for example. Sponge down the victim with water. Give him sips of fluid fortified with an electrolyte supplement or salt.

Be careful that in initiating the cooling process you don't send the victim into a hypothermic state.

### Heatstroke

*Heatstroke* is far more dangerous than heat exhaustion, and its onset is much more sudden. Confusion, irrational behavior, rapid pulse and respirations, hot and dry skin, and unconsciousness are common symptoms. To treat this condition, remove the victim's clothing and moisten his body with cool water. Fan him to increase air circulation and evaporative cooling. Again, beware not to cool his body into a hypothermic state. Evacuation to a hospital is necessary.

## Cold-related illnesses and injuries

It is through inadvertent exposure to the elements either by accident or poor planning that a person suffers cold-related illnesses such as hypothermia and frostbite. Prevention by dressing warmly and staying dry is the best approach; however, the unexpected can and does happen. The following sections help you to recognize and treat the various stages of hypothermia and frostbite.

### Hypothermia

*Hypothermia* is a state caused by the body's inability to generate enough heat to compensate for heat loss. The difference between mild and severe hypothermia is very difficult to recognize unless you have a low reading thermometer — one that reads below 94°F. Hypothermia is very difficult to treat and is much easier to prevent.

Eating a balanced diet; drinking adequate amounts of fluid; dressing appropriately for the weather; keeping your body and clothing dry by controlling sweating and preventing outside moisture from seeping in; covering your head, neck, and hands; and wearing clothes that maintain insulative properties even when wet are all ways to prevent hypothermia. Wearing wet clothing, sitting on snow, and exposing a body moist with perspiration to a cold wind can all bring on hypothermia.

A person with mild hypothermia may:

- Shiver and complain that she is cold.
- Have difficulty performing simple motor functions.
- Feel apathetic.
- Have a body temperature that falls to 95°F.

The first aid for mild hypothermia is to move the person from the cold into a warm environment, remove damp clothing or add warm insulation, and offer warm liquids and food if she is fully conscious and able to swallow easily.

A person with moderate to severe hypothermia may:

- Have slurred speech.
- Stumble.
- Be unresponsive.
- Have a decreased pulse and respiration.

✔ Experience mental confusion.

✔ Slip into unconsciousness.

✔ Have a body temperature below 95°F.

The first aid for moderate to severe hypothermia is to end the exposure immediately by covering the victim. Don't allow the victim to walk or move, and handle the victim very gently. Movement may force cold blood from the person's limbs into the core of her body, further complicating the situation.

Treat the victim very gently. Do check her for signs of frostbite. If you can't get her to a hospital quickly, then rewarming may be appropriate. Focus on applying warmth to her head, neck, armpits, and groin. Heat will most easily reach the body core from these areas. Use warm water bottles, warm blankets, or other warm bodies. Take great care that you do not burn the victim. In all situations of potential hypothermia, believe the signs and symptoms even if the victim is in denial.

### Frostbite

*Frostbite* occurs when circulation to the extremities is restricted or stopped. This reduction in circulation allows the water in the body tissues to freeze when the surrounding temperature is below 32°F. The primary goal in first aid for frostbite is to prevent additional freezing and further damage to the frozen tissue that could result from thawing and then refreezing. The signs and symptoms of frostbite include skin that is white, waxy, hard to the touch, and intensely cold and numb; restricted joint movement; and, in severe frostbite, hard underlying tissue.

The treatment is to give plenty of fluids and rewarm the part only if it is not going to bear weight and will not refreeze.

Do not rub or massage the frostbitten area. Evacuate the victim to a hospital immediately.

### Insect bites and stings

Unless the victim suffers an allergic reaction, insect bites and stings are usually more painful than they are serious. (Tick bites, on the other hand, can have more serious consequences — in fact, I devote an entire section just to treating bites from these nasty bugs. See "Ticks," later in this chapter.) For bee stings, use a knife edge or fingernail to scrape out the stinger. Do not use tweezers or try to grab the stinger — you may squeeze more venom into the sting area. Wash the affected area with soap and water and dab with hydrocortisone cream such as Cortaid, Lanacort, or Cortizone, or apply a natural paste mixture of baking soda and water. If the area begins to really itch, apply a lotion like calamine.

If the victim does suffer an allergic reaction, give him an antihistamine, keep him calm, keep his airway open, and evacuate him to a hospital. People who know that they are allergic often carry an anaphylaxis kit (brand names Epi-Pen or Ana-Kit), which contains a premeasured injection to fight the reaction. If you have to administer the shot for the victim, simply follow the directions on the case. In the event of a severe allergic reaction, called anaphylactic shock, and in the absence of a Ana-Kit or Epi-Pen which will inject life-saving epinephrine, use an asthma inhaler or nasal decongestant spray, or give a dose of antihistamine medication or nasal decongestant medication.

### Nosebleeds

Remain sitting and apply pressure on the side that is bleeding for at least five minutes. If this does not stop the bleeding, pack the nostril with soft cotton, gauze, or tissue. Sometimes combining this with cold packs on the bridge of the nose will help. After the bleeding stops, continue resting and do not blow your nose or pick at the encrusted blood. If the bleeding does not stop easily, then a visit to the nearest emergency room is recommended.

### Poisoning

If someone is poisoned, seek medical assistance immediately. Find out, if possible, what caused the poisoning and contact the poison control center for instructions. In the event that help is not immediately available, there are some steps you can take. First make sure that the person is breathing and that she has a pulse. If the victim doesn't have a pulse, begin CPR. Use caution in giving mouth-to-mouth since it's possible for the rescuer to become poisoned as well — especially if the victim vomits the poisonous substance into the rescuer's mouth, which does happen.

In general, you can induce vomiting as long as what was ingested is not a petroleum-acid-based or alkali-based product. In other words, if the substance burned on the way down, it will burn on the way up, so do not induce vomiting. Diluting this type of poison is not an option because that will make the victim vomit. For medicine or plant poisoning, dilution is acceptable, as is inducing vomiting.

The best first aid for poisoning is prevention. Teach your children not to eat plants or berries or put things into their mouths. Also, make sure that all substances are clearly labeled and easily identified. If a fuel bottle containing white gas and a bottle containing water look similar, you're asking for trouble.

### Poison oak, ivy, and sumac rashes

Signs of poison oak, ivy, and sumac exposure appear within one to two days of contact. Your skin will burn and/or itch, become blistered, and sometimes swell.

If you inhaled the plant's oils, breathing may become very difficult — this is an emergency that requires medical treatment. Get to a hospital.

If you suspect contact with a poison plant (see "Pointing out poisonous plants," earlier in this chapter, for help identifying this pesky greenery), first remove all contaminated clothing and wash it separately in hot water with laundry detergent. Second, wash your skin with soap (use a strong laundry soap or detergent) and water. Use warm, not hot water. Wipe down the affected area with rubbing alcohol.

If a rash develops, avoid scratching because opening the blisters can lead to a secondary infection. Contrary to popular belief, the oozing from a broken blister does not contain urushiol — the oil from the plant that causes the skin irritation — and will not spread the rash. Apply cold compresses and/or a soothing lotion containing hydrocortisone or a similar agent.

### Snakebites

The danger from snakebites is greatly blown out of proportion. In North America, there are five distinct poisonous snake species — the rattlesnake, copperhead, water moccasin, cottonmouth, and coral snake. These snakes will only strike if aggravated, scared, or surprised with no route of escape. For these snakes, biting a human is a defensive posture and not an offensive one — human beings are not and will never be food for a snake!

Learn to identify the snakes in your area and the habitats that they most often frequent. In over 20 years of exploring and hiking all over the U. S., Canada, and Baja, I have seen fewer than 20 poisonous snakes. Many recorded snakebites occurred because the snake was being handled, not because someone was traipsing through the wilderness on a family camping trip.

Most experts agree that you should treat a snakebite as follows:

1. **Try to identify the snake so the correct antivenin can be administered quickly, but don't spend time chasing the snake. Don't try to catch or kill it.**

2. **Clean the wound with soap and water.**

3. **Immobilize the injured limb below heart level and keep the victim calm.**

4. **Get the victim to a hospital as soon as possible.**

Snakebite kits are of little use. In most cases, more harm can be done by the first aid performed using a "slice and dice" kit than would have occurred had the victim just been taken to a hospital. If you insist on carrying a snakebite kit, get one that provides powerful suction and does not involve cutting — I recommend the Sawyer Snake Bite Kit. Never, ever, apply a tourniquet or ice, and never use your mouth to provide suction.

### Sprains

A sudden twisting or wrenching of a joint resulting from a hit or fall causes sprains. The most commonly sprained joints are the wrist, knee, and ankle. Because it is virtually impossible to distinguish between a break and a sprain without an x-ray, a first-aider should always assume that the limb is broken. Elevate and immobilize the injured limb to relieve pain and prevent further injury. The application of a cold pack is appropriate and will help minimize swelling.

### Strains

Strains are most often evidenced by sore muscles. Your back, neck, arms, and legs all get a workout from carrying a backpack — often more than your body is ready for if you spend most of your time in an office. Children seem less susceptible to strains, although they get them, too. Apply a cold pack or ice to the sore area. Massage and stretching of the affected muscles in combination with icing works wonders.

### Dislocations and bone breaks

Splint a suspected fracture or dislocation to immobilize the affected leg, arm, shoulder, or other body part. When in doubt, apply a splint and do not attempt to move, adjust, or reposition the injured body part. Get to the nearest emergency room for appropriate medical care. If, and only if, medical care is many hours or days away, you should consider attempting to straighten bones and deformities to restore circulation and minimize discomfort. This is another area where it is imperative that you obtain adequate wilderness medical skill so you can safely determine the best course of action.

### Sunburn

Sunblock or sunscreen should always be applied to all areas of exposed skin. Remember that the higher the elevation, the more intense the sun. Always use a lotion with an SPF (sun protection factor) of 15 or greater. For younger children and those with very sensitive skin, apply a product with an SPF of 25 or greater.

Wear a hat with a wide brim that protects your scalp, face, and neck. Always wear sunglasses, especially in higher altitudes and snowy conditions. Sunburned (snowblind) eyes are not only painful, they are dangerous.

If your skin becomes burned, keep the burned areas clean and covered with loose clothing. An application of aloe vera gel seems to soothe the discomfort quite effectively. Don't break blisters if they form — doing so can lead to infection.

## Ticks

Few things make my skin crawl more than mention of the word "tick," and I believe I'm not alone in my disgust for these blood-gorging little beasties. My anxiety about ticks stems from knowing they prefer to feast in those dark and moist places where I'd rather not have insect visitors, and that it can take them hours to get their fill. No wonder ticks worry us so much! (For tips on protecting yourself against ticks and other insects, from what to wear to which insect repellent to use, see "Repelling insects," earlier in this chapter.)

The two most common diseases transmitted by ticks in North America are Lyme disease and Rocky Mountain spotted fever. Here are some signs and symptoms of the two diseases:

- **Rocky Mountain spotted fever** occurs in all parts of the United States but is most common in the Appalachian region. Its signs and symptoms include headache, fever, severe muscle aches, and rashes on the palms of the hands and the soles of the feet that spread to other parts of the body. This disease must be treated with antibiotics.

- **Lyme disease** has occurred in every state except Alaska and Hawaii. Its signs and symptoms include fever, flu-like symptoms, a target-shaped rash at the point where the tick attached, and soreness and swelling, most significantly in the joint areas. This disease also must be treated with antibiotics.

If you find a tick on you, a partner, or a child, follow these steps:

1. **Getting as close as possible to its head, slowly pull the tick away from the skin without twisting or jerking.**

   Sawyer's Tick Plier, recommended by a number of experts, enables you to easily slide the plier's jaws beneath the tick's body and extract the tick without cutting or squeezing its body.

2. **If it becomes too difficult to remove the tick by pulling, try applying a heavy mineral oil directly to the upper and lower surfaces of the tick. Wait 15 minutes and then try pulling the tick out again.**

   The application of mineral oil clogs the tick's breathing passages and relaxes the tick's grip, making the insect easier to remove.

3. **Wash the bite area with soap and water.**

4. **Apply an antiseptic to the wound.**

5. **Try to identify the tick. If it is a Lone Star or deer tick, place it in a vial or plastic bag with a cotton ball soaked in alcohol to preserve it for analysis in case disease symptoms appear.**

# Part V
# The Part of Tens

The 5th Wave                    By Rich Tennant

## In this part...

No, I'm not David Letterman, but I do share my Top Ten picks for favorite campfire recipes, camping essentials, great camping destinations in North America, camping resources, and (modesty does not prevent me) Hodgson's laws about camping. Yes, the list is very subjective.

# Chapter 14

# Ten + One Survival Essentials

∙ ∙ ∙ ∙ ∙ ∙ ∙ ∙ ∙ ∙ ∙ ∙ ∙ ∙ ∙ ∙ ∙ ∙ ∙ ∙ ∙ ∙ ∙ ∙ ∙ ∙ ∙ ∙ ∙ ∙ ∙ ∙ ∙ ∙ ∙ ∙ ∙ ∙ ∙ ∙ ∙ ∙ ∙ ∙ ∙ ∙ ∙ ∙ ∙

*O*utdoor safety isn't so much a game of survival as it is an exercise in preparation. Knowing your limits, understanding your environment, and packing the right equipment and knowledge to aid you during your outing is crucial. Knowledge and equipment must go hand in hand. It is useless to build an arsenal of kits and gadgets and not have the knowledge to be able to use them.

Most emergencies involve only hours and not days or weeks. With basic equipment and an understanding of how to use the equipment, most situations should end happily.

I suggest that you pack the following ten items in a compact kit that travels with you on every outdoor adventure — even on a short hike.

## Metal Cup

Mountain Safety Research (MSR), a company famous for its backpacking and mountaineering stoves, also makes a large titanium cup that sports a lid. Not only is the cup very lightweight, but it is extremely durable, and the lid fits securely on top, making it a suitable container for many of the smaller items on this list. Best of all, it sits nicely perched between two rocks over a small bed of coals, quickly heating any liquid you pour inside to a steaming and calm-restoring boil. Cup of tea, anyone?

## Firestarter

You won't be doing much heating of water or warming of cold tootsies if you can't light a fire. Sure, there are books about starting fires by rubbing two sticks together, but think about it, gang: If that were so easy, we wouldn't have invented matches, now would we? You can purchase waterproof/windproof matches at most outdoor specialty stores. They light even in a downpour. Add to the kit a small candle and a few sticks of firestarting material, also available at most outdoor specialty stores.

# Parachute Cord

I suggest packing a 50-foot length of cord. With this, you can bear-bag food, lash poles together for an emergency shelter, repair broken boot laces, secure equipment to the outside of a pack — the list is as endless as your imagination should be. You should be able to purchase this by the foot or in prepackaged 50-foot lengths at most outdoor specialty stores.

# Flashlight

I prefer a waterproof headlamp and am partial to those made by Petzl. With headlamps, you keep your hands free for cooking, climbing, playing cards, and digging catholes. Be sure you always have at least one set of spare and fresh batteries and an extra bulb. Whatever light you select, be sure that it has a secure on/off switch that doesn't have a tendency to switch on while the lamp is being toted along, illuminating the pack for your journey but fading to black when you need it most.

# Compass and Map

I recommend you carry a compass with a sighting mirror, known as a prismatic compass. In a pinch, and with practice, the mirror can be used for signaling. A topographic map of the area you are in is also immensely useful. Assuming you are in trouble and must try to find water or even find your way back to camp or help should you become separated from your group, your best chance of success is with a topo map of the area and a compass — and the requisite skills necessary to use them, of course.

# Knife

Make this a multi-tool choice (such as Leatherman), placing a sharp blade, a saw, and a useful assortment of tools at your disposal should you need them. Tie a cord to your belt and to the knife's lanyard hole so that you can use the knife when needed but are not in jeopardy of losing it inadvertently.

# Emergency Blanket

Sometimes called a space blanket — or in the more deluxe version, a space emergency bag — these foil blankets are critical when sealing in the heat is essential. Although it may seem remarkable that such a thin barrier of foil can insulate anything, emergency blankets are often the only difference between a cold night of survival and a hypothermic night of falling into a sleep from which there is little chance of awakening.

# Basic First-Aid Kit

Your first-aid kit should contain enough supplies to enable you to provide care for most wilderness emergencies in a manner that will stabilize the injured person enough for evacuation to proper medical attention. The size of the kit will vary depending on the length and type of your journey (see Chapter 13 for some suggested items). At the bare minimum, it should include moleskin, butterfly bandages, a few safety pins, a roll of adhesive tape, small adhesive bandages, gauze pads, and some topical antiseptic ointment.

# Water Purification System and Two Water Bottles

If you use chemical water purification treatments such as Potable Aqua iodine tablets, remember that they have a shelf life. Always check expiration dates before leaving for your outdoor adventure. I also carry two wide-mouthed water bottles when using chemicals — one contains water that is already pure and ready to drink, and one contains water that is in the process of being purified. If you use a filter instead, that's fine, but it will be bulkier and, like anything mechanical, can fail right when you need it most. Although I favor filters, I never leave without a bottle of Potable Aqua tablets tucked into my emergency kit. (See Chapter 13 for more information about water purification.)

# Emergency Food

A one-day supply of extra food is appropriate. I pack some beef or turkey jerky, hard candy, a few Powerbars, a couple of granola bars, a packet of instant soup, some dried apricots, and a few tea bags. Although hydration is your most important survival issue in an emergency, staving of the pangs of hunger is not only comforting but also helps you to think more clearly.

# Someone Responsible — the Eleventh Essential

Okay, I know I'm stretching things a bit here, but frankly, this is a key factor in your personal well-being and potential to survive what disaster might befall you. If no one knows where you are or when you're supposed to return, who's going to alert the search-and-rescue team? I realize that you can't fit the person in your kit, but make him a part of your emergency planning! The responsible party can be a neighbor, close friend, or family member. Whoever he is, he should be someone you can trust and someone who has a vested interest in your return — either because he loves you or because you owe him money — and lots of it (just kidding). When you return home, don't forget to let him know that you're back safe and sound, either. When I worked search-and-rescue many years ago, my team got called out on a number of "false alarm" rescues by concerned family members who alerted the authorities, only to discover — sometimes several days later — that the person we were trying to "rescue" was safe at home, sipping hot tea and eating scones.

# Chapter 15

# Ten Low-Impact Camping Tips

• • • • • • • • • • • • • • • • • • • • • • • • • • • • • • • • • • • • • • •

As our wildlands and rivers become destinations of more and more campers, promoting and adopting a uniform environmental ethic is of increasing importance. "Leaving no trace" and "treading softly" are no longer cute terms for practicing minimum impact — they have become rules to live by. The following are suggestions to rely on when you travel through wildlands. They will make your wandering more pleasant and ensure that your passing is as light as a breath of wind upon the land.

## Discover Your Place in the Woods — Don't Create It

The perfect campsite is never made — it is discovered. Trenching, cutting branches, and leveling or removing vegetation are inappropriate camping techniques. Look for a level site that has naturally adequate drainage and is not in a sensitive area that will be irreparably damaged by your presence. Whenever possible, select campsites that have already been used — this will eliminate the creation or expansion of unnecessary camping areas. Always camp out of sight of others and the trail. Practice no-trace camping.

## Lose the Trappings of Civilization

Although campgrounds seem to be the antithesis of wilderness, they often serve as preferred — and excellent — base camps for families, photographers, mountain bikers, climbers, and many other wilderness seekers desiring a central location from which to day-hike and explore. Many state and national park campgrounds are, however, becoming nothing more than miniature cities, subject to air pollution, noise pollution, overcrowding, traffic jams, and more. Don't drive when walking is a suitable alternative. Leave the television and radio at home, and consider using ice or propane power to cool food, thereby eliminating the need to run a generator.

# Practice Proper Campsite Sanitation

Don't clean fish, dishes, clothing, or yourself in streams or lake water. Use soap at least 20 feet from the nearest natural water source. Never feed the wildlife, and be extra vigilant when disposing of food scraps, cleaning up, and storing food. Many campgrounds and park areas have specific rules and provide food storage areas when animals are a potential problem. Never bury food scraps. They will get dug up and scattered. Burn or pack out all leftover food. Fish entrails also must be burned or packed out. A consistent food source around campsites is an attraction to animals and a danger to other campers if the attracted animal is a bear. Follow the sanitation rules without deviation.

# Don't Use the Wilderness as Your Personal Toilet

Use established latrines when they are available. Otherwise, dig a hole six to eight inches deep in organic soil and at least 200 feet away from the nearest water source. Use toilet paper sparingly, and use only the undyed, non-perfumed variety. Pack out your toilet paper in a plastic baggie. If you have a campfire, burning the toilet paper there is acceptable. Feminine hygiene products must never be buried! They are slow to decompose and are often dug up by wildlife and left scattered about. Pack them out in double resealable plastic bags.

# Save a Tree: Use a Stove

Use a camp stove whenever possible. Campfires have romantic appeal, but they cause extreme impacts on the environment. Cutting down trees or using available deadfall wood only serves to completely strip the natural environment around the campground of its vital resources. If the obvious visual and ecological impacts aren't enough to dissuade you from building campfires, keep in mind that their dancing firelight all but destroys your night vision, obscuring the larger world outside the boundaries of a flame.

# Choose a Time and Place Least Crowded

Planning your wilderness trips to avoid major holiday rushes is a first step in minimizing your impact on the land. Trailheads and campgrounds often become so packed with humanity that the water, air, and noise impacts become severe. Travel only in small groups — four or fewer people make the ideal camping party.

# Follow the Path Most Traveled

When hiking on the trail, walk in a single file and in the center of the trail. Resist the urge to shortcut across a meadow or down a switchback. Doing so will only encourage severe erosion and trail damage. Take your rest stops only in areas where your presence will not damage the vegetation. Be careful to replace all gear in your pack — the most common time to forget gear or inadvertently litter is during a rest break.

# Pick Up after Yourself — Mother Nature Is Not Your Maid

Carry out all that you carry in. This includes fishing line, lures, spent cartridges, and cigarette butts. Pick up litter as you find it (although sometimes the practicality of doing this is questionable because of weight). And since you probably don't toss scraps, litter, and trash on the floor at home, don't do it in Mother Nature's house, either.

# Respect Other Cultures

Cultural sites are places of ancestral importance to Native Americans and other cultures and demand to be treated with respect and reverence. Look but don't touch or collect.

## Seek to Blend

Blend in with the environment at all times. Wear clothing that is muted in color — not a fabric billboard. There is no need to douse yourself with cologne or perfume and consequently subject all those around you to olfactory reminders of your presence. Portable game players, radios, CD players, and tape players become barriers to your enjoyment of the natural world and often create disturbances for others seeking quiet. Leave the trappings of civilization at home for a few days. Games and fun are wonderful, but temper the rowdiness, lest you disturb not only your camping neighbors but your wildlife hosts as well. Always be considerate of others and your hostess, Mother Nature.

## Learn about Leave No Trace

Leave No Trace (LNT) is a nonprofit organization whose mission is to promote and inspire responsible outdoor recreation through education, research, and partnerships. To find out more, you can visit the Web site at www.lnt.org or contact LNT at headquarters: P.O. Box 997, Boulder, CO 80306, 303-442-8217, 1-800-332-4100, fax 303-442-8217.

# Chapter 16

# Ten Camping Recipes

· · · · · · · · · · · · · · · · · · · · · · · · · · · · · · · · · · · · · · · · · · ·

*N*o, camping does not mean having to eat burnt food flavored with sand and the odd bug or two. Cooking over a fire or stove at the campground is really no different from cooking at home. What — you mean you don't cook at home? Regardless of your culinary expertise, campground cuisine can be downright delectable. For this chapter, I culled 10 of my favorite recipes accumulated through years of being a parent, a professional guide, and a participant in guided trips. Each recipe was selected for its simplicity and universal appeal — even to the most discriminating child palates. As a bonus, I close this chapter with "A Winter Picnic" — broccoli forest soup and ginger tea, which you can fix at home and take out hot for winter day trips.

## Hot Breakfast Cereal

A hot breakfast is the perfect start to a perfect day of camping. This hot cereal wakes up even the grumpiest early risers — and it's good for you, too!

**Tools:** *Grill, campfire, or camp stove; 4-quart saucepan*

**Preparation time:** *About 10 minutes*

**Yield:** *4 servings*

*3½ cups water*

*2½ cups quick-cook oats*

*Up to ¼ cup dried cranberries (optional)*

*Up to ¼ cup blueberries (optional)*

*Up to ¼ cup sliced bananas (optional)*

*Brown sugar or honey*

*¼ cup chopped walnuts (optional)*

*1* Bring water to a rolling boil.

*2* Add quick-cook oats.

*3* Move the pot to a cooler spot on the grill or turn down the heat on the stove so that the water-and-oats mixture continues to simmer but doesn't boil for one minute.

*4* Remove from the heat and let sit for two to three minutes.

*(continued)*

**5** If you want to add a tart taste to your cereal, add the dried cranberries to the mixture when you add the quick oats so the fruit has a chance to soften.

If your palate craves a sweeter taste, add blueberries after you stop cooking the oats. You can also add bananas at this time.

**6** Stir in brown sugar or honey to flavor.

*Gourmet flourish: For a really deluxe addition, sprinkle each serving with chopped walnuts before serving.*

## Grilled Muffins with Cheese and Egg

Okay, so it's not an Egg McMasterpiece, but at the campground, this does bring smiles, and it's sooooo easy to make.

**Tools:** *Grill, campfire with grill, or camp stove; griddle or frying pan; saucepan*

**Preparation time:** *10 minutes*

**Yield:** *1 serving*

| | |
|---|---|
| *1 sourdough English muffin* | *1 egg* |
| *½ tablespoon margarine or butter* | *1 strip bacon (optional)* |
| *1–2 slices American or cheddar cheese, depending on taste* | *1 tomato slice (optional)* |

**1** Slice the English muffin in half.

**2** Butter each muffin half with margarine or butter.

**3** Place a cheese slice on each muffin half and reassemble the muffin.

**4** Place the muffin directly on the grill, far enough from the direct flame that it won't burn.

You can use a griddle over a camp stove, too. Just keep the burner at low to medium so the muffin doesn't burn.

**5** Heat the muffin until the cheese melts — about one to two minutes.

**6** While the muffin is heating, prepare the egg by either hard-boiling it in a saucepan of water or frying it on a griddle. If you want to add bacon to the sandwich, cook it at this time as well.

*7* Open the muffin (be careful — the cheese is hot!) and add the egg.

*8* Close the muffin halves and serve.

>*Gourmet flourish: If you want to go deluxe, add bacon and tomato to the sandwich — yummy!*

## Eggs Benedict

This is the quintessential breakfast dish of breakfast gourmands, and it's not that difficult to make at the campground, either. The only difference is that you prepare a white sauce instead of a Hollandaise sauce (Hollandaise sauce requires a double boiler, and you just don't want to go there outdoors).

**Tools:** *Camp stove, 2- or 4-quart saucepan, cup, griddle*

**Preparation time:** *About 15 minutes*

**Yield:** *1 serving*

**Simple White Sauce:**

*2 tablespoons flour*

*¼ cup warm water*

*¼ cup whole milk*

*1 tablespoon margarine or butter*

*Dash of salt and pepper*

**Poached Egg:**

*1 cup water*

*1 teaspoon white vinegar*

*1 egg*

**Garnish:**

*1 slice Canadian bacon*

*1 toasted English muffin*

*⅛ cup grated cheese (optional)*

*1* Mix the flour with the warm water in the cup.

*2* Combine the milk and margarine in the pot and heat over a medium flame while stirring constantly.

*3* Slowly add the flour mixture to the pot and continue stirring as the mixture thickens.

*4* Add a dash of salt and pepper for flavor.

*5* After the sauce has thickened sufficiently, remove it from the heat.

*(continued)*

**6** Bring a pot of water to boil.

**7** Add the white vinegar to the water.

**8** Using a wooden spoon, stir the water hard enough to create a whirlpool, taking care not to splash boiling water and vinegar all over yourself.

**9** Add one egg to the water mixture while it's swirling. (The swirling prevents the egg from spreading out.)

**10** Swirl the water periodically until your poached egg is cooked to the desired hardness — typically about three minutes.

When you get good enough with one egg, you may be able to poach up to four eggs in one pot at the same time, but work up to this challenge.

**11** While the egg is cooking, toast an English muffin and fry a slice of Canadian bacon on the griddle.

**12** Place the Canadian bacon on the English muffin.

**13** Place the poached egg on top of the bacon.

**14** Pour the white sauce over the entire creation and serve.

*Gourmet flourish: Top it all off with a few sprinkles of grated cheese if you're feeling frisky.*

## Mexican Spoon Bread

Not too long ago, a sales rep for Lodge, a cast iron skillet and Dutch oven manufacturer, shared this recipe with me. It quickly became a must-have for all camping trips. Serve as a side dish to any meal where flavorful bread is a must.

*Tools: Charcoal briquettes, grill or campfire, 10-inch Dutch oven (of course, I recommend the Lodge Dutch oven), large mixing bowl, medium mixing bowl, grill*

*Preparation time: 45 minutes*

*Yield: 8 to 10 wedges*

⅝ cup shortening or butter

1 cup all-purpose flour

17-ounce can cream-style corn

¾ cup whole milk

2 eggs

¼ cup coarsely chopped onions

1¼ cups cornmeal

1 teaspoon salt

1 teaspoon baking powder

½ teaspoon baking soda

1 teaspoon sugar

4-ounce can chopped and drained green chilies

2 cups grated cheddar cheese (I prefer sharp)

**1** Grease the sides and bottom of the Dutch oven and then dust it well with flour.

**2** In the large bowl, mix together the corn, milk, shortening (melt it first), eggs (lightly beat them first), and onions.

**3** Blend in ¾ cup of the flour and the cornmeal, salt, baking powder, baking soda, and sugar.

**4** In the medium bowl, mix the chilies and the cheese.

**5** Pour one-half of the batter prepared in Steps 2 and 3 into the Dutch oven and top it with half of the chili-and-cheese mixture prepared in Step 4.

**6** Pour in the rest of the batter and top it with the remaining chili-and-cheese mixture.

**7** Cover the Dutch oven with its lid and place the oven directly onto the bed of hot coals. Cover the lid with a layer of hot coals and bake for about 20 minutes.

**8** Remove the Dutch oven from the bottom coals and place on a nonflammable surface, such as the dirt adjacent to the grill or campfire. Leave the layer of coals on the lid. Continue baking until the bread is done — approximately 5 to 10 minutes. Bread is done when the top springs back lightly to the touch.

**9** Allow the bread to cool slightly before serving.

### French Onion Soup

When I served this in the backcountry on weeklong backpacking trips, my clients' eyes would open wide. You can't quite do a French onion soup like a fancy restaurant does, but you can come close.

*(continued)*

*Tools:* *Camp stove or grill, 2- to 4-quart pot, frying pan*

*Preparation time:* *20 minutes*

*Yield:* *4–6 cups*

*1 package Knorr brand French Onion Soup Mix*

*Water — according to directions on package*

*1 coarsely chopped yellow onion*

*Dash of salt*

*1 French baguette*

*Several tablespoons olive oil*

*2 cups mozzarella cheese*

**1** In the pot, prepare the soup mix according to the package directions.

**2** Add the onion and a dash of salt to the soup as it cooks.

**3** While you're waiting for the soup to finish cooking, make croutons by slicing the bread into one-inch-thick pieces.

**4** Lightly coat both sides of each bread slice with olive oil.

**5** Place the bread slices in the frying pan and brown both sides over medium heat.

**6** Once the soup is boiling, carefully remove it from the heat and pour it into cups.

**7** Add the croutons to the cups and then generously top with the shredded mozzarella cheese. The cheese should melt immediately.

## Tabouli Salad

As a side dish, as a main meal for vegetarians, or stuffed into pita bread for a flavorful lunch, this is a great staple dish.

*Tools:* *Cup or mug, camp stove or grill, 2- to 4-quart pot*

*Preparation time:* *1.5 hours*

*Yield:* *2 servings*

*3 mint tea bags*

*2 cups water*

*2 cups bulgur*

*¼ onion, coarsely chopped*

*½ cup mixed vegetables (I like to use corn, tomatoes, celery, and fresh peas — this is also a great chance to use leftovers)*

*Chopped fresh mint leaves — to taste (sold by the bunch in grocery stores).*

*5 tablespoons fresh lemon juice*

*½ cup olive oil*

*Salt and pepper to taste*

*1* Steep the tea bags in ½ cup of water (bring it to a boil first) for about 5 minutes.

*2* Boil 1½ cups of water in the pot.

*3* Add 2 cups of bulgur to the boiling water.

*4* Add the onion and the mint tea (toss the tea bags first, of course!) to the boiling water.

*5* Cover the mixture and remove it from the heat. Allow it to sit for approximately 30 minutes.

*6* Stir in the mixed vegetables.

*7* Mix in the mint leaves, lemon juice, and olive oil.

*8* Add salt and pepper to taste.

## Baked Steak Surprise

The surprise part of this dish is the smiles you get when you open the steaming pot and begin serving.

**Tools:** Camp stove or grill, medium bowl, frying pan, 10-inch Dutch oven

**Preparation time:** 50 minutes

**Yield:** 4 servings

*(continued)*

1 pound top round steak, cut into strips

1 cup Worcestershire sauce

Splash of red wine vinegar

1 teaspoon garlic powder

Dash of liquid smoke (available in the condiment section of grocery stores)

½ cup chopped green onions

2 sliced green peppers

1 sliced red pepper

2 large tomatoes

2 sliced cloves garlic

2 tablespoons olive oil

½ to 1 teaspoon chili powder — depending on taste

Dash of salt

**1** Combine the Worcestershire sauce, red wine vinegar, garlic powder, and liquid smoke to create a marinade for the steak. (Alternatively, you can use any marinade you choose, but this is my favorite.)

**2** Marinade the steak strips for about one hour prior to cooking. The easiest way to do this is to pour the liquid you prepared above into a large resealable plastic baggie, add the steak, squeeze out the air, and seal the bag.

**3** In the frying pan over medium flame, sauté the green onions, red and green peppers, tomatoes, and garlic in the olive oil until the vegetables are tender.

**4** Grease the sides and bottom of the Dutch oven.

**5** Remove the meat from the marinade and add the meat and cooked vegetables to the Dutch oven.

**6** Sprinkle the mixture with the chili powder and add a dash of salt.

**7** Stir the mixture until all the vegetables and meat strips are well-coated with the seasonings.

**8** Place the Dutch oven on the coals and cover it with the lid.

**9** Cover the lid with hot coals and bake the steak dish for 25 to 35 minutes.

## Fried Rice Whatever

Rice is easy to make if you can follow simple cooking directions, and you can flavor it so that it takes on an attitude all your own. Enter Fried Rice Whatever!

**Tools:** *Camp stove or grill, iron or nonstick skillet*

**Preparation time:** *60 minutes*

**Yield:** *2–4 servings*

*1 tablespoon sesame oil*

*1 tablespoon peanut oil*

*2 cups cooked rice*

*1 teaspoon powdered ginger — more or less to taste*

*1 teaspoon Chinese mustard — more or less to taste*

*Black pepper — to taste*

*3 sliced cloves garlic*

*¼ cup tofu or cooked meat of your choice*

*2 eggs (optional)*

*⅛ cup pine nuts (optional)*

*⅛ cup chopped pecans (optional)*

*1 tomato (optional)*

*Dash soy sauce — more or less to taste*

*1* In the skillet, mix a little sesame oil and peanut oil — just enough to lightly coat the bottom of the pan — and begin heating over a medium to high heat.

*2* Add the rice, powdered ginger, Chinese mustard, black pepper, garlic, and tofu or cooked meat.

   Tofu works well if you're a vegetarian. I like to toss in shredded chicken breasts. My friends swear by freshly caught fish that has already been cooked.

*3* Keep stirring the mixture so that nothing burns while the rice is browning.

*4* If desired, add an egg or two to the mixture as it cooks.

   One of my friends likes to add pine nuts, chopped pecans, and tomatoes. Be creative and add whatever strikes your fancy.

*5* When the dish seems complete and thoroughly cooked, flavor it with soy sauce and enjoy.

## Roasted Apple Dessert

This was a favorite of mine when I was a Boy Scout, and it became a favorite of count-less kids I guided at camp.

*(continued)*

**Tools:** *Campfire or grill, metal hot-dog skewers*

**Preparation time:** *20 minutes or more depending on how hot the coals are and on your patience*

**Yield:** *Depends on the number of apples and people you bring along!*

*1 cooking apple per person*

*White or brown sugar — 1 cup will coat about 4–6 apples*

*Ground cinnamon — about one teaspoon per apple — more or less to taste*

*1* Wash the apples well.

*2* Firmly insert a skewer into each apple.

The old way meant hunting down suitable sticks that were 2 to 3 feet long, but I discourage this practice because it impacts the land unnecessarily, and cutting branches is a no-no except in case of an emergency — and frankly, the sticks can burn through unless they are green.

*3* Make sure that your campfire has generated a good bed of cooking coals.

You can roast the apples over a charcoal grill, too, but that's not as fun, and the results aren't nearly as tasty.

*4* Hold the apples 2 to 3 inches above the coals, turning them frequently to prevent burning.

Each person should be responsible for his own apple since this is a full-time job.

The skin will start to brown and juices will begin to flow as the apple cooks. After the apple has cooked, the skin becomes very loose and can be peeled off.

*5* Remove your apple from the flame and peel off the skin, but don't remove the apple from the skewer yet.

Use caution — the apple and skewer will be extremely hot.

*6* Hold the apple over a plate and generously sprinkle it with sugar and cinnamon.

*7* Place the skewered apple back over the coals, where the heat will bake the sugar and cinnamon into a tasty crust.

*8* Slide the apple onto a plate and eat it with a fork — it's too hot to bite into or break apart with your fingers.

## Popcorn

Yes, it is not only possible but highly encouraged to pop up some fresh popcorn while in the wilderness.

**Tools:** *Campfire or camp stove, frying pan with securely fitting lid*

**Preparation time:** *5 to 10 minutes depending on how hot the coals or stove is.*

**Yield:** *2–4 servings*

*1 tablespoon vegetable oil — margarine will work if you don't allow the frying pan to get too hot.*

*½ cup popcorn*

*Salt — optional. I like to sprinkle about a quarter teaspoon over my popcorn.*

*Melted butter or margarine — optional. Between ⅛ and ¼ cup is about right.*

**1** Heat the oil in the frying pan.

**2** Add several kernels of popcorn to the pan.

**3** Place the pan over the hot coals or on the stove set at a medium flame.

**4** After the first kernels pop, add the rest of the popcorn and cover the pan with the lid.

**5** Shake the pan until the popping subsides.

**6** Remove the pan from the heat.

**7** Remove the lid and immediately salt the popcorn to flavor. Add melted margarine or butter if desired and serve.

# A Winter Picnic

Whether you are outdoors enjoying a brisk winter's hike through local woods or gliding among snow-laden mountain pines on skis, steaming hot soup, a chunk of sourdough bread topped with cheese, and a hot drink will go far in chasing the chill away at lunch. Pack the hot liquids along in a thermos or have them awaiting your return to the car. Remember to always pack additional water. Hot drinks and soup are no substitute for preventing dehydration. The following are two of my favorite recipes, given to me by a friend, David Strumsky, when I guided for a company in southern California.

## Broccoli Forest Soup

**Tools:** *Blender, large pot, measuring cups, large spoon*

**Preparation time:** *30 minutes*

**Yield:** *4 servings*

*2 heads broccoli*

*2 tablespoons butter or vegetable oil*

*1 yellow onion, diced*

*4 cups cashew milk (Soak two cups roasted, no-salt cashews in four cups water for 15 minutes. Puree in blender until lique- fied. The sweet, nutty flavor blends out- standingly well with the broccoli)*

*2 tablespoons soy sauce*

*1 bay leaf*

*2 tablespoons cornstarch mixed thoroughly with 2 tablespoons cold water (optional)*

**1** Cut broccoli into small flowerets and steam until tender (don't overcook). Set aside.

**2** Sauté onion with butter in large soup pot over low heat until onion is clear and tender. Add cashew milk and soy sauce.

**3** Measure out two cups of liquid and puree in blender with half of the broccoli.

**4** Dice the remaining broccoli.

**5** Combine puree, bay leaf, and diced broccoli with the liquid in the large soup pot.

**6** Warm to serving temperature — do not boil. Add cornstarch mixed with cold water to thicken if desired.

## Ginger Tea

**Tools:** *Grater, medium pot with lid*

**Preparation time:** *45 minutes*

**Yield:** *4 servings*

*2 one-inch cubes of fresh ginger*

*3 or more tablespoons honey to taste*

*4 cups water*

*1* Peel the ginger and grate it.

*2* Place all the ingredients in a pot and bring to a boil. Cover and simmer for approximately 25 minutes.

*3* Uncover and cook on medium-low heat for 15 minutes. Strain and serve.

*An instant version of this sold in a box of individual packets is available at many health and Asian markets. If ginger tea is not to your liking, try adding one drop of extract (almond, vanilla, peppermint, orange, and so on) to a cup of coffee, hot chocolate, or tea.*

# Chapter 17

# Ten or So Camping Resources

*E*verywhere you turn, be it in a bookstore, at a newsstand, at the library, or on the Internet, there are more bits and pieces of outdoor where-to and how-to information tossed at you than there are grains of sand on a beach — well, maybe not that many, but close. For this chapter, I pulled together a brief listing of what I feel are some of the most useful sites and magazines to get you started. Where you go from here is entirely up to you.

## *Adventure Network*

I founded Adventure Network (www.adventurenetwork.com) in 1995 to provide an online resource for camping, adventure, and fitness enthusiasts. With a simple point and click (Figure 17-1), you can access unbiased, detailed information on products; thorough how-to advice on camping, adventure, and fitness activities; and well-researched, complete answers to specific questions from readers. A network of links to market-leading manufacturers and quality guide services enhance the services Adventure Network offers. Adventure Network's selection of product buying guides and activity checklists are the best in the business, created from years of hands-on product testing and retail and field experience. Recognized as a 1999 *USA Today* Hot Site, a 1999 XpertSite.com Featured Expert award winner, and a 1999 Golden Web award winner, Adventure Network is well-respected for the quality and quantity of information it provides.

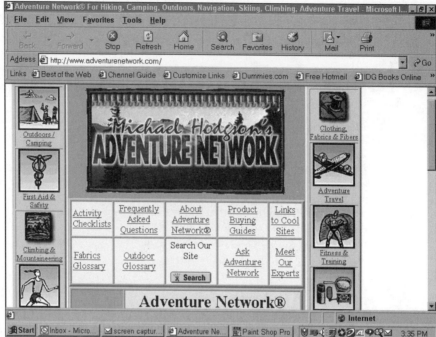

**Figure 17-1:**
Adventure
Network
home page.

# Mailing Lists and Newsgroups

Experts are great, but often the best information can be gleaned by simply talking to others who have been places, tried gear, and created recipes from personal experience. Subscribing to bulletin boards and participating in newsgroups is a bit like heading out to your local bar or coffee shop for some casual repartee. Bulletin boards typically require you to register these days, simply so they can effectively regulate who enters their space to join a discussion thread or post a message. You can opt to be notified by e-mail whenever someone responds to a query you may have posted or a discussion you may have chimed in, but beware — join too many bulletin boards and you may find yourself buried under an avalanche of e-mail notifications. To test the bulletin board waters, I would point your mouse to `www.adventuresports.com/newsgrp/newsgrp.htm`. Newsgroups are another great source of information. (If you have questions about accessing and participating in newsgroups, check with your Internet Service Provider, refer to the Help menu in your Web browser, or check out *The Internet For Dummies,* published by IDG Books Worldwide.) My favorite newsgroups include `rec.outdoors.national-parks` and `rec.outdoors.camping`.

# Finding the Gear You Need

Fogdog Sports (`www.fogdog.com`) offers a feature called The Search Squad which will help you find the North Face jacket that everybody seems to be sold out of, the hiking boots in extra narrow, and the sleeping bag with a left zip that you can't find anywhere. Two other e-tailers of note are Planet Outdoors (`www.planetoutdoors.com`) and REI (`www.rei.com`). If you are seeking new product information or looking for a retailer who might carry a product you need, head to GearTrends (`www.GearTrends.com`).

# Outside Magazine

A great magazine for the all-around outdoor adventurer, *Outside* often features articles highlighting the best places to camp or get away from it all. Two annual special issues, the *Buyer's Guide* and *Outside Family Vacations,* are wonderful resources. In addition, Outside Online (`www.outsidemag.com`) features original editorial content supplemented by an extensive archive of past magazine articles, product reviews, and excellent chat and question-and-answer forums with experts such as the Interactive Gear Guy, the Adventure Advisor, and Mr. Fit.

# Backpacker Magazine

Considered the backpacker's bible by many, *Backpacker* magazine is the best choice for wilderness adventurers seeking solid how-to advice along with some of the best gear-testing and evaluations I've read. Their annual Buyer's Guide is a superb who's-who resource highlighting companies selling tents, backpacks, sleeping bags, boots, and more in the world of backpacking.

# Riverworld.com

Riverworld.com (`riverworld.com`) is operated by Cascade Outfitters, an online and physical store sharing space with Maravia Rafts in Boise, Idaho. The store's mission for RiverWorld is to make the site a "virtual community for river users throughout the country." So far, the company has done an admirable job, considering the site has only been up and running since late

1998. The site features links to weather conditions (courtesy of the Weather Channel online), data on river flows and levels (for Maine, Washington, Montana, Oregon, Idaho, Wyoming, Colorado, California, Pennsylvania, and Tennessee), travel information (courtesy of the book *Western Whitewater* by Cassady, Calhoun, and Cross) and, of course, an online store. With its pleasing design, helpful features, and easy navigation, Riverworld.com is definitely worth bookmarking.

## Princeton Outdoors

Princeton University has offered an extensive outdoor education program for some time now, so the school has accumulated a wealth of knowledge about the outdoors, gear, and team-building processes. Now anyone — even those who don't harbor warm fuzzy feelings for ivy — can access the site at `www.princeton.edu/~oa/oa.html`. You can find links to first aid and safety information, equipment advice, gear lists, selected outdoor resources, weather information, and natural history files. One word of warning: The site is vast and so interesting that you're likely to disappear and not come out for weeks.

## Find-A-Guide

Find-A-Guide (`www.findaguide.com`) maintains a worldwide directory of professional guides, outfitters, and charters for outdoor adventures. This site is a good starting point if you're interested in trying something new or have a specific destination in mind and want to include an experienced professional in your plans.

## Adventure Sports Online

Adventure Sports Online (`www.adventuresports.com`) is perhaps the ultimate resource for any outdoor activity. Here you can find advice and directories on gear, outfitters, shops, and events for your favorite adventure sport as well as links to great outdoor resources, how-to and equipment information, and much, much more!

# Tubbs Snowshoes

The Tubbs site (www.tubbssnowshoes.com) embodies all that is fun and fitness about snowshoeing. Pleasing graphics guide a willing cyber-surfer through an online trail directory, facts about snowshoeing and fat burning, a how-to-get-started tutorial, and a guide for choosing the best shoe for the activity, as well as the standard company fare of product information, special events listings, and Team Tubbs appearance schedules. Any good Web site works hard to create a sense of belonging or community, and Tubbs succeeds here by encouraging visitors to register their favorite snowshoeing trails for the trail directory in return for a free "Tubbs TrailNet Advisor" T-shirt. Two thumbs up — and a five snowball salute!

# Recreation.gov

Chances are that at some time in the next year, you'll recreate on public lands. But what if you have a question about camping resources, facilities, permits, or other details? Which agency, which office, and which department should you query? To help you wade through the maze of information available on our nation's public regions — and avoid a lot of government bureaucracy — the half-dozen federal agencies charged with the stewardship of these wide-open spaces teamed up to create www.recreation.gov. This amazing database of nearly 2,000 recreation sites — including parks, forests, and other public resources — is searchable by state and activity. The site provides thumbnail sketches of each recreation site along with contact numbers, maps, weather forecasts, and links to many other pages maintained by individual jurisdictions. Verrry cool!

# Chapter 18

# Ten Best Outdoor Destinations

● ● ● ● ● ● ● ● ● ● ● ● ● ● ● ● ● ● ● ● ● ● ● ● ● ● ● ● ● ● ● ● ● ● ● ● ● ● ● ● ● ● ● ● ●

*T*rying to limit the selection of great outdoor camping adventures to ten is a bit like being asked to choose only ten favorite desserts from a table laden with hundreds of chocolatey and creamy concoctions: At best, you can sample only a few. Knowing too that many of us have limited time on our hands these days, I tried to select a variety of places where outfitted and guided trips were equally enjoyable as planning the trips yourself. For more ideas, look at current and back issues of outdoor magazines such as *Canoe and Kayak*, *Backpacker*, *Outside*, and *National Geographic Explorer*. I also encourage you to visit my Web site, www.adventurenetwork.com, and read about or post your own ideas for great trips in the bulletin board area.

## Lightning Lakes: British Columbia

For scenic value alone, this park is worth a visit — and is perhaps one of the best places to introduce a newcomer or young family to the world of back-packing. Four lakes are linked by a trail system that meanders along the eight-mile-long Cascade Mountain valley floor. Fishing in the lakes is memorable, and the backdrop of jagged, towering peaks is unforgettable. The best time to visit is June through September. Contact the British Columbia Park Visitor Center at 604-840-8836 for more information.

## Picture Rocks National Lakeshore: Michigan

Picture Rocks National Lakeshore along Lake Superior is perhaps one of the ultimate adventures for the snowshoer. Hidden deep in the woods are ice caves and frozen waterfalls that are stunning in their enormity and color. Overnight visitors stay in the warmth and comfort of a heated lodge — although you can camp, too, if you choose. (See Chapter 2 for information about planning a winter camping trip.) January and February are the best times to visit. For more information, call Great Northern Adventures at 906-225-8687 or visit the company's Web site at www.merchantfind.com/gna/gna/htm.

# Glacier National Park: Montana

Glacier National Park, located along the Canadian/U.S. border in Montana, is full of grizzlies, glaciers, alpine meadows weighted down with colorful blooms, and mountain peaks that seem to reach for the sky. Sound appealing? It is — and then some! Some of my favorite hikes are along the Iceberg Lake and Grinnell Glacier trails that begin near the Swiftcurrent Picnic Area on Many Glacier Road. Grinnell Glacier is perhaps the most difficult of the hikes, but you won't find a finer show of flowers, meadows, and glaciated views. Take a boat from the Many Glacier Hotel to the head of Swiftcurrent Lake to shorten the hike somewhat. When hiking, do keep a sharp eye out for grizzlies because they do own the place. Rangers close trails on occasion when grizzlies are sighted patrolling a meadow or two through which a trail passes. For more information on backcountry and campground reservations, contact the park visitor center at 406-888-7800 or visit its excellent Web site at www.nps.gov/glac.

# The Temagami: Ontario, Canada

Dozens of classic freshwater paddling trips leave folks speaking in superlatives for days on end: Okeefenokee Swamp in Georgia and the Boundary Waters in Minnesota are two that come to mind. But for a real wild experience that winds and mends its way through a puzzle-like network of lakes, streams, and rivers, head to the Temagami, located on the border of Quebec and Ontario north of Toronto. Over 1,500 miles of paddling trails are etched into this rocky and forested section of the Canadian Shield, and it is unlikely that you'll find yourself repeating a section in your lifetime. Novice to epic paddling trips — full of numerous portages and challenging paddling conditions — are possible. Call the Ontario Recreational Canoeing Association at 416-426-7170 for more information.

# All 'Round Ranch: Utah

All 'Round Ranch, located in Jensen, Utah, specializes in backcountry trips to the wilder parts of northeastern Utah — with a twist: You are assigned a horse as your partner and become a working cowpoke for the week (see Figure 18-1). When I took my daughter Nicole (then 12 years old) with me, we slept in canvas tents, ate around the campfire spinning tales, worked the range, and spent one of the most gloriously adventurous weeks of our camping lives together. The ranch is open to guests from April 1 to October 1, with a 12-person limit on each outing. It's worth spending a few extra days either before or after your adventure to explore Dinosaur National Monument. Call 800-603-8069 for more information, and tell Al hello for me — the horseshoe nail he bestowed on me at the end of the week as an award sits clipped to my truck visor as a daily reminder that details do matter.

**Figure 18-1:** Cowpokes at All 'Round Ranch.

*Photo courtesy of All 'Round Ranch.*

# Cumberland Island National Seashore: Georgia

There's a bit of pirate or Robinson Crusoe in all of us, and this is best discovered whilst camping along a seashore. Cumberland Island is the largest and most southerly of Georgia's 15 ocean islands: 16 miles long yet only 3 miles across at its widest point. The side of the island that faces the Atlantic is more windswept naturally, and as a result, the beaches are more scoured. The westerly side of the island boasts remarkable saltwater marshes. Inland, you can wander through live-oak forest adorned with curtains of Spanish moss. The only way to reach the island is by private boat or ferry, and the government restricts the number of visitors. For more information on boat reservations and camping permits, contact the Cumberland Island National Seashore at 912-882-4336.

# Gates of Lodor, Green River: Utah

A float trip with a light smattering of rapids for smiles and thrills is a great way to escape for a few days of camping and relaxation. A number of outfitters run super trips down the Green River that wind their way down the historic route John Wesley Powell took back in 1869. The rocky shoreline, numerous pictographs etched on the red rock, and willowy groves tucked into narrow slot canyons inspire the imagination while sandy beaches, warm swimming holes, and interesting side day hikes create the feeling of memorable adventure at a relaxed pace. ARTA (800-323-2782) and Adrift Adventures (800-824-0150) are just two of the outfitters that run excellent trips on the Green.

# King Range National Conservation Area: California

The King Range rises abruptly from sea level to 4,087 feet, the summit of King Peak, in less than three miles. Steep streams cascade into the ocean, and the eroding cliffs create huge rockslides and talus piles — rock debris that breaks away from cliffs and mountainsides and gathers in heaps. Wildlife is abundant here. Offshore, expect to see seals, sea lions, and a variety of shore birds playing in the kelp beds and tidal areas. In the Douglas fir and chaparral-covered coastline, black-tailed deer and black bear make their homes. The Lost Coast Trail is a beautiful 24-mile trek through one of the most pristine areas on the Pacific Coast. Bounded by the ocean and steep mountains and cliffs, the trail follows the beach most of the way, crossing numerous streams and grassy flats. Hiking the entire trail requires a shuttle, unless you're in the mood for a 48-mile round-trip. Allow for at least three days for the one-way trek. The terrain varies from fine-grained sand to large boulders. The walking is fairly level because it follows the beach most of the time. There are occasions when the trail wanders onto grassy flats above the beach and through Douglas fir, cypress, chemise, and possibly poison oak. Two areas, Sea Lion Gulch and Shipman Creek, require the use of a tide table — a schedule that shows high and low tides each day — because the trail is completely cut off by the incoming tide at times. You can find good camping areas at Cooskie Creek, Spanish Flat, and Shipman Creek. Driftwood is readily available for campfires, but you must obtain a campfire permit prior to the trip. Also, watch out for rattlesnakes when collecting wood! You can visit King Range year-round. This region is typically the wettest area on the Pacific Coast, with an average of 100 inches of rainfall annually. Summer is typically cool and foggy along the coast and warm to hot at the higher elevations inland. For more information, contact the BLM Arcata Resource Area at 1125 16th Street, Room 219, Arcata, CA 95521; 707-822-7648.

# Monongahela National Forest: West Virginia

Mountain biking overnights can become a bit, well, epic, especially if you have to tote along all the camping paraphernalia. However, in West Virginia, one outing gaining in popularity encourages mountain bikers to ride from cabin to cabin along dirt roads and converted rail beds through the deep valleys and densely wooded mountains of Monongahela National Forest. A quick call to Camp Monongahela at 888-245-3982 secures reservations at the camp's private cabins along the route. Each is stocked with food, sleeping bags, bunks, and a wood stove. If you want all the trip planning to be done for you, the camp will do that, too, for a higher fee.

# Strathcona Park Lodge: Vancouver Island

Okay, so it isn't camping in the strict sense of the word, but it is a lodge and it is remote — smack in the middle of Vancouver Island, Canada. They welcome families with open arms and have a smorgasbord of adventures to fill your days — rock climbing, paddling (whitewater or flat), orienteering, sailing, hiking . . . the list goes on. If an overnight in a tent is what you desire as well, simply let the good folks know and they'll undoubtedly arrange it for you. Call 250-286-3122 for more information.

# Chapter 19

# Ten Times Two: Hodgson's Twenty Laws of Camping

· · · · · · · · · · · · · · · · · · · · · · · · · · · · · · · · · · · · · · · ·

1. The one item you are going to need the most is the one that has migrated to the bottom of your pack.

2. Whatever weight you lose on a camping trip is sure to find you when you get back home.

3. Emergencies never seem to happen when the sun is shining — be prepared.

4. The one spot you are planning to visit will most likely be located right at the corner of four USGS topographic maps.

5. If your tent is going to spring a leak, it will always be on your side.

6. The first time your camping partner mentions a bad back or trick knee is when you are dividing the gear at the trailhead.

7. No matter where you set up your tent, you will always be the one sleeping with your head downhill.

8. Rainstorms always seem to occur when you have packed your raingear in the most inaccessible corner of your pack.

9. Rainstorms always seem to let up just after you have struggled for 20 minutes to find your raingear and put it on.

10. If you can drink it without grimacing, it isn't real camp coffee.

11. It's best to cook under the cover of darkness. That way, no one can see what they're eating.

12. The only one in your group who will be inspired to break into song around the campfire is the one person who can't carry a tune, even with a handle.

13. It takes a box of matches and five gallons of gas to start a sputtering campfire, but only one spark to ignite a forest fire in a rainstorm.

14. Flashlights always work perfectly until you really need them — when it's dark and you've dropped a contact.

15. Undercooked or burned, it's all camp cooking and guaranteed to taste good if you are hungry.

16. Hiking in the outdoors without wearing sunscreen is a bit like reaching into the oven without an oven mitt — you're going to get burned!

17. A bad attitude is contagious — if you acquire one, keep it to yourself so that everyone else can enjoy the trip.

18. Unbreakable means unrepairable. Unrepairable means unusable. Nothing in this world is unbreakable. Count only on what is repairable.

19. Expect and prepare for the worst, and inevitably you will experience the best.

20. Camping adventures have their roots planted in the world of the unexpected. If you look for a positive side to the unexpected and seek opportunity in the face of a challenge, you will discover lasting memories of accomplishment.

# Part VI
# Appendixes

## In this part...

**M**ost appendixes are useless pieces of anatomy. Not this one! Part VI contains helpful references and lists to speed you on your camping trip, whether it's your first or 101st. Appendix A is a glossary of outdoor lingo, from altimeter to yogiing (betcha never saw that word before — check it out). Appendix B is a countdown check-list to help assure that your camping gear is in good shape, your home-base in good hands, and your vehicle packed and ready to roll. Appendix C tells you where to find information for planning a camping trip — names, addresses, 800 numbers, and Web sites.

# Appendix A

# Understanding the Outdoor Lingo

• • • • • • • • • • • • • • • • • • • • • • • • • • • • • • • • • • • • • • • •

**altimeter:** An instrument that measures elevation by using barometric (air) pressure.

**azimuth:** The degree of bearing from your current position to a landmark or destination. Reversing the bearing is known as a *back azimuth* or *back bearing*. See also **bearing, back bearing**.

**azimuth ring:** The rotating part of a compass that holds the damping fluid and the magnetic needle and has degrees ranging from 1 to 360 engraved around its edge. Also called the *housing*. See also **damping fluid, compass**.

**back bearing:** The 180-degree opposite of the **azimuth** or **bearing**. Also known as *back azimuth*.

**back sighting:** Establishing a back bearing. See also **bearing, back bearing**.

**base plate:** The transparent plate of an orienting compass onto which the compass housing is mounted.

**berm:** A lip or edge of debris that builds up on the downhill side of a trail, preventing water from flowing off the trail and leaving a puddle or muddy area to form.

**bearing:** The direction of travel from your current position to a landmark or destination, expressed in degrees from 1 to 360. Also called *azimuth*.

**bench mark:** A permanent (well, as permanent as things can be in this world) object that is either natural or man-made with a known elevation that can be used as a reference point when navigating.

**blaze:** A trail marking that can be a painted symbol on a tree, a sign, or a rock cairn. See also **cairn**.

**box canyon:** A canyon that is surrounded on three sides with an entrance but no separate exit. See also **canyon**.

**boulder field:** An area that is so densely covered by large boulders that you are obliged to walk over them — which is risky — or around them.

**boxing the needle:** A term that refers to placing the red end of a compass's magnetic needle exactly over the red end of the orienting arrow when determining a bearing. Because the orienting arrow is slightly larger than the magnetic needle, navigators refer to "boxing in" the magnetic needle. Some books or manuals refer to this as "red on red" or "centering" the needle. See also *compass*, *magnetic needle*, *orienting arrow*.

**buffer zone:** A protective strip of land on either side of a trail or waterway that insulates the wilderness traveler from development, mining, or logging.

**bushwhack:** To travel off-trail, often in very overgrown areas.

**cache:** A placement of food and/or supplies along or near a trail or route of travel for future use.

**cairn:** A stack or mound of stones that provides a visible marker of a trail's location through areas that are devoid of trees.

**compass:** A mechanical device that uses the earth's magnetic field to help a navigator plot a course, stay on course, determine the location of a landmark or destination point, or follow a course determined by a guidebook or friend.

**canyon:** A deep, narrow valley with steep sides that often features a seasonal stream or year-round stream or river flowing along the bottom.

**carabiner:** An aluminum or steel oval or other modified "D" or "O" shape with a hinged gate that is either locking (a screw-down ring keeps the gate from opening) or not. The device is used in rock climbing or mountaineering situations to attach ropes to climbers and anchored points of protection.

**cardinal points:** The four main points of direction on a compass: north (360 degrees); east (90 degrees); south (180 degrees); and west (270 degrees).

**clevis pin:** A metal pin that is held in place by a split ring and used to attach packs to their frames.

**clinometer:** A feature found on some compasses that allows the compass to be used to measure vertical angles (such as the slope of a hill). A clinometer can also be used as a level.

**col:** A pass between two peaks or a gap in a ridge line.

**contour interval:** The difference in elevation (height) between one contour line and the next on a topographic map. This interval is expressed in either feet or meters. See also *contour line, topographic map*.

**contour line:** On a topographic map, each contour line comprises an often irregular closed loop that connects points of equal elevation. The line with a darker shade of brown, typically every fifth line, is called an *index contour* and usually has the elevation printed on it. Elevations refer to elevation above sea level. See also *contour interval*, *topographic map*.

**coordinate:** A series of numbers that indicate on which map and in which grid a position is located. Latitude and longitude and UTM eastings and nor-things are nothing more than coordinates on a grid. A GPS (Global Positioning System) relies on coordinates. See also *latitude*, *longitude*, *GPS*, *Universal Transverse Mercator*.

**crevasse:** A fissure or break in glacier ice that may or may not be covered by a thin layer of snow. These can appear or disappear on active glaciers and can be deadly to the glacier traveler who is not prepared with the requisite safety tools — ropes, ice axe, ascenders, harnesses — and the knowledge needed to use those tools.

**damping fluid:** The fluid contained in the compass housing. Typically, this fluid is either a light oil or alcohol and is designed to minimize swing or excessive motion of the magnetic needle. Compasses that are not adequately damped, meaning the needle appears to shake and shift back and forth before settling, are hard to work with and quite unreliable.

**declination:** The difference in degrees between magnetic north (the direction the magnetic needle on a compass points) and true or geographic north (the direction maps are printed towards). See also *magnetic north*, *geographic north*.

**depression:** A natural or man-made hole in the ground that may or may not have a wet bottom. Depressions are shown on topographic maps by a contour line with small hachure marks pointing inward. See also *hachure*.

**direction-of-travel arrow:** Engraved or painted on the front of the base plate of a compass, this arrow indicates the direction in which you should hike when you have established a bearing or the direction in which you should point the compass to establish a bearing.

**double blaze:** Two painted blazes or markings on a tree that announce a change in direction or junction along a trail. See *blaze*.

**duff:** A layer of dead plants, needles, and leaves covering the ground in forested areas.

**eastings:** These are a part of the UTM coordinate system and are numbers printed along the top or bottom edge of a map that allow the navigator to determine an exact position. Increasing easting numbers indicate the navigator is moving east; decreasing easting numbers indicate a westerly heading.

**equator:** An imaginary line that divides the globe into two parts: northern hemisphere — north of the equator; southern hemisphere — south of the equator.

**Expanded Vinyl Acetate (EVA):** The closed-cell foam in the midsole of many athletic, trail running, and hiking shoes. EVA is used for its cushioning qualities since it is lighter and softer than other major midsole ingredients such as polyurethane.

**freshet:** A sudden overflow of a stream caused by heavy rain or nearby thawing of snow or ice.

**geographic north:** The north pole. Also known as *true north*.

**geographic poles:** Refers to the geographic points on the earth termed north pole at the northernmost point of the globe and south pole and the southernmost point of the globe.

**giardia:** More properly known as *giardiasis,* an infection of the lower intestines caused by the amoebic cyst *Giardia lamblia,* giardia lives in water, so you should always chemically treat or filter your water before drinking. Symptoms include stomach cramps, diarrhea, bloating, loss of appetite, and vomiting.

**GPS:** Short for Global Positioning System. This is typically used to refer to the handheld units that utilize the GPS system of 24 satellites orbiting the earth twice a day to precisely determine a navigator's position anywhere on earth.

**grid:** A pattern of squares on a map that fix your position. Coordinates provide numbers that help you find a horizontal line and a vertical line and then follow them to the point of intersection, placing you within that particular grid. See also *coordinates*.

**grommet:** A brass eyelet used in tarps, garments, and backpacks.

**guy line:** A cord from the side of a tent used to secure the tent to the ground using stakes.

**hachure:** Short lines on a topographic map used to represent relief features that lie in the direction of the steepest slope.

**housing:** See *azimuth ring*.

**index line:** The point at which the direction-of-travel arrow meets the housing and where the degree reading should be read to establish a bearing. See also *direction-of-travel arrow*, *housing*, *bearing*.

**knob:** A prominent rounded hill or mountain.

**latitude:** The distance in degrees north and south from the equator. Latitude lines run laterally (horizontally) around the globe and parallel the equator. One degree of latitude is divided into sixty smaller measurements called minutes. Each minute, in turn, is divided into even smaller measurements called seconds. One degree of latitude equals 69 statute miles or about 1.15 miles for every minute. One degree of latitude equals 60 nautical miles. One minute of latitude equals one nautical mile.

**layover day:** A rest day during an extended paddling, backpacking, or adventuring trip.

**longitude:** The distance in degrees east and west from the prime meridian established in Greenwich, England. Longitude lines run vertically (lengthwise) around the globe and connect the north and south poles.

**magnetic lines:** Lines drawn on a topographic map by the user to indicate the direction of magnetic north and to allow the map to speak the same directional language as the compass. See also *compass*, *magnetic north*, *topographic map*.

**magnetic needle:** The magnetized needle floating in the compass housing with one red end and one white end. The red end of the needle will always point toward magnetic north. Word of caution: since the needle is magnetized, it will also point toward metal surfaces or other magnetized items.

**magnetic north:** The geographical region toward which all magnetic needles point. This point is approximately 1,300 miles south of true north and moves slightly each year due to the earth's rotation and the friction created between its solid crust and liquid center. See also *true north*.

**map datum:** The reference point from which all maps are drawn. GPS is based on a grid for the entire earth called WGS-84. Unfortunately, many maps were published before GPS existed, so they utilize different datums. In North America, the datum is called the North American Datum 1927 or NAD27. Make sure that your GPS can interpret the map datums for the areas you will be in. See also *GPS*.

**map projection:** The process of transforming a round object (the earth, for example) into a flat object (a map) with the least amount of distortion. Some distortion always results from this process — that's why grid lines on a map are not perfectly parallel. See also *grid*.

**meridian:** An imaginary line circling the earth and passing through the geographic poles. All points on any meridian have the same longitude. See also *geographic poles*, *longitude*.

**mineral soil:** Dirt that contains mostly minerals and very little organic matter.

**moleskin:** A thick adhesive patch that is fuzzy on one side and sticky on the other. This first-aid kit essential is used to reduce friction (from hiking boots, for example) that can cause blisters.

**northings:** These are a part of the UTM coordinate system and are numbers printed along the side edges of a map that allow the navigator to determine an exact position. Increasing northing numbers indicate the navigator is moving north; decreasing northing numbers indicate a southerly heading.

**organic soil:** Dirt that contains a high percentage of organic material. This kind of soil is poor for constructing trails through since it rots, breaks down, compacts, and holds water.

**orienteering:** Using a map and compass in the field to determine your route of travel. The term has commonly come to mean a type of competition at which competitors try to navigate across challenging terrain from point to point and arrive at the finish line first.

**orienting a map:** Turning the map so that it represents a two-dimensional image that comes as close to exactly paralleling the three-dimensional world you are standing in.

**orienting arrow:** The north-south pointing arrow engraved into or painted in red or black on a compass housing. The orienting arrow is slightly wider than the magnetic needle and is used to "box" or surround the magnetic needle when establishing a bearing. See also *bearing*, *compass*, *housing*, *magnetic needle*.

**orienting lines:** The lines on the bottom of the compass housing that parallel the orienting arrow. See also *compass*, *housing*, *orienting arrow*.

**outslope:** The downhill slope of a well-constructed trail that allows water to drain.

**parallel of latitude:** An imaginary line that circles the earth parallel to the equator. All points on a given parallel have the same latitude. See also *equator*, *latitude*.

**pink snow:** Nature's laxative, this snow is filled with algae that is actually green in color but has coated itself with a pink gel for protection from the sun. Eat some and spend the next day worshiping the porcelain throne.

**position fix:** Sometimes referred to as *fixing your position*, this term means establishing your exact position on a map in terms of a coordinate system such as latitude/longitude or Universal Transverse Mercator. See also *coordinate*, *latitude*, *longitude*, *Universal Transverse Mercator*.

**prime meridian:** The meridian that runs through Greenwich, England, at a longitude of 0 degrees and is used as the position of origin for measurements of longitude. See also *longitude*.

**prismatic compass:** A compass designed with a mirror to allow a user to see both distant objects being sighted and the compass face at the same time. See also *compass, sight.*

**protractor:** Sometimes built into a compass, this instrument allows you to determine and measure angles in degrees and is most useful when projecting magnetic lines across your map. See also *compass*, *magnetic lines*.

**puncheon:** A log bridge built over fragile terrain that is wet.

**quadrangle:** A four-sided section of land bounded by parallels of latitude and meridians of longitude depicted on or by a topographic map. Topographic maps are sometimes referred to as "quads." See also *latitude*, *longitude*, *topographic map*.

**ravine:** A deep narrow indentation in the earth's surface, usually caused by runoff. See also *runoff*.

**relief:** Changes in terrain.

**relief shading:** The process of shading a map so that it takes on a three-dimensional look. Typically, maps are shaded as though the light source casting the shadow is coming from the northwest.

**rock flour:** A fine, silty sediment from glacially ground rock that causes creeks and mountain tarns to appear milky or greenish in color. See also *tarn*.

**runoff:** Rainfall that is not absorbed by the soil.

**saddle:** A ridge between two peaks.

**scale:** The distance between two points on a map as they relate to the distance between those two points on the earth.

**scree slope:** A slope with an angle of at least 30 degrees that is covered with small rocks and gravel that have broken away from the cliffs above.

**sight:** The notch or notches on a compass used by the navigator to line up a landmark to follow or obtain a bearing accurately.

**sighting line:** Sometimes called *line of sight*, this term refers to the imaginary line that you sight along to take your bearing. See also **bearing**, **sight**.

**skirt:** To work your way around a mountain or obstacle.

**slick rock:** A common name for southwestern sandstone made slick by the rubbing and grinding action of sand.

**slot canyon:** A narrow canyon carved into sandstone or slick rock by centuries of rain and flash flooding. Slot canyons are often filled or partially filled with water and can be extremely dangerous to navigate through. See also *canyon*.

**snow bridge:** A layer or "bridge" of snow that can be inches or feet thick spanning a creek or crevasse. Snow bridges can and will collapse when walked on, so use extreme caution. See also **crevasse**.

**spur ridge:** A side ridge that branches off a main ridge.

**stile:** A structure built over a fence that allows hikers to cross over without having to deal with a gate. Common in Great Britain.

**switchback:** A zigzagging trail up the side of a steep ridge, hill, or mountain that allows for a more gradual and less strenuous ascent.

**talus slope:** Talus slopes are more angled, sloping at 45 degrees or more, than scree slopes. Talus slopes are also larger than screes, and their rocks have sharper edges, all of which make talus slopes far more dangerous to cross and difficult to scramble up or down than scree slopes. See also **scree slope**.

**tarn:** A small mountain lake.

**Time To First Fix (TFF):** The amount of time it will take your GPS receiver to make its first position fix after it has been in the off position for over a month, lost its memory, or been moved for over 300 miles without an interim fix. Typically, this won't amount to more than 15 minutes. See also **position fix**, **GPS**.

**topographic map:** A map that reveals the topography of an area using contour lines. Also referred to as a *topo*. See also **contour line**.

**traverse:** To go up, down, or across a slope at an angle.

**tread:** A trail's surface.

**true north:** See **geographic north**.

**Universal Transverse Mercator (UTM):** The system grid that divides the entire world into 60 zones that are each 6 degrees wide. The zones begin at east/west longitude 180 degrees and continue at 6-degree intervals. Each zone is then removed from the globe and flattened, losing its relationship to a sphere and introducing a certain amount of distortion. Because UTM projections distort the regions above 84 degrees north latitude and below 80 degrees south latitude far too much, they are not used on maps referencing the UTM grid. The meter and grid lines on the UTM grid are always spaced 1 kilometer (0.62 miles) apart, making it much easier to estimate distance on a map. UTM coordinates are printed on a map in an east/west and north/south position. Numbers along the right side of a map are called *northings* (indicating the exact position in a north/south relationship). Numbers along the top of the map are called *eastings* (indicating the exact position in an east/west relationship). Making sense of the numbers is quick and easy: Increasing easting numbers indicate that you are heading east; decreasing easting numbers indicate that you are heading west. Increasing northing numbers indicate that you are heading north; decreasing northing numbers indicate that you are heading south.

**waypoint:** A checkpoint used as a point of reference for GPS. See also ***GPS***.

**whiteout:** A condition of zero or extremely limited visibility. Fog, thick clouds, or rapidly falling snow creates a situation in which light from above is of the same intensity as the light being reflected off the snow so that there are no shadows and no visible horizon.

**yogiing:** The despicable habit of dipping into others' picnic baskets when they aren't looking. Scheming campers have traditionally used this technique to steal food, but teens are increasingly using the technique to search for booze.

# Appendix B

# Before You Leave Home: Countdown Checklist

The following checklists will help you to be sure you are prepared to leave home and begin your adventure — your gear is good to go, mail and pets taken care of, appliances unplugged, thermostat set — nothing to worry about.

## Camping Gear Preparation

- Check boats to be sure they have no holes.

- Check boots to see if the leather needs to be conditioned and/or waterproofed.

- Check electronic gear (handheld radios, electronic compasses, GPS units, etc.) to see if they are working properly. Do they need batteries? Do they need technical care from a professional? Do they need to be retired and new ones purchased?

- Check flashlights to see if bulbs and/or batteries need replacing.

- Check packs for:

  - Rips or tears in the fabric

  - Sticking or broken zippers

  - Worn or torn seams

- Check sleeping bags for sticking or broken zippers.

- Check stoves for:

  - Fuel (do you have enough?)

  - Leaks (do any gaskets or seals need to be replaced?)

  - Lighting (does anything need to be cleaned or replaced?)

✔ Check waterproof gear to be sure it has no tears.

✔ Set up your tent to check for:

- All necessary stakes and guy lines

- Mildew

- Sticking zippers (lubricate them with dry silicone)

- Tears

# Home Care, Pet Care, Itinerary

✔ Schedule a neighbor or close family friend to house-sit or check in on the home each day to water plants, feed pets, take out garbage, take in newspapers, and pick up mail.

✔ Leave written instructions on pet care.

✔ Leave written instructions on plant care.

✔ Leave emergency contact information and vet name, address and phone number.

✔ Be sure pet food is well stocked and won't run out.

✔ Unplug appliances that don't have automatic turn-off features.

✔ Set the water heater temperature control and furnace/air conditioner thermostat.

✔ Leave a detailed itinerary and map of where you are going and where you will be at what estimated time. Be sure to leave the name and number of the nearest ranger station or campground manager for contacting should you not return on time. And when you do return home safely, *remember* to let everyone know so that needless search-and-rescue efforts are not begun.

# Planning Ahead: Did I . . . ?

✔ Get maps and directions to where I am going and pack them?

✔ Get the necessary camping permits and pack them?

✔ Get the necessary fire permits and pack them?

✔ Get the necessary fishing licenses and pack them?

✔ Get the necessary wilderness permits and pack them?

# In-Vehicle Essentials

- ✔ Clean clothes for the drive home
- ✔ Drinking water and bowl for pet
- ✔ Games, books, and entertainment for the drive
- ✔ License and car registration
- ✔ Litter bag
- ✔ Meals and snacks for the drive
- ✔ Suitable music for the drive
- ✔ Sunglasses

# Vehicle Preparation

- ✔ Check battery connections, belts, and hoses for wear.
- ✔ Check brake lights, headlights, and trailer connections.
- ✔ Check oil and fluid levels.
- ✔ Check spare tire for proper inflation and readiness.
- ✔ Check tires for wear and proper inflation.
- ✔ Check to be sure your tire-changing gear — jack and lug wrench — are in place and ready to use.
- ✔ Fill tank with gas.
- ✔ If you have a roof rack to install, put it on to ensure all parts are in working order.
- ✔ Prep vehicle emergency kit with flares, jumper cables, tire chains, snow shovel, and so on.
- ✔ Check windshield wipers and fluid.

# Appendix C

# Connections

● ● ● ● ● ● ● ● ● ● ● ● ● ● ● ● ● ● ● ● ● ● ● ● ● ● ● ● ● ● ● ● ● ● ● ● ● ● ● ● ● ● ● ● ● ●

## *Map Resources*

**Canada Map Office**
Offers topographic maps for all of Canada and the Northwest Territories.
Phone: 613-995-4921
Fax: 613-947-7948
E-mail: topo.maps@NRCan.gc.ca.
Web site: www.maps.NRCan.gc.ca

**DeLorme Mapping**
Offers topographic atlases for most of the 50 states. Excellent resource for planning purposes.
Phone: 207-865-4171
Web site: www.delorme.com

**MapTech**
Produces CD-ROM maps that cover the entire United States.
Phone: 800-627-7236
Web site: www.maptech.com

**National Geographic Maps Trails Illustrated**
Offers waterproof and, in my opinion, the most up-to-date topographic maps of our nation's national parks, as well as many recreation and wilderness areas.
Phone: 800-962-1643
Web site: www.trailsillustrated.com

**Tom Harrison Cartography**
Offers excellent topographic maps of parks and wilderness areas in California.
Phone: 415-456-7940
Web site: www.tomharrisonmaps.com

**United States Geological Survey (USGS)**
Offers topographic maps covering almost all of the United States.
Phone: 888-ASK-USGS, 888-275-8747
Web site: www.usgs.gov.

**Wilderness Press**
Offers topographic maps that coincide with their excellent field guides for
California and, more recently, other states.
Phone: 510-843-8080
Web site: www.wildernesspress.com

**Wildflower Productions**
Offers CD-ROM maps of US National Parks. Excellent!
Phone: 415-282-9112
Web site: www.topo.com

# Planning and Research Resources

## National Park Service

You should always plan ahead. You can either write or call for general information or specific park brochures. For specific park information, contact the
parks in advance about reservations, permits, regulations, activities, and services. A listing of NPS site phone numbers is available by visiting the National
Park Service Web site.

The Department of the Interior
National Park Service, Office of Public Inquiries
P.O. Box 37127, Room 1013
Washington, DC 20013-7127
Phone: 202-208-4747 (Monday–Friday 9 a.m. to 3 p.m. EST)
Web site: www.nps.gov.

The following additional publications are also useful.

*National Parks Visitor Facilities & Services* ($4.50)
The National Park Hospitality Association
1331 Pennsylvania Ave. NW, Suite 724
Washington, DC 20004-1703
Phone: 202-662-7097

*The Complete Guide to America's National Parks* ($14.95)
National Park Foundation
1101 17th. St., NW, Suite 1102
Washington, DC 20036
Phone: 202-785-4500
This publication is also available in most bookstores.

# Forest Service and Army Engineers Site Reservations

The National Recreation Reservation Service (NRRS) — www.reserveusa
.com — bills itself as "North America's largest camping reservation service,"
offering over 49,500 camping facilities at 1,700 different locations managed by
the USDA Forest Service and the U.S. Army Corps of Engineers. It is currently
the official campground reservation service for both the Forest Service and
Army Corps of Engineers. You will use this service if you are seeking to reserve
a campsite either in a campground or a wilderness area.

## One-stop research

Click your browser to www.recreation.gov, a partnership among federal
land management agencies aimed at providing a single, easy-to-use Web site
with information about all federal recreation areas. The site allows you to
search for recreation areas by state, by recreational activity, by agency, or by
map. Recreation.gov includes information about the following:

- 371 National Parks
- 114 National Forests
- 422 National Wildlife Refuges
- 260 Bureau of Land Management sites
- 457 Army Corps of Engineers sites
- 241 Bureau of Reclamation sites

## Wilderness resources

Wildnerness.net provides links to all 626 wilderness areas in the United States.
Web site: www.wilderness.net/nwps/all_wilderness.cfm

## State park and agency resources

Adventure Sports Online has a great listing of state agencies and
departments of tourism, complete with Web links that can be a major
help when trying to plan your trip.
Web site: www.adventuresports.com/service/state_service.html

# *Canadian National Park resources*

The following are the contact addresses, numbers and, in most cases, e-mail addresses for the information centers for the Canadian National Park system — one of the finest national park systems in the world. You can research your visits and make camping reservations by beginning with the following resources:

**Parks Canada National Office**
25 Eddy Street
Hull, Quebec
Canada K1A 0M5
Phone: 888-773-8888 (toll-free for North America only)
E-mail: parks_webmaster@pch.gc.ca

**Parks Canada — Halifax Service Center**
Historic Properties
1869 Upper Water Street
Halifax, Nova Scotia
Canada B3J 1S9
Phone: 902-426-3436 or 800-213-7275 (toll-free for North America only)
Fax: 902-426-6881
E-mail: atlantic_parksinfo@pch.gc.ca

**Parks Canada — Québec Service Center**
3 Passage du Chien d'Or
P.O. Box 6060 Haute-Ville
Québec City, Québec
Canada G1R 4V7
Phone: 418-648-4177 or 800-463-6769 (toll-free for North America only)
Fax: 418-649-6140
TDD: 418-648-5099
E-mail: parkscanada-que@pch.gc.ca

**Parks Canada — Ontario Service Center**
111 Water Street East
Cornwall, Ontario
Canada K6H 6S3
Phone: 800-839-8221 (toll-free for North America only)
Fax: 613-937-1331
E-mail: ontario_parkscanada_info@pch.gc.ca

**Parks Canada — Calgary Service Center**
(for Manitoba, Saskatchewan, Alberta, Northwest Territories, and Nunavut)
Room 552, 220 4th Avenue SE
Calgary, Alberta
Canada T2G 4X3
Phone: 403-292-4401 or 800-748-7275 (toll-free for North America only)
Fax: 403-292-4408
E-mail: NatlParks-AB@pch.gc.ca

**Parks Canada Information — British Columbia**
Box 129, 23433 Mavis Avenue
Fort Langley, BC
Canada V1M 2R5
Phone: 604-666-1280
Fax: 604-513-4798
E-mail: Parks_Infobc@pch.gc.ca

**Parks Canada — Yukon**
Suite 200, 300 Main Street
Whitehorse, Yukon
Canada Y1A 2B5
Phone: 800-661-0486 (toll-free for North America only)
Fax: 867-393-6701
E-mail: whitehorse_info@pch.gc.ca

# Index

• Z •

# IDG BOOKS WORLDWIDE BOOK REGISTRATION

Register This Book and Win!

## We want to hear from you!

Visit **http://my2cents.dummies.com** to register this book and tell us how you liked it!

- ✔ Get entered in our monthly prize giveaway.

- ✔ Give us feedback about this book — tell us what you like best, what you like least, or maybe what you'd like to ask the author and us to change!

- ✔ Let us know any other *For Dummies*® topics that interest you.

Your feedback helps us determine what books to publish, tells us what coverage to add as we revise our books, and lets us know whether we're meeting your needs as a *For Dummies* reader. You're our most valuable resource, and what you have to say is important to us!

Not on the Web yet? It's easy to get started with *Dummies 101*®: *The Internet For Windows*® *98* or *The Internet For Dummies*® at local retailers everywhere.

Or let us know what you think by sending us a letter at the following address:

*For Dummies* Book Registration
Dummies Press
10475 Crosspoint Blvd.
Indianapolis, IN 46256

™

BESTSELLING
BOOK SERIES